P9-CJS-978

SECOND EDITION

ASSESSING EDUCATIONAL LEADERS

For James

SECOND EDITION

ASSESSING EDUCATIONAL LEADERS

Evaluating Performance for Improved Individual and Organizational Results

DOUGLAS B. REEVES

CORWIN PRESS
A SAGE Company

Copyright © 2009 by Douglas B. Reeves

All rights reserved. When forms and sample documents are included, their use is authorized only by educators, local school sites, and/or noncommercial entities who have purchased the book. Except for that usage, no part of this book may be reproduced or utilized in any form or by any means, electronic or mechanical, including photocopying, recording, or by any information storage and retrieval system, without permission in writing from the publisher.

For information:

Corwin Press
A SAGE Company
2455 Teller Road
Thousand Oaks, California 91320
www.corwinpress.com

SAGE Ltd.
1 Oliver's Yard
55 City Road
London EC1Y 1SP
United Kingdom

SAGE India Pvt. Ltd.
B 1/I 1 Mohan Cooperative
 Industrial Area
Mathura Road, New Delhi 110 044
India

SAGE Asia-Pacific Pte. Ltd.
33 Pekin Street #02-01
Far East Square
Singapore 048763

Printed in the United States of America

Library of Congress Cataloging-in-Publication Data

Reeves, Douglas B., 1953-
Assessing educational leaders : evaluating performance for improved individual and organizational results/Douglas B. Reeves. —2nd ed.
    p. cm.
Includes bibliographical references and index.
ISBN 978-1-4129-5117-3 (cloth)
ISBN 978-1-4129-5118-0 (pbk.)
   1. School administrators—Rating of—United States. 2. Educational leadership—United States. I. Title.

LB2831.652.R44 2009
371.2′01--dc22   2008020251

08   09   10   11   12   10   9   8   7   6   5   4   3   2   1

Acquisitions Editor:	Arnis Burvikovs
Associate Editor:	Cassandra Harris
Production Editor:	Eric Garner
Copy Editor:	Edward Meidenbauer
Typesetter:	C&M Digitals (P) Ltd.
Proofreader:	Taryn Bigelow
Indexer:	Molly Hall
Cover Designer:	Michael Dubowe

Contents

Preface to the Second Edition

In the first edition of *Assessing Educational Leaders*, I claimed that leadership evaluation was a mess. Our research revealed that the evaluations of educational leaders were frequently inconsistent, ambiguous, and unrelated to the strategic objectives of the school system—and that was when evaluations happened at all. In almost 20 percent of the cases we studied, leaders had never been evaluated in their present position. Finally, we found that the longer the tenure of leaders in their current position and the greater their responsibilities within a school system, the less likely they were to receive accurate and constructive evaluations. The response to these findings from a broad range of educational leaders, policymakers, advisers, and researchers suggested that it was time to update the book, add new resources for readers, and provide case studies of success.

In this new edition, I offer evidence that a growing number of school systems are making significant improvements in their leadership evaluation procedures, providing models for the educational world to consider. Moreover, researchers and scholars offer practical insights into the key distinction between *evaluation* of leaders—a process sometimes fraught with politics, subjectivity, and relationship-poisoning judgment—and *assessment* of leaders—a process designed to provide feedback that will improve leadership performance. That distinction is at the heart of the new content in this edition, including

- Principal Evaluation Rubrics (Resource E), an exceptionally creative contribution to the field by Kim Marshall, leadership coach for New Leaders for New Schools and the editor of *The Marshall Memo* (www.marshallmemo.com). Marshall not only brings a singular grasp of educational research to this project but provides the most practical method of principal evaluation I have found.
- Hallmarks of Excellence Leadership Research (Chapter 10), a cutting edge leadership assessment and coaching tool designed to provide confidential feedback to senior leaders.
- Planning, Implementation, and Monitoring (PIM) Research (Chapter 11), revealing the specific actions of educational leaders that are most linked to improved student achievement.

- Examples of real-world applications of the Ascension Parish Leadership Professional Growth Matrix found in Resource F.

While the new evidence in this edition offers some cause for optimism about the potential for improved leadership assessment, there is also considerable cause for caution. First, in the United States alone, we are about to witness a leadership turnover of unprecedented proportions, with the American Association of School Administrators (Davis, Darling-Hammond, LaPointe, & Meyerson, 2005) estimating that more than 40 percent of school leaders will be eligible for retirement within the next four years. Worse yet, the schools and districts most in need—poor, urban, and exceptionally challenging—are those least likely to retain effective leadership. Even among the nation's leading urban school systems, according to the Council of the Great City Schools, superintendent tenure averages only 3.1 years (2006), and cases of urban schools and districts with revolving doors in the executive suite are common.

Some of these challenges are systemic—high-need schools and districts can burn leaders to a cinder with unsustainable hours and extraordinary stress, and therefore higher turnover might come with the territory. But many of the challenges causing leadership turnover are self-inflicted wounds. In particular, boards of education place demands on superintendents and, in turn, superintendents place demands on subordinate leaders, that range from the unreasonable to the ridiculous: The superintendent reprimanded by the board for failure to attend the right service club meetings; the principal called on the carpet for attending the birth of twins rather than the right basketball game; the academic dean raked over the coals for requiring a student to participate in a reading intervention that prevented a failure but irritated an activist parent. If this book can be reduced to a single sentence, it is the following: *Leadership assessment must be focused on effectiveness, not popularity.*

Improvements in student assessment are a hallmark of the past two decades of educational research and practice. From a tradition dominated by multiple-choice tests and norm-referenced assessments, the work of Wiggins (1998) and Wiggins and McTighe (2005), Darling-Hammond (1997), Stiggins (2000), and Stiggins, Arter, Chappuis, and Chappuis (2004) have brought authentic assessment and assessment *for* learning into the mainstream. It is therefore deeply ironic that the part of the educational establishment where advanced degrees predominate—building administrators and senior leadership—has failed to keep pace in the use of assessment that is designed to improve performance. If first-year teachers provided feedback to students in a manner that was ambiguous, inconsistent, and unrelated to performance goals, then their jobs would be in jeopardy. But if elected officials and administrators with terminal degrees commit the same offenses with their evaluations, then the too common reaction is resigned acceptance. Thus this edition of *Assessing Educational Leaders* is a clarion call to action. We should expect no less of policymakers and senior administrators than we require of novice teachers—evaluation, assessment, and feedback that is accurate, specific, and clear. Most important, we must change the fundamental purpose of assessment of leaders, following the pattern of recent changes in the assessment of students. The purpose of assessment is not to rate, rank, sort, and humiliate. The purpose of assessment is to improve performance. Only when leadership assessment achieves that goal will this book have achieved its purpose.

—Douglas B. Reeves
Salem, Massachusetts
January 2008

Acknowledgments

Collaboration is the hallmark of any worthy endeavor. My colleagues at The Leadership and Learning Center are my constant source of intellectual challenge and stimulation. In the past year in particular, they have inspired me with their commitment and determination. Eileen Allison played a major role in support of the National Leadership Evaluation Survey. She gathered examples of leadership evaluations from school systems throughout the nation, searched the Internet with dogged determination, and lent her unique blend of persistence and gentility to the project, moving it from concept to reality. Cathy Shulkin transferred thousands of pieces of data from survey responses to the computer and thus made my life much easier. The survey respondents, whose candor made me fully recognize just how awful leadership evaluation is, deserve my particular appreciation. In addition, hundreds of superintendents and personnel directors shared their leadership evaluation forms, knowing full well that they might be critically examined. I hope that the constructive suggestions in this book justify the risk that they took in sharing their work with me. Every example—even the ones I excoriate—represents a triumph of learning over secrecy, and for that I am most grateful.

Rachel Livsey of Corwin Press provided encouragement and support, as well as extremely helpful suggestions on the manuscript. Esmond Harmsworth of Zachary Schuster Harmsworth Literary Agency once again channeled my ideas into a completed book. Rachel and her colleagues challenge their authors to accept the advice of blind reviewers. These reviewers, whose contributions are almost invariably anonymous, deserve public credit in the case of this book. Dr. Libia Gil, Dr. Susan Kessler, and Suzanne Fonoti provided insightful, challenging, and much needed editorial advice. They confronted my prejudices and challenged my assumptions. They are more than editors and reviewers; they are good teachers, and there is no higher compliment I can offer. Toni Williams provided far more than the copyediting with which she is credited, but provided clarity and common sense where my original manuscript failed on both counts. Challenging authors is a difficult but necessary task, and readers can thank Toni for those moments in which they say, "I think I've got it." Despite the help of so many insightful colleagues, I remain responsible for the text. The failings in the pages that follow are more likely to be due to my obstinacy rather than their failure to offer good advice.

Footnotes are always inadequate to acknowledge the intellectual debt an author owes to others. My thinking on leadership evaluation has been particularly influenced by five people. Charlotte Danielson's (2002) pioneering work in teacher evaluation has had a profound and widespread impact on improving teacher evaluation. My fondest wish for this book is that it can do for leaders what Danielson has done for teachers. Linda Darling-Hammond, perhaps the preeminent scholar of teacher research of our age, has provided the intellectual structure and passionate advocacy that may yet transform teaching into the profession it must become. Her work is the example that those seeking to professionalize educational leadership must follow. Grant Wiggins has transformed the way we look at student assessment from a merely evaluative exercise into an educative one. The clarity, rigor, and constructive approach he brings to assessment of student performance represent the ideal toward which we should strive in leadership assessment. Robert Marzano has forced every leader to supplant opinions with research, prejudice with fact. In choosing the ways in which we evaluate leaders, Bob reminds us that our illusions of what great leaders look like must be replaced by the reality of what great leaders do. Mike Schmoker has wisely focused on the power of teachers and leaders at the building level. His careful documentation of school success in the most challenging of circumstances reminds us that diligence, focus, and building-level leadership are more powerful than grandiose visions and perplexing strategies.

Most of all, I am indebted to my daily encounters with some of the nation's best organizational leaders in education, business, and government service. Some of these leaders are named, but many of them are anonymous in the pages that follow, particularly when I dissect their failings. The willingness of these leaders to discuss not only their successes but their vulnerabilities is a mark of courage and confidence. Their ability to embrace accountability rather than fear it sets an example for us all.

This book, as with the 23 that preceded it, is written at the sufferance of a family who tolerates my absences and preoccupations. They are, most of the time, as happy to have me cheering on the sidelines, helping with homework, accompanying music practice, listening to their tribulations, or offering encouragement as they are to have me arrive so late in the evening that I can offer only my silent companionship. Their pictures, notes, and love sustain me through every journey. I am fortunate beyond words that they do not conduct the rigorous evaluation of me that I recommend to readers in the pages that follow. Shelley, Alex, Julia, James, and Brooks teach me many lessons: Fifty is beautiful, teenagers can be fun, tears are made to be shared, and childhood is brief. James, the young man to whom this book is dedicated, among the world's more worldly fourth graders, recoils at my fond recollections of his first years of life. During every midnight cry and noontime expression of wonder, he taught me more than I could possibly teach generations of my own students. His tenacity and tears, his toughness and tenderness, and above all his decency and generosity, are models I strive to emulate. Along with his mother and siblings, he defies Wilde's maxim that the lessons most worth learning cannot be taught. For the rest of my life, I will try to be a student worthy of these wonderful teachers.

The contributions of the following reviewers are gratefully acknowledged by Corwin Press:

Libia Gil, PhD
Chief Academic Officer
New American Schools
Alexandria, VA

Suzanne "Chris" Fonoti
Principal
Cromer Elementary School
Flagstaff Unified School District
Flagstaff, AZ

Susan Kessler, EdD
Principal
Williamson County Schools
Franklin, TN

About the Author

Douglas B. Reeves, PhD, is the president of The Leadership and Learning Center an organization that works with governmental organizations and school systems to improve standards, assessments, and accountability systems. The author of more than 20 books and many articles, he is the author of the best-selling *Making Standards Work,* now in its third edition. Other recent books include *The Daily Disciplines of Leadership: How to Improve Student Achievement, Staff Morale, and Personal Organization* (Jossey-Bass, 2002), *The Leader's Guide to Standards: A Blueprint for Educational Excellence and Equity* (Jossey-Bass, 2002), *Reason to Write: Help Your Child Succeed in School and in Life Through Better Reasoning and Clear Communication* (Simon & Schuster, 2002), and *Holistic Accountability: Serving Students, Schools, and Community* (Corwin Press, 2002). He has twice been named to the Harvard University Distinguished Author's Series and is the recipient of the Parent's Choice Award for his writing for students and parents.

Beyond his work in assessment and research, he has devoted many years to classroom teaching with students ranging from elementary school to doctoral candidates. His family includes four children ranging from elementary school through college. He lives near Boston and can be reached at dreeves@leadand learn.com.

Why Leadership Evaluation Is Broken 1

Changing leadership evaluation is going to be only slightly less difficult than those most insurmountable school challenges of revising the schedule and altering the grading system. Because schools persist in the use of schedules and grading systems with which they are most comfortable (that is, which most resemble the grading systems and schedules of previous eras), the prognosis for effecting change in leadership evaluation is grim. Why then do I persist in tilting at these windmills? Because leadership evaluation at present is a mess. In the course of researching this book, I reviewed hundreds of leadership evaluation systems and descriptions of leadership evaluation procedures from active educational leaders. In general, I found prevailing leadership evaluation systems to be the "perfect storm" of failure. In his book by that title, Sebastian Junger (1998) defined the perfect storm as one in which many different variables come together at the same time to create particularly destructive consequences. The perfect storm in leadership evaluation is in evidence when there is a combination of a national leadership crisis occasioned by an acute and growing shortage of educational leaders, accompanied by a leadership evaluation system that simultaneously discourages effective leaders, fails to sanction ineffective leaders, and rarely considers as its purpose the improvement of leadership performance. I studied thousands of pages of documents in search of an example worthy of emulation. These leadership evaluation systems do not come from the pens of incompetent bureaucrats. These are intelligent and thoughtful people. In many cases they are my friends. But in almost every case, the evaluation systems they use are deeply flawed. These systems fail to recognize excellence, give encouragement to bad practice, tolerate mediocrity, turn a blind eye to abusive practice, accept incompetence, and systematically demoralize courageous and committed leaders. The examples that follow will clearly show that these descriptions are not hyperbole, and my willingness to challenge the present form of leadership evaluation represents my confidence that friends and colleagues would rather forgive my candor than condone a continuation of leadership evaluation as we know it.

How bad is it really? Some educational research is equivocal in tone and circumspect in conclusion. This will not be such a book. The plain truth is that educational leadership evaluation is a failure in the vast majority of cases we studied. More than 18 percent of leaders we studied had never received an evaluation in their current position. In the words of one of our research subjects, "The worst evaluation experience was no evaluation at all. The message was that I was not important enough for my supervisor to take time to give me an evaluation." What of the 82 percent of leaders who did receive at least some evaluation? The vast majority of respondents found leadership evaluation to be inconsistent, ambiguous, and counterproductive. Thus, although we know that feedback is one of the most powerful mechanisms to influence performance (Hersey, Blanchard, & Johnson, 2000; Marzano & Pickering, 2001), educational organizations use this powerful tool badly or not at all.

The research at the heart of this book, the National Leadership Evaluation Study, was conducted in 2002 by the Center for Performance Assessment. The study was based on interviews, surveys, and documentary reviews. More than 500 leaders from 21 states were included in the survey, and more than 300 leadership evaluation instruments were reviewed. Respondents had the opportunity to elaborate on their answers, and the combination of objective and extended responses forms data on which the conclusions of the study are based. In collecting leadership evaluation instruments, there was no desire to find egregious examples of poor evaluation practice. Schools shared with us the best evaluations that they had, and many of these evaluations were established as the result of thoughtful consideration and, in the case of very large systems, collective bargaining between administrator associations and the district. Despite our best efforts, this (and any study) has some limitations that should be acknowledged from the outset. The study certainly is not comprehensive and does not represent every school system in the nation. There are, to be sure, examples of excellent leadership evaluation instruments. Since the study was completed, two notable school systems, Virginia Beach, Virginia, and Omaha, Nebraska, have shared with me particularly strong leadership evaluation policies. Nevertheless, the preponderance of the evidence suggests that, at the very least, school systems should critically examine their own leadership evaluation instruments and compare them to the best practices in assessment. Where standards are ambiguous, feedback is late, and evaluation is destructive, no national study is required to suggest that change is necessary. The details of the National Leadership Survey, including the narrative comments of the respondents, are in Resource B.

THE KNOWING-DOING GAP

One recent survey of educational leaders revealed the growing chasm between what we know to be important and how leaders actually behave. This gap provides clear evidence that the evaluation systems that are now in place display an intellectual understanding of what needs to be done, but lack the fundamental ability to act on that knowledge. For example, the North Carolina Center for School Leadership Development (2001) found that while 60 percent of leaders strongly agreed that leaders must present evidence that their leadership vision is shared, only 30 percent of respondents performed this function. More than two-thirds of the leaders thought it important to manage time to be an instructional leader, but only 28 percent actually did so. Three-fourths of them knew it was important to collect data to develop instructional strategies and improve the effectiveness of classroom instruction, but only 40 percent strongly agreed that they performed such a function. Sixty-eight percent of the respondents strongly agreed that leaders must use the vision to guide and define decisions, but only 31 percent expressed a similar level of agreement that they performed this function. Seventy percent agree that leaders should "maintain a steady flow of two-way communications to keep the vision alive and important" and only 27 percent devoted time to such an important objective. The disconnection between expectation and reality was brilliantly captured by Jeffrey Pfeffer and Robert Sutton (2000) in their landmark book in which the title matched the subject: *The Knowing-Doing Gap*. The remainder of the survey pointed to enormous gaps between what leaders know and what they actually do. The only instance in which the gap was closed was, of course, the area that consumes the attention of most leaders—procedures and discipline. Seventy-five percent of leaders know that they should "develop and distribute student handbooks with information about rules, requirements, and expectations for student conduct and potential consequences" and 73 percent did the deed. Instructional leadership, indeed. The results of the North Carolina survey are summarized in Resource D.

Lest readers be too harsh on the state of North Carolina, it is worthy of note that the leaders in the state department of education have the courage and integrity to report these findings and work toward the creation of an improved leadership evaluation system. Many other states continue in a pattern of leadership analysis and evaluation in which they ignore glaring deficiencies. The responses by our national sample of leaders were strikingly consistent with the North Carolina findings, with the worst ratings related to the specificity of the evaluation and the relevance of the evaluation to improving student achievement.

PROGRESS IN LEADERSHIP EVALUATION

Despite the generally deplorable state of evaluation in educational leadership, there have been some notable efforts in the right direction. The Interstate School Leaders Licensure Consortium (1996) articulated standards that have now been accepted by the majority of states, and several states have created ambitious leadership evaluation systems. Almost all of these represent an advance over previous evaluation systems and are certainly better than the utter absence of systematic leadership evaluation. It is also fair to note that the criticisms leveled at some of these systems could only take place because the authors and sponsors had the courage to publicize their systems and expose them to reviews by outsiders. Those whose leadership evaluation systems are secret or nonexistent are safe from direct criticism in this book, but their risk is far greater than that undertaken by their colleagues who had the commitment, vulnerability, and integrity to put their work on the Web and allow researchers like me to comment on it. I offer the comments in the following paragraphs in the spirit of constructive improvement and with the comment that our harshest criticism should be reserved for leadership evaluation that is shrouded in mystery, politics, and guesswork.

AMBIGUOUS LEADERSHIP STANDARDS

The problem starts with what we call leadership, particularly in the context of education. At best, the expectations are ambiguous. At worst, the expectations are contradictory, impossible, or at great variance to common values and mountains of research. The primary problems are poorly defined standards of leadership and undefined standards of performance. There are four separate issues that plague our definition of effective leadership. First, there are poorly defined standards of leadership in which ambiguity, typically confounded by educational jargon, replaces clear expression. The second problem is undefined standards of performance, a problem that prevails even in those cases where the evaluation system has purged itself of offending jargon and ambiguity. Even the most crystal clear standard is impotent if the evaluation system does not provide a continuum of evaluation so that the adequate performance is clearly and consistently differentiated from the performance that is making progress and the performance that is exemplary. The third problem, the responsibility–authority disequilibrium, is familiar to most leaders. They are responsible for the actions of others, ranging from the most recalcitrant employee to the most disinterested community member, yet they have the authority to compel the actions of neither of these stakeholders.

In the vast majority of the leadership evaluation documents I reviewed, one of two problems prevailed. Either the standards themselves were ambiguous or the performance expectations were unclear. The following statements have been gleaned from local, state, and national expectations for school leaders. After each statement is a challenge that any leader being evaluated by such a standard would want to consider.

Expectation	*Challenge*
"The administrator facilitates processes and engages in activities ensuring that curricular, co-curricular, and extra-curricular programs are designed, implemented, evaluated, and refined."	What in the world does this mean? How would we know if this standard has been met? Does evaluation and refinement have to do with what is popular or what is effective?
"Stays current with research and theory regarding theory and motivation. Keeps abreast of the latest developments in the field of education."	*Any* research and theory? Much of it is awful and contradictory to the goals and values of the school system. This goal appears to endorse a collection of fads, the proverbial "flavor of the month" in which school leaders fail to distinguish what is current from what is important, valid, tested, trustworthy. When someone announces with breathless enthusiasm that he has found the True Path in a recent discovery, such as interdisciplinary instruction, I am compelled to ask, "Didn't we call that 'humanities' 30 years ago?" When I listen outside the doors of national conventions or local staff development meetings, I hear ideas—including some good ones—that are of the vintage of Socrates or Dewey, yet are promoted as if they are copyrighted by a 21st century guru with exceptional insight. The point is not the elevation of one era over another, but rather the application of research and thinking of millennia with judicious caution, appropriate skepticism, and historical context.
"Provides information on curriculum/instruction."	The issue is not whether the leader provides information, but rather whether the information is of sufficient quality to be understood and whether the information is used to make good decisions to improve student achievement.
"Expects and coaches effective classroom practices and a service orientation."	I have an idea of what effective classroom practices are, but unless they are specified, the definition of effectiveness can vary wildly from one administrator to the next. The variations are as likely to be based on opinion as on research. I do not know what a service orientation means in this context.
"The administrator facilitates processes and engages in activities ensuring that relevant demographic data pertaining to students and their families are used in developing the school mission and goals. Diversity is considered in developing learning experiences."	Does this mean that good leaders have different goals for poor schools than for rich schools? Is it a good idea to have different goals for schools based on their ethnic composition? Does this mean that if the families have a culture of low expectations that schools should mirror those expectations?
"Demonstrates effective organizational skills."	What skills? What does effectiveness mean in this context?
"Participates in professional development activities."	My fourth grader's hamster can participate in professional development activities. What does this tell us about the impact of using new knowledge and skills to become a more effective leader?

(Continued)

(Continued)

Expectation	*Challenge*
In the same leadership evaluation instrument, one district requires that its effective leader "carefully weighs consequences of contemplated action" and, a few sentences later, requires the same leader to be "action-oriented; presses for immediate results. Decisive; doesn't procrastinate on decisions."	As if this were not sufficiently problematic, the rating scale for the 21st century Solomon who is to occupy a leadership position in this district has only two possible ratings: "Meets Standard" and "Does Not Meet Standards." It is no surprise that the same evaluation form requires the leader to simultaneously "hold to personal opinions," "exhibit a need to control most situations," and "demonstrate adaptability and flexibility." One might gently suggest that an administrative certificate and a doctorate are not the criteria sought by this district, but rather some combination of divinity and multiple personality disorder.

INCOHERENT LEADERSHIP EVALUATIONS

Not every leadership evaluation instrument is so deeply flawed with regard to the establishment of clear leadership standards. But even where I found clarity in the standard, I discovered ambiguity with regard to the description of performance levels. Typical of the language of performance evaluation was "exceeds expectations" or "meets expected performance levels" or "superior" or "average"—without any clear indication of which specific leadership behaviors deserved such labels. In the absence of specification, the only criterion available is the idiosyncratic judgment of the evaluator. However wise and insightful an individual evaluator may be, these judgments are doomed to be inconsistent and of little use for coaching. The recipient of the evaluation only knows that one evaluator regarded her as "outstanding," but the same leadership traits and behaviors merited a rating of "meets standards" from another evaluator while yet a third evaluator looked at the same performance and said that it "exceeds expectations." Out of such linguistic mire one should not expect leadership wisdom to emerge.

Effective evaluation systems allow both the evaluator and the one being evaluated to understand clearly the difference between various levels of performance. Michael Jordan, for example, is acutely aware of the difference between putting the ball in the basket and hitting the rim. His fans share his perceptions of clarity in evaluation. Sarah Chang, along with the vast majority of her audience, knows the difference between an F-natural and an F-sharp. But do school leaders, to whom we entrust our children and billions of dollars in resources, know the difference between performance that is exemplary and that which is deplorable? Descriptions of performance—even if the standards themselves are clear—devolve into the linguistic quicksand of "sometimes" compared to "seldom" or "frequently" compared to "often" or "exceeds expectations" compared to "satisfactory." Intelligent people of good will can disagree about what any of these descriptions mean. Perhaps the least helpful are the descriptions such as "growth needed"—invariably a negative comment in the context of evaluation, yet I strain to think of a single leader, from Alexander the Great to Napoleon to Churchill to the very best school leaders I have observed in more than a million miles of travel who would not enthusiastically check a box called "growth needed" when describing themselves. To put it bluntly, when is growth not needed? Presumably when one is dead.

It's really not as bad as all that—it's worse. Consider the following examples of descriptions of performance:

Expectation	*Challenge*
"The principal always meets and sometimes exceeds expectations for performances in this position requirement."	Whose expectations? How frequently? What does "sometimes" mean? What is the difference between "meeting" and "exceeding" expectations? If the expectation is fair and ethical behavior, how does one exceed it? If the expectation is that the principal provides equitable opportunities for 100 percent of students, how is it possible to exceed such a standard?
"Students using technology or products of technology. Yes or No."	By such a binary standard, students gain the same credit for an insightful analysis of literary criticism of Hemingway discovered on the Internet as they do for playing Nintendo or e-mailing a friend.
"No disruptions. Yes or No."	Are these people serious? When is the answer "yes?" In the summer? At midnight? In the cemetery? In a school without students?

I could go on, but the point has been made. Schools are succeeding in spite of, rather than because of, these tainted leadership evaluation instruments. If they could continue to depend upon a generation of leaders who would persist, learn, and succeed without any meaningful coaching, reinforcement, or sanctions from their evaluation system, then this book would be unnecessary. But in a nation in which a growing number of leadership positions are unfilled and an alarming number of leaders are leaving the field of education, it is well past time for fundamental reform in a system that is not merely broken, but shattered. The nation needs a new form of leadership evaluation and it needs it now.

AUTHORITY-RESPONSIBILITY DISEQUILIBRIUM

We wish our leaders to be some mythical combination of folk heroes, in which they have the insight of Lao-Tzu, the courage of a New York firefighter, the risk tolerance of Amelia Earhart, and the work ethic of Paul Bunyan. For the purposes of rhetorical flair and savvy marketing, publishers cast as wide a net as possible, offering us models for leadership who include, in alphabetical order, Attila the Hun, Catherine the Great, Churchill, Elizabeth I, Jefferson, Jesus, Machiavelli, Moses, Napoleon, Nixon, Rasputin, Roosevelt (Teddy and Franklin), Washington, and untold numbers of yet to be reconstructed historical leaders whose biographers have found some link between personal traits and organizational effectiveness. In the real world of school leaders, however, the relationship between demands and authority leads to more prosaic results. This does not stop the authors of leadership evaluations from the grand presumption that the school principal or district superintendent enjoys monarchical powers.

The most glaring examples of the authority–responsibility disequilibrium occur when the administrator is held responsible for the actions of others. One set of leadership standards, for example, requires that the leader "ensures that staff and community understand the analysis of student data." The leader can provide information to the staff and even assess the staff's knowledge, but cannot "ensure" understanding. Certainly the leader can share information with the community, but that is a long way from guaranteeing comprehension or even interest by the general public. Another leadership evaluation requires leaders to "ensure a balanced budget." This might require controlling the weather in New England, the price of oil in Iraq, the impact of hail on the roofs of schools in Kansas, and the number of snow days in Idaho. A host of natural events can affect the budget in ways that are far beyond the control of school leaders.

A BETTER WAY: MULTIDIMENSIONAL LEADERSHIP ASSESSMENT

There is an alternative to the vacuous exercises now called leadership evaluation. Building on the best practices in performance assessment, this book offers a new model of leadership evaluation: multidimensional leadership assessment (MLA). In assessing any human performance, whether a student leaning to read or a superintendent leading a complex system, there is a complex set of variables that must be assessed. Imploring students to read well is of little more value than exhorting the superintendent to be a better leader. Improvement requires feedback that is specific, accurate, and timely. Thus, rather than making evaluation an event that occurs once every year (or in the case of senior leaders, every three or four years, always after it is too late to influence performance), MLA provides frequent feedback with multiple opportunities for continuous improvement. Rather than providing performance levels that are meaningless ("meets expectations," "above average," or "progressing toward standards"), MLA describes in specific terms the difference between performance that is distinguished and performance that is proficient, progressing, or failing to meet standards.

Finally, MLA is not merely a retrospective approach to leadership evaluation. MLA can be used to improve the performance of a 30-year veteran and to coach the newest assistant principal. It can also be used to train new leaders and identify prospective leaders who will become the next generation of educational leadership. Most important, MLA will force school systems to establish clear, coherent, and fair expectations for present and future leaders. In the past three decades, tremendous strides have been made in every area of educational assessment. It is well past time that we apply those lessons to the assessment of educational leaders.

Reframing Leadership Evaluation 2

Topics Presented in Chapter 2 Include

✓ The Risks and Rewards of Evaluation

✓ A New Vision of Educational Accountability

✓ Criteria for Multidimensional Leadership Assessment (MLA)

✓ Implications of a New Vision for Leadership Evaluation

PATRICK'S CHOICE: THE RISKS AND REWARDS OF EVALUATION

"It feels as if you are evaluating me," Patrick* complained, "and I don't like it." I was astonished at this reaction from an experienced and successful school leader. The feedback he was receiving was nonthreatening, constructive, and reciprocal. He had devoted several days to learning more about effective assessment in the classroom and school, and participants were reviewing one another's work using a scoring rubric. An essential skill for every educational leader, after all, is to coach teachers and other instructional leaders to improve their performance. Practicing this essential skill in a workshop seemed natural, even necessary, for an effective workshop. Nevertheless, Patrick would have none of it. His experiences with evaluation, both as the evaluator and as the one being evaluated, had been largely negative. Staff development workshops were supposed to be a break from the stress of the day, and now all that stress came flooding back. In other conversations with him, I discovered one of his highest accolades for another person was that the person was "nonjudgmental."

AUTHOR'S NOTE: *Unless specifically noted, all names are pseudonyms based on a composite of actual conversations.

This attribute was closely associated in Patrick's mind with skills such as empathy, attentive listening, and resonance, all of which he knew to be associated with effective leadership in successful organizations (Goleman, Boyatziz, & McKee, 2002). In his selective perception of leadership research on the subject, Patrick had excluded the need for confronting facts, receiving and providing feedback, and engaging in a continuous process of evaluative learning as part and parcel of the leadership skills he so admired. A computerized doll, after all, can respond to every statement of a colleague with, "That's great. I understand. Of course. It sounds as if that means a lot to you. I understand. That's great. I understand. . . ." Such vain repetitions are neither empathetic nor resonant. They are, in the most precise sense of the term, nonjudgmental and, as a result, without the ability to be either constructive or destructive. The absence of malevolence is not necessarily the presence of benevolence. It is rather simply benign, without any positive or negative impact. Perhaps, in Patrick's view, this is better than being destructive, but I would offer a different point of view.

Consider the two risks involved. Risk 1 we shall call *Patrick's choice.* On one side of the balance is the risk that an effective leader like Patrick will receive the same nonjudgmental feedback as his colleague who is incompetent, disorganized, and burdened by a history of low expectations of his students. The reward is that Patrick is neither offended nor discouraged, and due to his personal commitment to his students and his principles, he persists in his job, at least for now. The risk of Patrick's choice is that his counterpart sinks deeper into the mire of incompetence and bigotry, unchallenged by the reality of the consequences of his actions. Moreover, Patrick will ultimately grow weary of being lumped into the same category as every other school leader, irrespective of dedication and competence. "I love these kids and I used to love this job," Patrick sighs. His colleagues and subordinates recognize the signs of burnout and know intuitively that Patrick will not last very long. If he's lucky, he'll find another position or return to the classroom. If he isn't, he will precipitate a crisis that may cost him his career and reputation.

Risk 2 is the *leader's gambit.* Leaders welcome coaching, feedback, and evaluation because they know that they will learn something from it. In fact, they are disappointed if they do not receive feedback, including suggestions for improvement, because the absence of feedback implies that mentors are not paying sufficient attention to their needs. The reward of the leader's gambit is a cadre of motivated and empowered leaders that sets an example for every student, teacher, and community member with their dedication to lifelong learning. The risk, of course, is that sometimes the leaders' feelings are bruised. "She could have told me that my assessment skills were progressing rather than saying that my sample performance assessment tasks were silly and cryptic." Some senior leaders will be impervious to the emotional needs of their colleagues and provide evaluations that are clumsy and, to put it mildly, undiplomatic. Other leaders in the healthy organization shrug this off by saying, "That's just Laura!" and accept the feedback for what it is—badly stated but true. "She could have said it better," Laura's subordinates conclude, "but the fact is that my assessment models could use some work, and I can hardly expect my teachers to excel in standards-based assessment if I don't set a superlative example for them." In the leader's gambit, we have judgment, the very judgment that Patrick eschews. We also have the risk of hurt feelings, the very risk that Patrick regards as nearly cataclysmic. Why then do the most successful leaders accept this risk? Because the rewards of feedback far outweigh the emotional cost imposed by the revelation of imperfection. For every imperious and demanding Laura there is an encouraging and motivating Anne, Charles, and Ramona, each of whom observes the same frailties in leadership and uses the evaluation system to improve leadership performance.

Neither choice is perfect. Both Patrick's choice and the leader's gambit have risks. The only question is this: Which choice has the greater reward and the smaller risk? If Patrick were right, then this book would not even have the word *evaluation* in the title, as it is simply too hot to handle. After all, as Patrick's reasoning goes, the risk of offense is the highest risk of all. The leader's gambit, by contrast, responds that educational leaders are much tougher and more intelligent than we give them credit for. These leaders seem to be saying, calmly but clearly,

> It's not the 1970s anymore and we do not expect to have a world in which we are guaranteed freedom from offense and emotional injury. Sure, there are jerks out there, but that is no reason to stop the free flow of information, including the essential feedback that will make us better leaders.

Figure 2.1 illustrates the choices on the risk–reward matrix that every leader must confront when considering the issue of evaluation. On the horizontal axis we find the risks and rewards associated with demands for high educational performance, and on the vertical axis we find the risks and rewards associated with the focus on the perceived emotional needs of the leader and staff. Patrick occupies the upper left-hand quadrant, as he seeks to nurture his staff and himself, insulating them from reality, feedback, criticism, coaching, or anything that would threaten their satisfaction with the status quo. He is, above all, very *frustrated*. Patrick's staff of veteran teachers has seen several principals come and go, so Patrick reasons that he probably could not change them if he wanted to. Therefore, the path of least resistance and greatest comfort for everyone concerned is to focus on the emotional needs of the adults. When educational performance suffers and Patrick is criticized by the superintendent, he can always count on his teachers, he believes, to console him and assure him of how unfair the world is. Faculty meetings frequently devolve into gripe sessions about the central office, the world of education, parents, and students. Every demand for performance is avoided, even actively resisted. The very words *evaluation* and *accountability* are regarded as epithets that are beneath contempt, and those who attempt to implement evaluation and accountability clearly are organizational savages who do not value people as individuals. The strange thing is that for a group whose emotional needs Patrick so assiduously massages, they certainly do not seem very happy. In fact, some of Patrick's best teachers have requested transfers to another building. They said something about wanting more professional development and intellectual challenge, but to Patrick they seem most ungrateful for all he has done to protect them. The leaders in this quadrant are not only frustrated themselves, but their frustration is contagious and spreads throughout the organizations they lead.

Figure 2.1   Evaluation Risks and Rewards

	Frustrated	Effective
High	• Low organizational performance and therefore a high risk of demoralizing the most effective leaders • Low risk of offense to feelings of other adults, at least in the short term	• High reward of exceptional organizational performance, motivation of great leaders, and honest identification of problem leaders • High regard for emotional needs of staff, including the emotional need for truth, consistency, and membership on a winning team • Students and staff feel that they are successful because they are successful
	Indifferent	Threatening
Low	• Risk of failure • Risk of personnel dejection and demotivation • Low risk of change fatigue	• High risk of organizational meltdown • High risk of eliminating next generation of leaders and teachers • High risk of out-migration of parents and students of promise • High reward of short-term gains in test scores

Focus on Emotional Needs

Low   **Performance Demands**   High

In the lower right-hand quadrant, the *threatening* leader is willing to accept high emotional risks, driving his staff, berating his students, and relentlessly pursuing his vision of excellence which, it turns out, is the average score on the state test. Threats, intimidation, and tantrums are his favorite management tool. In the short term, it worked. Teachers who did not accept the threatening leader's vision moved out, more time was devoted to academics and test preparation, and during the first year scores improved. Of course, this leader has not matched wits with very many students who are, it turns out, quite expert in undermining the authority of adults. Once they learned that their success would make the leader look good, the students made sure that their state test results would do no such thing.

The *indifferent* leader dwells in the lower left-hand quadrant, where she neither cares for the emotional needs of her staff nor responds to demands for emotional performance. She is a firm believer in the "leader as victim" school of thought (Reeves, 2002b) in which she can only respond to the externalities in the system—families, home environment, income, television, video games, unions—and hopes to survive to retirement. Her staff meetings are quick and sullen readings of official announcements, and her other interactions with staff reflect a belligerent indifference to their needs. She says in word and deed, "Let's just get out of here with the least possible pain and bother for all of us." Indifferent leaders typically rotate through multiple assignments as administrators, as they have typically never done anything bad enough to justify termination, but their low performance and toxic emotional style combine to make them a regular participant in the annual ritual described by the personnel office as *the dance of the lemons.* In this destructive dance, ineffective leaders are reassigned to other buildings or departments, but the underlying performance issues are never addressed.

Standing far apart from the other three quadrants is the space occupied by the *effective* leader. The symmetrical appearance of the four quadrants does not do justice to how far removed the effective leader is from her colleagues who fail to match her rare combination of high demands for performance and great care for the emotional needs of her staff. When they were teachers, the effective leaders understood that true self-esteem in their students never arose from the lies of adults in which they would provide false praise for inadequate work. In the classroom, their favorite word was *yet,* as they simultaneously goaded and reassured their students that any time an assignment was less than stellar, whether that judgment was made by the students themselves, a parent, or a teacher, the assessment must be followed by the word *yet.* When a student would examine a piece of work and conclude sternly, "I don't think this is proficient," the effective leader would quickly reply with a smile, "not proficient *what?*" "It's not proficient *yet,*" the student would quickly reply. The effective leader brings the same unremitting optimism to her role as an educational leader, confronting the fact that neither her school nor any other institution is perfect and yet making every observation of imperfection an opportunity for encouragement and coaching. Her teachers, including those who have received some intensive coaching for improved professional performance, feel that they have learned more from the effective leader than in any college class they ever took. Like the great teacher that she is, the effective leader expects a great deal from her faculty, and teachers report that they work hard both in and out of the classroom. Each faculty meeting is a seminar devoted to examination of student work, lessons, or research, and every teacher has responsibility for regularly leading those seminars. By dealing with announcements and administrative announcements in writing, the effective leader not only saves time, but also conveys the unmistakable sense to her colleagues that she trusts them. "You really don't need to read aloud to grownups, you know," explains the effective leader, "and I don't need to pass along administrative requirements with any threats or explanations—we're too busy helping our students." It is telling that the highest compliment the effective leader's colleagues bestow on her is that "she's a real teacher." This perhaps explains why the effective leader's school not only shows exceptionally high levels of performance, but why the school she left three years ago that is now led by a young and inexperienced principal continues to be successful.

A NEW VISION OF EDUCATIONAL ACCOUNTABILITY

Accountability has the potential to be either a constructive or a destructive force in education. Leaders recoil from the common practice of educational accountability systems that are superficial (dependent solely on test scores), infrequent (announced once a year), and destructive (fulfilling a political agenda without shedding light on how the system can be improved). When it comes to the decisions of legislators, federal policymakers, and local school board members, leaders rarely express any hesitancy about exposing the defects of deeply flawed accountability systems. A few school systems have provided a constructive alternative, creating holistic accountability systems (Reeves, 2001) that are constructive, comprehensive, and focused on system improvement. While the transformation of an accountability system represents an enormously important step toward improved system performance, the process remains incomplete unless leadership evaluation becomes as multifaceted and constructive as the best accountability systems.

The fundamental purpose of effective accountability systems is not the rating, ranking, evaluating, sorting, and humiliating of students, schools, teachers, and leaders. The fundamental purpose of effective accountability systems is the improvement of teaching and learning. Similarly, the fundamental purpose of effective leadership evaluation is neither the fulfillment of an administrative burden nor the wielding of a bureaucratic stick to grab the attention of the person being evaluated. Rather, the fundamental purpose of leadership evaluation is the improvement of teaching and learning through the building of the knowledge and skills of current and prospective educational leaders. While it is true that there remains a necessary administrative component to evaluation—documenting particularly good and bad practices to provide administrative support for rewards and sanctions—those purposes are secondary to the fundamental purpose of improving leadership skills. As Collins (2001) has noted persuasively, by the time any organization realizes that it needs to evaluate people in the hope of improving their performance, it is usually too late. Given the punitive, threatening, and destructive nature of most evaluations, it is little wonder that the language of performance improvement is replaced by the language of defensiveness and blame.

Thus, evaluation and accountability are inextricably linked. Both have the potential for organizational renewal through insights into individual and group performance. Through the systematic identification of effective practice and the careful measurement of both student results and leadership actions, systemwide accountability and individual evaluation can transform random acts of good and bad practice into the brains of a learning organization. Each good decision can be systematically replicated, and each poor decision can be analyzed and serve as a learning opportunity for leaders throughout the organization. The same powerful tools of accountability and evaluation can, of course, have the potential for disaster through their misuse as destructive and demotivating management tools. In this type of evaluation, results are viewed without the context of causes, and thus the leader fortunate enough to be present when good results occur is presumed to have caused them, whether or not the decisions for which the leader is responsible are sound. In destructive accountability systems, the only consideration is a set of numbers, typically test scores, and the systematic consideration of cause variables is missing. If test scores are low, then there is a search for blame rather than a search for causes.

In such an environment, errors are the source of fear rather than the source of learning. A fundamental thesis of this book is that effective leadership assessment depends on the candid acknowledgment of every leader's successes and mistakes and the clear association of those leadership practices with organizational results. Those who evaluate educational leaders can find great value in an analysis of both superior leadership practices and leadership errors. Such a candid understanding of leadership practices and organizational results provides those who assess educational leaders with a deep understanding of the antecedents of leadership excellence. Without such an understanding, the organization will validate Santayana's prediction that those who fail to remember the past are condemned to repeat it.

There is not a simple dichotomy between leadership evaluation practices that are enlightened and those that are wretched. The third alternative is avoidance. In this more typical model of leadership evaluation, we have the worst of both worlds, even as the practitioners of avoidance delude themselves into believing that they are avoiding risk. The mindless approval of poor leadership is an inherent part of the avoidance strategy, as mediocre practice gains acceptance through the failure of anyone in the organization to identify and sanction it. Sanctions, it becomes clear, are reserved for the most egregious acts of misconduct, and thus mere mediocrity can thrive. Excellence is neither identified nor rewarded. In extreme examples of avoidance, leadership evaluations simply do not exist. In some school systems, principals, central office administrators, superintendents, and board members never receive formal evaluations. If they avoid extraordinary malfeasance, they continue their employment, receive annual raises, and lead their professional lives in a state of less than blissful ignorance. The more common avoidance strategies of evaluation contain the illusion of evaluation, with periodic pieces of paper bearing the word *evaluation* and perhaps even a few meetings with the topic of evaluation as the nominal agenda. A closer inspection of the documents and meetings, however, reveals the truth: Neither the evaluation documents nor the evaluation meetings are related to the values and mission of the school system. Take this challenge in your own system. Ask a colleague to find a dozen or so leadership evaluations and eliminate any references to names, schools, or other text that would specifically identify the person being evaluated. Then read the evaluations and attempt to identify the most and least effective leaders based solely on the words contained in the evaluation. My experience suggests that the same phrases creep into each evaluation (sometimes with the help of a computer program). The specific identification of exceptionally good or bad performance is a rarity, and the utility of the evaluation document for personal coaching and performance improvement is nil. When discussing individual leaders, the author of the evaluations has no difficulty in differentiating between the principal who is a future superintendent and ready for immediate promotion and specialized professional development opportunities and the principal who has had three successive years of chronic failures in personnel management, community relations, and student achievement. Yet when the written evaluations of these two principals are reviewed, they are scarcely distinguishable from each other.

CRITERIA FOR
MULTIDIMENSIONAL
LEADERSHIP ASSESSMENT (MLA)

Clearly leadership evaluation and its organizational counterpart, accountability systems, can be constructive or destructive. Because the very act of evaluation can be emotionally laden and influenced by interpersonal dynamics between the person receiving the evaluation and the one rendering it, one might regard the primary differences between effective and ineffective evaluation as the intangibles of the personalities of the people involved. I dissent. Intelligent, charming, and thoughtful people are capable of participating in dreadful evaluation systems just as such delightful colleagues are capable of avoiding evaluation altogether. Effective leadership evaluation systems must be *robust*, a term with two important meanings. As it is commonly used, robust is a synonym for healthy, vigorous, and strong. Researchers use the term robust to refer to a measurement that is responsive to different conditions. Typical evaluation schemes are suited for a singular purpose, typically conformity with a bureaucratic requirement. A few special-purpose evaluation schemes are used to get the attention of a recalcitrant employee, to threaten someone who is belligerent, and perhaps even to reward someone who has done a good job. A multidimensional assessment system, however, must suit all of these purposes and more. Of greatest importance, a robust system is sufficiently dynamic that it will change as the employee and system change. Because the fundamental purpose of leadership evaluation is the improvement of individual and organizational performance, only an evaluation system that adapts to these improvements and changes will offer lasting value to the organization. What does it take for an evaluation system to be multidimensional? The language of music offers a useful acronym for the characteristics of robust evaluation systems. Music students typically learn a few terms for the volume of compositions, such as *forte*, meaning loud, and *pianissimo*, for very soft. Composers also indicate their desire for the appropriate pace of a musical piece by using either metronome markings, typically indicating the number of beats in a minute, or, more frequently, the composer describes in words the expected pace. Thus, *andante* suggests a walking tempo, while *largo* suggests a very slow and deliberate pace. By contrast, the words used to describe exceptionally fast paces are *vivace* and *presto*. The pace of change, the dynamic nature of great music, and great organizations require the ability not only to work, but also to operate, when appropriate, at *tempo presto*. When amateur musicians attempt to perform at the presto level, they sometimes allow haste to supercede clarity. That is not at all what the tempo marking means. No matter how quickly the music is played, each note has meaning, each phrase conveys a melody, and each harmony contains essential structure, even if the notes linger for but fractions of a second.

When we say that leadership evaluation systems must meet the criteria for *presto*, it is a reference not only to speed but to clarity and adaptability. Each letter in the word presto serves to remind us of an important characteristic of

P	*Proactive.*	It starts before the first day on the job.
R	*Reciprocal.*	It gives the leader the opportunity to provide feedback to the organization.
E	*Empowering.*	Leaders have authority to make decisions that will improve their effectiveness.
S	*Standards based.*	Success is not a guessing game, as the standards for proficient and exemplary leadership are clear.
T	*Truthful.*	Feedback is honest and accurate.
O	*Objective.*	Leadership behaviors are a matter of description, not conjecture.

robust evaluation (see Figure 2.2). First, the evaluation is proactive. This characteristic is perhaps the most distinctive quality of presto evaluation—it is completed before the leader's first day on the job. By rendering an evaluation before the job has started, both the leader and the employer must acknowledge some important truths. However joyous the love-fest surrounding the hiring decision in which the victorious candidate is identified as the best person for the job, this ego-fueled euphoria can be tempered with the knowledge that even the best person for the job is not perfect. By acknowledging those imperfections in the first proactive evaluation, both parties avoid the shocking recognition that usually comes after a year or two of employment that the candidate falls short of perfection. The leader expects to grow, develop, learn, and improve, and guided by a proactive evaluation, the leader can identify specific areas in which development and growth are most needed.

Second, the presto evaluation is reciprocal. When a leader discusses how the organization plays a role in improving the leader's performance, particularly after a critical evaluation, the idea that there are multiple causes for both successes and failures strikes some observers as little more than excuse-making. Good leaders, the reasoning goes, share credit generously and take responsibility personally when things go badly. While personal responsibility is an admirable trait, this characteristic is most laudable when it is accurate. In the complex world of educational organizations, most results, both good and bad, are the result of the leader's actions and a host of other influences within and outside the organization. During the process of recruiting and hiring a leader, the organization is acutely aware of how it influences the leader's future success and thus there are numerous conversations about resource support, professional development, and the need to take care of the leader's health and nurture the leader's family. These ideals become faint memories when later evaluations turn to the issues of school finance, student achievement, and organizational politics. If, by contrast, each leadership evaluation is, by design, reciprocal—each party to the evaluation contributing ideas how the other party can change, improve, and make better decisions that lead to individual and organizational success—then the evaluative process is of necessity more collaborative and productive. The act of evaluating involves not only rendering judgments, but listening to another view of how one's own decisions affect organizational success. We dispense with the common evaluation fantasy in which the evaluator presumes that changes in the acts and decisions of the person being evaluated will, by themselves, change the system.

The third criterion of robust evaluation is closely linked to the first two. The letter *e* in presto represents the empowering characteristic of effective evaluation. Unfortunately, the language of psychology, not altogether unfairly labeled psycho-babble by its critics, has associated empowerment with a feeling rather than an accurate description of the relationship between a person with power and the ability to exercise that power. If evaluation is to be empowering, it is not that the leader being evaluated feels good, feels powerful, has heard reassuring words about the importance of empowerment, or even possesses a colorful empowerment poster prominently displayed in the office, hallway, or conference room. Empowerment in a robust evaluation system is precisely what we mean it to be—a system that allows, indeed requires, the person being evaluated to become an active participant in the evaluation process rather than the passive recipient of the critiques of others. If there are leadership successes worthy of celebration, then other stakeholders in the system had a role in those successes and their contributions must be acknowledged and understood. If there are challenges, then it is unlikely that the leader or any other individual is singularly responsible for the difficulty but that the decisions and actions of others contributed to each challenge. Empowering evaluation requires both the leader and those conducting the evaluation to cast a wide net to identify the sources of successes and failure. There is, of course, a thin line between the acknowledgment of multiple causes of failure and the generation of excuses. Psychiatrist M. Scott Peck noted in his best-selling book, *The Road Less Traveled* (1978), that neuroses and character defects are two sides of the same coin. The neurotic leader assumes too much responsibility, presuming that every error is his or her own personal responsibility. The leader with a character defect, by contrast, assumes that all problems are caused by others and thus assumes the mantle of the permanent victim. Neither extreme is productive or allows the leader or the organization to improve. Empowered leaders, by contrast, have a healthy understanding that they are not the sole causes for success or failure and they use that knowledge not for the avoidance of responsibility but for the constructive understanding of the links between individual and organizational actions and successful results.

The fourth characteristic of robust evaluation is that it is standards based. The case for academic standards in schools is clear. In contrast to an evaluative system that pits one student against another, the use of academic standards compares the performance of each student against objective standards. Thus standards-based evaluation does not fall prey to the fallacy of false complacency, in which nonproficient students are reassured because they are better than other students, or the error of inaccurate disparagement, in which proficient students are labeled as inferior because other students are more proficient. Without standards, evaluations are constantly subject to the shifting sands of relative performance rather than the bedrock of clear, fair, and immutable standards. Every student knows what the definition of *success* is and understands that the key to success is hard work, deep understanding, and the pursuit of a specific goal—not merely the ability to be a little bit better than a colleague. When viewed in this light, standards are not merely a nice idea or passing educational fad, but the very foundation of fairness, a value that endures throughout time. Fads change; values do not. Because standards-based evaluation is essential for the fair and accurate evaluation of student performance, the use of standards also provides the opportunity for fair, accurate, and comprehensive evaluation of educational leaders. In evaluating leadership performance, the question is not, Who is the best leader? but rather, How does this particular leader perform compared to the organization's explicit expectations? Much of the rest of this book is concerned with the establishment of standards for leadership performance, but there will be no easy recipe for leadership evaluation. An essential component of effective leadership is the development of a mutual understanding between the leader and the organization about the specific behaviors and professional practices that are associated with exemplary leadership. The language suggested in this volume is only a starting point. Ultimately, the language of exemplary leadership must be developed locally, so that board members, leaders, parents, community members, teachers, and all stakeholders are comfortable articulating what success means. This is directly analogous to the need of teachers and students to collaborate to create standards that are meaningful in the language of students. While state standards are frequently laden with pedagogical terminology and educational jargon, the academic performance standards articulated by students tend to be specific and clear. By allowing students to interpret and articulate state academic standards, ambiguity is reduced, clarity enhanced, and student performance improved. Similarly, by using the leadership standards in this book as a starting point for further interpretation and clarification by the reader and the reader's colleagues, ambiguity will be reduced and clarity enhanced. Only when leaders know what is expected and only when that knowledge is broadly shared throughout the organization can there be a reasonable expectation that leadership performance will improve.

One of the most important characteristics of standards-based leadership evaluation is that it provides a continuum of evaluation. Many leadership evaluations fall prey to the binary fallacy in which the evaluator must respond yes or no to a series of questions regarding leadership performance. In virtually every case of leadership performance, however, such a binary response does not do justice to the complexity of leadership behavior. If the criterion is successful communication with parents and community members, there are few instances in which a leader is either successful or unsuccessful. Some leaders are proactive communicators, using multiple channels of communication. Moreover, these exemplary leaders conduct frequent checks for the effectiveness of their communication and make mid-course corrections throughout the year to improve the quality and effectiveness of their communication. These leaders also recognize that an important component of communication is listening as well as speaking, and thus they create many opportunities for parents and other community stakeholders to know that their voices are heard, understood, and respected by educational leaders. Finally, these leaders regularly share their insights and effective practices with colleagues, spreading their effectiveness throughout the organization.

This exemplary level of performance stands in contrast to the leader who is proficient, meeting all legal requirements for communication, complying with all board policies on the subject, getting reports out on time, holding scheduled conferences, and following the stakeholder communication plan. The proficient leader is significantly different from the leader who may have a plan and is aware of district communication policies, but fails to implement those policies consistently or effectively. This *progressing* leader understands what is required and, with coaching and supervision, can become proficient. This is quite different from the leader at the lowest level, the one failing to meet the standard. This leader does not have a communication policy for stakeholders, has no method of monitoring it, shows little awareness of district communication policies, and displays little or no ability to understand and implement those policies. Whereas the progressing leader can be coached to improve effectiveness, the leader failing to meet standards requires intensive intervention, assignment to different job responsibilities, or termination. Because each level of performance is clearly specified with both labels and unambiguous descriptive terms, the leader and the evaluators know in advance what the expectations are, and they both know after the evaluation precisely what is necessary to proceed to the next higher level of performance or how to maintain the highest level of performance. The typical leadership evaluation that might have a criterion, such as stakeholder communication, followed by ratings such as outstanding, very good, satisfactory, below average, and failing, are unhelpful, unclear, and ultimately destructive. They neither motivate the effective leader to thrive and share wisdom throughout the organization nor motivate the ineffective leader to improve performance.

The fifth characteristic of effective leadership evaluation is that it is *truthful*. Perhaps it is obvious—of course evaluation must be truthful. Unfortunately, this elemental demand for accuracy and honesty is absent from an astonishing number of leadership evaluations. The research on which this book is based suggests that the lack of honesty is not necessarily the result of malice, but of ambiguity. Honesty, whether it involves praise or admonition, is an essential part of effective feedback. Just as accurate feedback is essential to improved student performance, honesty is an essential element of improved leadership performance. Unfortunately, honesty is frequently associated with negative feedback. The phrase "I've got to be honest with you" is too frequently a qualifier for criticism, implying, apparently, that when appreciation and affirmation are provided, it is not necessary to say, "I've got to be honest." How much more effective it would be if every comment on leadership performance were accurate, with no protests about the honesty of the statements necessary.

The sixth and final characteristic of robust leadership evaluation is that it is *objective*. The mere presence of standards does not necessarily indicate objectivity. The language of standards varies widely from the objective ("this leader provides evidence of multiple channels of communication with parents") to the subjective ("this leader communicates effectively with parents"). Leadership literature is littered with phrases that demand that leaders be insightful, wise, empathetic, and action oriented, but none of these descriptions provides explicit direction to the leader who aspires to these qualities. What specific behaviors are associated with empathy? How can the evaluation and the leader herself objectively state that she does or does not meet the criteria for empathy? The demand for objectivity strikes some people as impossible. "Either you've got it or you don't—it's an art, not a science, and you can't describe effective leadership with precision." The same has been said of writing, teaching, and for that matter, the practice of medicine. But in each of these disciplines, it has been possible to acknowledge that there is an element of elusive art, but there are also objectively described characteristics that are either present or absent in the best writers, teachers, and physicians. That is why we can have standards for writers, teachers, and doctors. We preserve their creativity, while providing a safety net of effective practice that we agree constitutes proficient practice. Similarly, leaders can vary widely in their decision-making style, while all agreeing that decisions must be based on evidence. Leaders can vary widely in their approach to teaching and curriculum, while agreeing that students must know in advance what they must know and be able to do in order to be successful.

The risk in a commitment to objectivity is that a set of leadership guidelines will become so hyperspecific that the leader has no room for creativity, discretion, and the exercise of authority based on changing circumstances. Such a risk is an argument against poor leadership standards, but not an argument against objective leadership standards. We must challenge the presumption that, in the absence of an attempt at objectivity, we will have educational nirvana, in which leaders instinctively do the right thing. Good motives and noble intentions are not sufficient for effective practice. Leaders—all of us— need to know what the expectations are if we are to meet those expectations.

In sum, just as the term *presto* indicates speed and clarity in music, robust leadership evaluation provides feedback that is quick, clear, and constructive. Effective leadership evaluation is

- *Proactive.* It starts before the first day on the job.
- *Reciprocal.* It gives the leader the opportunity to provide feedback to the organization.
- *Empowering.* Leaders have authority to make decisions that will improve their effectiveness.
- *Standards based.* Success is not a guessing game, as the standards for proficient and exemplary leadership are clear.
- *Truthful.* Feedback is honest and accurate.
- *Objective.* Leadership behaviors are a matter of description, not conjecture.

IMPLICATIONS OF A NEW VISION FOR LEADERSHIP EVALUATION

If educational systems embrace robust leadership evaluation, there are immediate and profound implications for policymakers, the leaders of today, and the leaders of the future. For policymakers, robust evaluation requires an extraordinary amount of specificity with regard to their expectations of educational leaders. The fuzzy descriptions infused with the jargon of the past will not substitute for the precision required in robust evaluation. Moreover, policymakers must not only identify the characteristics that they expect leaders to meet, but board members and legislators must also examine their own decisions and behavior, acknowledging that they, too, will be evaluated in a reciprocal leadership evaluation system. If policymakers take this matter seriously, they cannot place a want ad for a new school administrator without fundamentally rethinking the responsibilities of that position and the role that the system, including the senior leaders and policymakers, play in making that new administrator a success or failure. For example, if the board intends to hire or promote a leader who is expected to have an influence on student achievement, then the board must ask, Will this person have authority over the matters that we know will profoundly influence student achievement, including curriculum; schedule; teacher assignment to courses; teacher hiring, transfer, and dismissal; and student intervention programs? In my experience, policymakers are long on expectations of leaders and short on providing the authority, resources, and policy support necessary for leadership success.

The implications for the leaders of today and tomorrow are similarly significant. In the past, leadership evaluation has lurched between the two extremes of ambiguity and hyperspecificity. In the former, an undefined mix of good intentions, savvy community relations, and a grasp of central office politics was sufficient to provide security, if not success.

> Sure the school has lousy achievement—what do you expect? He's been there for 18 years and is about the only person who wants that job—do you think we could get anybody else to volunteer for that school? He comes to meetings and gets the paperwork in on time. Let him retire with dignity.

In the latter, a single two-hour test could undermine a decades-long career. The hyperspecific evaluation abandons every leadership responsibility for a focus on a single indicator.

> I don't care how much you have improved, how many children you have saved from dropping out, or how many teachers you have recruited and developed. You're history if the fourth grade reading scores don't rise by two more points.

School leaders will insist, sometimes through collective bargaining agents or leadership professional associations, that the shifting sands associated with the terms *accountability* and *evaluation* are insufficient. They will require clarity of expectations and authority to be successful. They will expect to regularly communicate their expectations and provide feedback to other elements of the school system and community, just as they will routinely receive feedback from multiple sources. With more than 40 percent of principals retiring in the next five years and a growing number finding opportunities outside of education, leadership talent is a seller's market. The best leaders of today and the most promising leaders of tomorrow will not accept an interview for a position that fails to provide an evaluation system that is constructive, fair, and clear—that is, in brief, robust.

The rest of this book is concerned with the development and implementation of a leadership evaluation system for your organization. You can use it for second grade team leaders, secondary school department heads, central office division directors, superintendents, principals, or any other leadership position. Because leadership can mean so many different things to different people, we will take care to define what leadership is and what it is not. Too many qualities and characteristics masquerade as leadership in the popular imagination and much of the literature on the subject. Thus, in the next chapter we will consider those qualities that are often conflated with genuine leadership.

Moving Beyond 3
One-Dimensional
Leadership Evaluation

Topics Presented in Chapter 3 Include

✓ The Prevalence of One-Dimensional Evaluation

✓ Leadership Is More Than Test Scores

✓ Leadership Is More Than Popularity

✓ Leadership Is More Than Obedience

THE PREVALENCE OF
ONE-DIMENSIONAL EVALUATION

One might think that one-dimensional evaluation is so obviously flawed that few leadership evaluation systems would depend upon a single indicator. In theory, those conducting leadership evaluations can produce a long list of dimensions for leadership competence. In practice, however, one-dimensional evaluation is strikingly common. It begins with federal and state accountability systems that are almost entirely focused on test scores. In 2002, only 18 states provided reading assessments for every grade from Grades 3 through 8 as required by the No Child Left Behind Act signed by President Bush early in 2002, and only half a dozen states meet the new federal requirements for testing in mathematics (General Accounting Office, 2002). Thus the primary emphasis in educational accountability will be, for the vast majority of states, the implementation of a more comprehensive testing program. For those states already in compliance with the testing provisions of the law, there is considerable flexibility in the definition of "adequate yearly progress," so that states may take into account not only student performance on test scores, but also other accountability indicators in teaching, learning, curriculum, and leadership.

A consideration of many dimensions of leadership success and a judgment made on the preponderance of the evidence would create what I have described elsewhere as a holistic view of educational accountability (Reeves, 2001). To be fair, the federal legislation clearly allows states to avoid an exclusive reliance on test data, particularly when the sample sizes are small, mobility is high, or other factors affect the validity and reliability of the data emerging from the testing program. Few if any states, however, appear to be poised to take advantage of this flexibility. Only one state, Nebraska, has seized the opportunity to use the federal testing mandates as a device for improving teacher-created classroom assessments (Christensen, 2001). Unless policymakers significantly shift their understanding of educational success, then *progress* means higher test scores, and the failure of test scores to rise is a self-evident indicator of failure. The message to current and aspiring educational leaders is therefore clear: Whatever else you think leadership success is supposed to be, it is really only the extent to which your average test scores increase.

With the foregoing comments, I do not join the antitesting chorus that demands that all standards-based tests should cease and leaders should heed the teachers' plea to "just close the door and let me teach." In fact, academic standards have little meaning if students, parents, teachers, leaders, taxpayers, and other stakeholders do not know the extent to which students are proficient in achieving those standards. Moreover, fairness and equity are fundamental values that are not served when the performance expectations for children are governed by neighborhood and personal preference rather than academic standards. My concern is that the emphasis on a single indicator will inevitably lead to unintended and undesirable consequences. For the teenager who focuses only on the indicator of weight, an eating disorder is a distinct possibility, as other data on deteriorating health are ignored as long as the weight declines. An example of the danger of one-dimensional evaluation is the case of Enron, a company that formerly commanded billions of dollars in assets and employed thousands of people. The single-minded focus on stock price and reported earnings led to a series of decisions at the energy giant which then led to the largest corporate failure in U.S. history, disrupting the lives and ruining the retirement savings of tens of thousands of people. Just a year before the collapse, however, Enron's numbers looked good and the company was thus applauded in virtually every corner of Wall Street. We will have an "educational Enron" when a school system is found to have focused myopically on test scores to the point that dropout rates have increased, special education classifications have soared, and post-testing reviews and corrections of student answer sheets become a part of the ethical cesspool that once was known as school culture.

The problem of an excessively narrow definition of leadership success is hardly restricted to the current fixation on test scores. In other times, the single dimension on which leaders were evaluated might have been attendance at central office meetings, relationships with the teacher's union, popularity with parents, or successful engagement in organizational politics. In fact, leaders ignore these factors at their peril. Successful leaders need to have a positive impact on student achievement while maintaining good relationships with parents and staff members. While leaders need not be obsequious, a decent respect for central office colleagues and an understanding of organizational culture and politics is not inappropriate. Leadership evaluation falls apart, however, when any one of these elements becomes the single defining feature of leadership success or failure.

In this chapter, we will examine three common themes associated with leadership success: student test scores, personal popularity, and obedience, particularly to prevailing cultural norms, as well as compliance with federal, state, and local policies. In fact, each of these themes plays a role for the successful school leader, but none of them is sufficient for sustained success. Nevertheless, when many educational leaders examine the areas on which they devote most of their time, these three themes recur with startling consistency.

LEADERSHIP IS MORE THAN TEST SCORES

A balanced approach to leadership and test scores has proven increasingly elusive among educational leaders. Some superintendents and many principals have become openly defiant of the current emphasis on testing, equating testing programs with the demise of educational values. Others have embraced the quantification offered by testing to measure school and teacher quality, and clearly define their successes and failures based on changes in test scores. One trend, however, is undeniable and has persisted throughout the decades that standardized tests have been fixtures of public education. This trend is the tendency of students and schools to improve as they and their teachers become more familiar with test format and content and for the same students and teachers to fail to improve when tests change and there is, as a result, a wider gap between the taught curriculum and the tested curriculum (Popham, 1999). The problem is not necessarily with the tests themselves, but rather with the presumption that individual tests measure educational quality. Leaders of schools where students arrive at kindergarten reading fluently may engage in unwarranted self-congratulation, while leaders in schools where students arrive at age seven or eight with no understanding of English and no exposure to the social norms of school or any other extra-familial group may accept an inaccurate view of their impotence in the face of overwhelming social, economic, and linguistic challenges. While the trend toward value-added accountability analysis may offer some potential to level the evaluative scheme between principals in rich and poor areas, even this sophisticated accountability tool relies exclusively on effect variables—student test scores—and fails to explore or even measure the decisions and actions of teachers and school leaders. The presumption of any model, whether using mean test scores or value-added models, is that the relationship between leader, teacher, and student is an imponderable black box and thus only the output can be examined. Any other discipline in the natural or social sciences that took such a facile approach would be subject to well-deserved ridicule.

The exclusive reliance on test scores is more than a methodological problem; It is a moral one. Consider the possibility that learning really is an imponderable black box beyond human understanding and that a commitment to scientific precision suggests that a reliance on test scores is just the best we can do and maintain any semblance of reliability in evaluation. Even if the proposition were true, the implicit message is that leaders should first find the effects (healthy kids with prosperous parents who speak English) and then supplant themselves into the situation. A migration of leadership talent away from students and schools most in need is then inevitable. It is as if the most successful heart surgeons leave their hospitals and commit their practice to giving blood pressure tests to professional athletes who are in perfect medical condition and who have already committed themselves to a regimen of diet and exercise. The surgeon will have a very high success rate because few of the patients will die of coronary disease. Never mind the fact that the physician was no more responsible for the health of the professional athletes than she had been for the illnesses of the patients who sought her treatment in the hospital. In an environment in which the effects are all that matters, responsibility goes out the window with logic.

Leaders should neither ignore test scores nor embrace them as the sole indicator of student learning, teacher ability, or school quality. Rather, leaders must use test scores as one strategic piece of the complex puzzle they must solve. As a weather forecaster considers data on wind, temperature, history, and personal experience, so also must those evaluating educational leaders consider test scores as an important piece of data, but not the only piece on which they will predict future leadership performance. Consider two leaders with identical test scores for their schools. The first says,

> I just don't understand it. We tried everything—new training programs, computer programs, and a mailing to all the parents. Nothing seems to work. The parents don't read what I send them and the kids just don't care. The staff is demoralized and frankly, so am I. But there's just not much I can do about it—I'm doing all that can possibly be done.

Another leader whose school had the same level of student achievement, as measured by test scores, offers a different insight:

> The average test scores are pretty discouraging, but I've discovered some very interesting things in the data. First, we had exceptional gains in math problem solving—an area where we really concentrated. We provided 90 additional instructional minutes each week, every teacher used the same strategy, and I reviewed student progress charts at least once a month. I personally met with students and parents for those students who were not achieving proficiency after a few months. Our kids really shined, showing double-digit gains in this part of the test. Unfortunately, I failed to provide the same kind of leadership in reading comprehension, writing, and vocabulary. Those scores caused our averages—the numbers posted in the newspaper—to look lousy. I'm not happy about it, but I've got a clear idea on how to build on our strengths and use that knowledge to directly address our challenges.

Next year, we'll see not only continued improvements in math problem solving, but we're going to knock it out of the park for reading, writing, and vocabulary.

In an evaluative system that rests entirely on test scores, both of these leaders receive identical treatment. They may be equally scorned, equally tolerated, equally transferred to different positions, or even equally terminated. But a moment's reflection on the analyses offered by these two leaders makes clear that they are dramatically different with respect to their understanding of the present and their potential for the future. These differences, obvious only to those who consider more data than test scores, create an exceptional opportunity for the organization to recognize excellence that may be hidden by temporarily poor test score data. Moreover, it will prevent the organization from recognizing ineffectiveness in those instances where the first leader coexists with adequate test scores. The scores mask the failures of the ineffective leader. The situation is even worse as prospective leaders may attempt to emulate the strategies—including helplessness, impotence, and cynicism—engendered by the first leader. Just as a society that values only weight loss will unwittingly validate anorexia and drug abuse, an organization that values only test scores will unwittingly validate mediocrity and ineffective leadership practices because it fails to differentiate among the many leadership variables linked to student performance.

LEADERSHIP IS MORE THAN POPULARITY

In some parts of the country, school superintendents are selected in popular elections. By definition, popularity is a requirement for the job. Although most school systems now select the superintendent through board appointment, and principals are always appointed by superintendent or board action, the personal popularity of the leader remains a key ingredient in both initial selection and ultimate termination. The demand for popularity is a conundrum, as there are both positive and negative attributes of leadership that are popular. Most people would agree that it is popular—that is, approved by the people—for one to be ethical, competent, and fair. However, popularity is not a quality bestowed only by a group, but by individuals. Thus while the group may approve of behavior that is ethical and competent, the individual may prefer behavior that serves the private interests of the few at the expense of the many.

Evaluators of educational leaders risk sending mixed signals when it comes to personal popularity. They want, for example, the leader to be an effective communicator and to have good relationships with students, staff, and community members. Does that mean that students, staff, and community members must always agree with the decisions of the leader? Does that mean that the leader must always consult with students, staff, and community members to achieve consensus and gain broadly based input on the decision? Leaders will inevitably make difficult decisions that are, at least with some stakeholders, unpopular. It is a very short leap from an individual decision being unpopular to the person who made that decision losing popular support. I have said to national gatherings of educational leaders with my tongue not entirely planted in my cheek, "You don't get to choose whether to be fired, but only how to be fired. So you had better make sure that you get fired for the right reason." One might think that most job losses by educational leaders would be matters of total incompetence or grave moral principle. The reality is that when popularity is the primary factor in leadership evaluation, then astonishingly trivial matters can become the lynchpin of leadership success and failure. The following is just a partial list of real leadership decisions that resulted in leaders losing their jobs or having them placed in jeopardy:

- Refused to fire the football coach after a losing season
- Hired a gay librarian
- Failed to attend voluntary district staff meetings, despite significant success in improved student discipline, building safety, and academic achievement
- Failed to reside in the district, despite dramatic increases in student achievement, an award for positive labor relations, and national recognition for excellence
- Supported a teacher who failed students for cheating
- Supported an athletic director's decision to hire a girl's basketball coach who was not the choice of a vocal board member
- Failed to provide personal support for a ballot issue on charter school initiatives
- Changed bus schedule to provide additional professional development for teachers

Veteran leaders who are reading this book will nod with recognition. It is neither the cataclysmic issues of the day nor profound matters of leadership principles that lead to job jeopardy, but the quotidian details of daily life that, when disrupted, cause the leader to be threatened with career disruption.

Does this mean that effective leaders should scorn popularity and strike a deliberately independent, even provocative, stance? Of course not. Effective leaders must choose their battles carefully. Popularity is not a bad thing unless purchased at the price of moral compromise. But universal popularity is neither possible nor desirable. The person who, it is claimed, is "loved by everyone" either has a constituency of clones or is not telling each element of that constituency the same thing. The leaders who attempt chameleon-like reflection of their surroundings will eventually be caught. School systems are like small towns in which every comment by current or aspiring leaders travels at the speed of light to others. With even the slightest divergence of opinion, leaders who attempt to be all things to all people will be caught in a trap of their own making. The only remedy to the vain (in both senses of the word) search for popularity is authenticity. The authentic leader looks his constituents in the eye and says, "Some of you will agree with this, some of you won't care, and others of you will vehemently disagree. But at least you know that I'm telling you all the same thing and that my position on this matter doesn't change based on who is in the room."

Authenticity has its price, as five 20th century leaders know well. The stories of Winston Churchill, Nelson Mandela, Gerald Ford, Indira Gandhi, and Jimmy Carter illustrate that authenticity can have tragic consequences for individuals, even as it provides opportunities for the nations they served. Churchill was revered as a war leader and then turned out of office after the victories of the Allies in World War II. President Nelson Mandela languished in a jail for decades after leading the fight for freedom and equality in South Africa. Only very late in life was his courage and persistence rewarded, and even after assuming his position as president, he was buffeted on all sides by critics who simultaneously accused him of doing too much and not enough.

One of the best examples in history of leadership authenticity is Gerald Ford, who succeeded Richard Nixon after he resigned the presidency. Although President Ford only served for two years in the tumultuous years after Watergate and the Vietnam War, he should be remembered for his moral courage. Comedians lampooned President Ford as the bumbling golfer whose errant shots hit bystanders and whose malapropisms were not the stuff of the polished professional politician. They even laughed at his earnestness, snickering at the Eagle Scout that he, in fact, was. While his presidency receives scant mention in the history books, a defining moment of moral courage was his choice of a venue for advocating an amnesty for those who protested the Vietnam War. This conflict, which had torn the United States apart and decidedly separated the World War II generation from the Baby Boomers, ended in 1975, early in the Ford administration. With images of people fleeing the U.S. embassy in Saigon flashing across television screens, the impact of the United States losing a war could not have been greater than among America's veterans who, until 1975, had never lost a war. In the economic, social, and political malaise that followed, those who had opposed the war in Vietnam may have been prescient, but they were hardly popular. Nevertheless, President Ford went before the American Legion, the nation's premier veterans' organization, to propose amnesty for those who had evaded service in Vietnam. "I want them to come home," President Ford said. Amid a crowd conditioned to deep respect for officers in command and certainly for the Commander in Chief came the astounded cries of, "No!" President Ford was defeated in 1976 by Jimmy Carter, who promised a government "as good as the American people," and he too was defeated after a single term in office.

Many political observers cited President Carter's downward spiral as beginning with his confrontation of the American people and his own cabinet to rise above the cynicism and despair of the day. In 2002, President Carter received the Nobel Peace Prize, recognizing the value of his work more than 20 years after his constituents turned him out of office. Prime Minister Indira Gandhi paid with her life for her commitment to leadership. Gunned down by a member of her own guard unit, she was a voice for women and traditionally disadvantaged groups in India. Remarkably, her stewardship of that nation coincided with a time in which Indian agriculture became self-sufficient, transforming a country that had been a perennial recipient of food from abroad into a net exporter of grain. She laid the groundwork for future development with commitments to technology, industry, and education, yet was never able to overcome the ethnic and political rivalries that eventually took her life. Churchill, Mandela, Ford, Carter, and Gandhi all illustrate the danger of honest confrontation of a difficult reality. These were all leaders who were willing to accept temporary failure for the right reasons. Their jobs were temporary. Their moral courage and willingness to confront difficult challenges were permanent. All had been enormously popular for a brief period of time. All lost their popularity when they preferred honor to obeisance. Every leader—certainly every educational leader—must make similar choices during a career. With good policymakers and enlightened senior leadership, honorable choices do not subject a career to permanent jeopardy. With morally bankrupt policymakers and intellectually vapid senior leadership, however, it is a certainty that no good deed will go unpunished. Whether those evaluating educational leaders are perceptive or pernicious, the standard of popularity is insufficient for the determination of leadership success and failure.

LEADERSHIP IS MORE THAN OBEDIENCE

At the military academies and private military schools in the United States, new cadets and midshipmen are put through rituals that are variously known as "beast barracks," "hell week," and "summer training." Whatever the label, the reasoning is the same: Leaders must learn to follow orders before they can give them. For some future military leaders, these experiences provide a nuanced view of leadership. For example, a military leader schooled in both the norms of obedience and the complexities of 21st century organizations might conclude, "I learned that some orders, such as those involving safety, are necessary. Some orders, such as those involving etiquette, are important in the context of tradition, respect, and continuity. And some orders, such as those requiring us to memorize nonsense rhymes, are just silly holdovers from an earlier era and if I'm given the opportunity to change those, I will in the fullness of time." For an unfortunate few, the nuance is lost and only obedience remains. Any order, whether vital or trivial, is an order. When confronted with a failure, analysis is supplanted with the obligatory "No excuse, sir!"

In the context of educational leadership, obedience is not the mindless trait of the amoral soldier, but a necessary component of an educational world that is governed by federal, state, and local regulations. Effective leaders must comply with laws, policies, and guidelines. But obedience is not enough. Thoughtful leaders must persistently identify, probe, and exploit flexibility in the rules. The objective is not compliance, but the achievement of the mission and values of the school system. While the rules cannot be flouted, neither must they be the only criteria by which the leader is judged: "Yes, it's true that students aren't proficient and that our values have been compromised, but I can assure you that I am in full compliance with the regulations." That is not the motto that will mobilize the exhausted and discouraged educators and school leaders I know.

We now know what effective leadership evaluation is not, and it is time to explore a specific system for developing and implementing leadership evaluation in your organization. In the next chapter, we will explore the essential building blocks of such a system, describing each element of leadership performance across four different levels of proficiency. We cannot have effective leadership evaluation if we are unwilling to articulate what it is. "I know it when I see it," does not pass the test. We are now called upon to transform theory into reality. What does the successful evaluation of educational leadership really look like? In the following chapters, we will describe in detail the behaviors and characteristics that separate exemplary leaders from those who are proficient, progressing, or failing to meet essential leadership standards.

Creating an Improved Leadership Evaluation System 4

We expect too much of leaders. In fact, our expectations are frequently impossible because success in one area may lead to a lack of success in another. For example, we expect leaders to create and maintain a positive climate within the organization, and this positive climate should be reflected in a staff that is cheerful, committed, positive, and enthusiastic. This general characteristic of staff satisfaction should be reflected in other indicators, such as low employee turnover and the absence of employee complaints or union grievances. At the same time, we expect the leader to implement new and challenging initiatives, some of which may be so upsetting to traditionalists who resent change that opponents may file grievances, complain loudly, and even leave the organization. Demands for universally popular change initiatives are unrealistic and silly, yet leadership evaluation contains many such potential contradictions. We want higher levels of student achievement and the rigorous standards required to attain such a goal, and at the same time we insist upon positive parent relationships. Complaints by a dozen parents to the central office may appear to be an avalanche of discontent, particularly when they all occur in the same day or at the same board meeting. Those complaints might come from parents who are being told, perhaps for the first time in many years, that their children need to work harder and are not proficient in some critical standards.

These challenges provide three alternatives to policymakers and senior leaders. First, they can throw up their hands and contend that the challenges of educational leadership are inherently contradictory and thus impossible. Second, they can choose the politically safe path that blends popularity with mediocrity, knowing that far fewer people complain about low standards and poor achievement than they do about schedule changes, modifications of tradition, and wounded egos. The third path is transparency, acknowledging that we do, in fact, have contradictory expectations. This calls for the specification of the critical areas of leadership performance, called domains of leadership, and the clear identification of performance levels for each domain. It is quite likely that a leader will exhibit exemplary performance in one domain of leadership while falling short of proficiency in another domain. The objective of the third path of leadership evaluation is neither the illusion of perfection nor the enticement of the apparently safe allure of popularity at the cost of achievement and innovation. A transparent evaluation system will state unambiguously that leaders must communicate with parents and faculty members in a respectful and open manner, gaining their trust and support. At the same time, leaders must make difficult decisions that will engender angry challenges from some parents and faculty members.

When an evaluation system makes a leader appear to be uniformly outstanding in every domain of leadership, it is quite likely that the evaluations are deeply flawed or that some domains are missing. Such distortions creep into leadership evaluation systems because grade inflation is as rampant for educational leaders as it is for students. The identification of flaws becomes the subject of defensive argumentation rather than a learning conversation. Effective leadership evaluations, by contrast, invite a conversation on the real-world challenges and contradictory demands that confront every leader.

It seems rational enough that leaders and those evaluating them could agree that perfection is not an option. Nevertheless, evaluations that fall short of glowing admiration are rare, and even the most oblique references to needs for improvement are overwhelmed by praise on other dimensions of leadership. One reason for this is the self-fulfilling prophesy effect. Boards want to believe that they made the right decision in hiring the superintendent, and thus (at least for the board members voting in favor of that decision) the evaluations of the superintendent tend to justify that decision. Superintendents want to believe that they made the right decision in hiring other leaders, and the same cascading effect takes place. Moreover, the national shortage of qualified leaders diminishes the likelihood that performance issues in leaders will be confronted directly, as there are other school systems ready to offer a contract to the school leader who feels insufficiently appreciated. These distortions all arise from the negative connotations associated with the word *evaluation.* Because any performance issue is, in this distorted view, a reflection of some inherent defect in the personal characteristics of the leader, those conducting the evaluation hesitate to say anything negative at all. Any attempt at performance improvement sounds, in this twisted interpretation of evaluation, like judgment, blame, and the association of a performance challenge with a personality defect.

Concerns over raising performance challenges are valid. Leaders who have been the recipient of awkward attempts to raise performance issues may recall how legitimate performance issues became, with a few strokes of the evaluator's pen, a personal attack. The leader who needs to develop more empathy and improve interpersonal relationships is described as "aloof and unfriendly." The leader who needs to explain more consistently the rationale behind decisions before issuing them is described as "imperious and demanding." Such descriptions are never helpful, because they focus on a component of personality rather than a changeable behavior. The challenge in leadership evaluation is to identify those characteristics that are essential for leadership success and then to associate those characteristics with specific behaviors. I may be, in fact, imperious and demanding. But I can learn to listen more before formulating an opinion, deliberately seek a wide range of views as part of a decision-making process, and fully communicate the rationale for important decisions rather than merely announcing them.

DOMAINS OF LEADERSHIP PERFORMANCE

Each organization must establish its own domains of leadership based on its cultural environment and unique needs. Although there are some common elements of leadership effectiveness, this chapter serves only to illustrate some alternatives the reader may consider, not to prescribe a singular approach that meets the needs of every educational organization. While the specification of leadership domains is a local task, the suggestions contained in this chapter may help to jump-start that process. When any group of stakeholders begins to brainstorm leadership domains, it is likely to think of a very long list of characteristics of leadership performance. Some of these characteristics are within the leader's direct control. Leaders can personally control the words they write on a faculty evaluation, the manner in which they conduct faculty meetings, their communications with students, faculty, and staff, and a host of other leadership practices that are directed by the leader. Other domains of leadership are subject to the leader's direct influence. In many schools, the assignment of teachers and approval of course material and daily schedule are influenced by the leader, but are not a matter of direct leadership control. Other domains, such as parent involvement and the professional development activities of the staff, are indirectly influenced by the leader. Finally, there are a large number of factors that are neither controlled nor influenced by the leader. For example, it is axiomatic that 21st century educational leaders are expected to improve student achievement, and we know that there are some actions that school leaders can control or influence that will have an impact on student learning as measured in achievement tests. There are other factors, however, including prenatal care and the nutritional choices made by students and parents, that extend far beyond the influence or control of even the most extraordinary educational leader. Figure 4.1 shows the four levels of influence into which each domain may fall.

When considering potential leadership domains for an evaluation system, it is important to consider the degree of influence the leader will exert over that

Figure 4.1 Leadership Domains: Degrees of Control and Influence

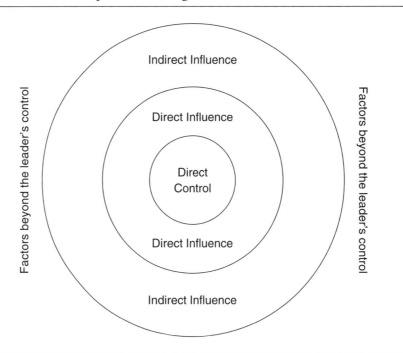

domain. A cardinal principal of leadership evaluation is that the evaluation system will have the greatest impact on improving individual and organizational performance when the evaluation is focused on those decisions and behaviors that are under the direct control of the leader. To a lesser but still important degree, evaluation should focus on those areas the leader can influence, but not directly control. However, the inclusion in an evaluation system of variables outside the control or influence of the leader is counterproductive, as it fails to distinguish between the leader who is genuinely effective and one who is merely lucky (Reeves, 2002a).

Figure 4.2 includes possible dimensions for inclusion in a leadership evaluation system. This is hardly an exhaustive list, but may serve to accelerate the brainstorming process for your school system.

The leaders, policymakers, and stakeholders in your school system might identify 100 or more areas in which a leader should be proficient, and persuasive arguments can be made in favor of including each one of those 100 domains in a leadership evaluation system. Nevertheless, a cardinal principle of measurement is that it is more effective to measure a few things frequently than many things infrequently. Thus the original list that is the result of group brainstorming must be pared down to its essentials. In the end, you should ask these questions to filter your list of leadership domains:

- Is this domain within the control or direct influence of the leader?
- Is this domain directly related to our mission and vision?
- Is this domain subject to objective description so that the people evaluating the leader have a clear and consistent understanding of what successful leadership in this domain really means?

Figure 4.2 Potential Leadership Domains

1. Resilience
   1.1. Constructive reaction to disappointment and failure
   1.2. Willingness to admit error and learn from it
   1.3. Constructively handles disagreement with leadership and policy decisions
   1.4. Constructively handles dissent from subordinates
   1.5. Explicit improvement of specific performance areas based on the previous leadership evaluation

2. Personal Behavior
   2.1. Integrity
   2.2. Emotional self-control
   2.3. Compliance with legal and ethical requirements in relationships with employees
   2.4. Compliance with legal and ethical requirements in relationships with students
   2.5. Tolerance of different points of view within the boundaries of the values and mission of the organization
   2.6 Organization, including calendar, desk, office, and building(s)

3. Student Achievement
   3.1. Planning and goal setting for student achievement
   3.2. Student achievement results
   3.3. Student achievement reporting to students, parents, teachers, and other leaders
   3.4. Use of student achievement data to make instructional leadership decisions
   3.5. Understanding of student requirements and academic standards
   3.6. Understanding of present levels of student performance based on consistent assessments that reflect local and state academic standards
   3.7. Decisions in teacher assignment, course content, schedule, and student curriculum based on specific needs for improved student achievement

4. Decision Making
   4.1. Factual basis for decisions, including specific reference to internal and external data on student achievement and objective data on curriculum, teaching practices, and leadership practices
   4.2. Clear identification of decision-making structure, including which decisions are made by consensus or by staff independently, by the leader after getting input from staff, or by the teacher alone
   4.3. Decisions linked to vision, mission, and strategic priorities
   4.4. Decisions evaluated for effectiveness and revised where necessary

5. Communication
   5.1. Two-way communication with students
   5.2. Two-way communication with faculty and staff
   5.3. Two-way communication with parents and community

6. Faculty Development
   6.1. Understanding of faculty proficiencies and needs for further development
   6.2. Personal participation in leading professional development
   6.3. Formal and informal feedback to colleagues with the exclusive purpose of improving individual and organizational performance

(Continued)

Figure 4.2 Continued

7. Leadership Development
    7.1. Strong assistant administrators who are capable of immediately assuming leadership responsibility in this school or other buildings
    7.2. Consistent identification of potential future leaders
    7.3. Evidence of delegation and trust in subordinate leaders

8. Time, Task, and Project Management
    8.1. Consistently maintains daily prioritized task list
    8.2. Choices for time management reflect a focus on the most important priorities
    8.3. Complex projects have clear objectives and coherent plans
    8.4. History of completion of projects on schedule and within budget

9. Technology
    9.1. Demonstrated use of technology to improve teaching and learning
    9.2. Personal proficiency in electronic communication

10. Learning
    10.1. Personal understanding of research trends in education and leadership
    10.2. Personal professional development plan
    10.3. Professional development focus
    10.4. Application of learning

Copyright 2009 by Douglas B. Reeves. All rights reserved. Reprinted from *Assessing Educational Leaders: Evaluating Performance for Improved Individual and Organizational Results* (2nd ed.), by Douglas B. Reeves. Reproduction authorized only for the local school site that has purchased this book.

Only if a leadership dimension meets all three of these filters should it be included in your final set of leadership dimensions. There are many lofty goals that appear as leadership standards, expectations, criteria, or other components of leadership evaluation, but if they do not pass through these filters, they waste time and divert attention. If the dimension is important, but not subject to the influence or control of the leader, then evaluation on such a dimension is a prescription for frustration on all sides. If the domain is popular with a vocal segment of stakeholders, but not part of the vision and mission of the entire system, then evaluation on this dimension will risk diverting time, energy, and resources away from the most essential priorities of the organization. If the dimension is full of rhetorical flourish and fine-sounding phrases, but is not subject to objective description, then a group of evaluators may have wildly different opinions about what the dimension really means. If such differences occurred in the evaluation of student performance, we would recognize it as an unreliable assessment and distrust its results. We should apply the same high standard of objectivity and consistency to leadership evaluation.

There will undoubtedly be characteristics of leadership that stakeholders and a legion of leadership experts and authors agree are important, but which fail to pass these three filter questions. Figure 4.3 provides a worksheet for a group to use in order to apply these filter questions to each prospective leadership domain.

Figure 4.3 Worksheet for Leadership Dimensions

Leadership Domain	Leader's Impact?	Relationship to Mission and Vision	Subject to Objective Description	Comments
	4 = Direct control 3 = Direct influence 2 = Indirect influence 1 = Beyond leader's control	4 = Essential relationship 3 = Clear relationship 2 = Indirect relationship 1 = No relationship	4 = Obvious distinctions between exemplary, proficient, progressing, and failing performance levels 3 = Distinction between proficient and nonproficient performance can be specified with clarity and consistency 2 = Performance distinctions can be clarified, but are inconsistent from one evaluator to the next 1 = Subjective and not amenable to objective description	
1. Personal Behavior				
2. Student Achievement				
3. Decision Making				
4. Communication				
5. Faculty Development				
6. Leadership Development				
7. Time, Task, and Project Management				

41

Figure 4.3 Continued

Leadership Domain	Leader's Impact?	Relationship to Mission and Vision	Subject to Objective Description	Comments
8. Technology				
9. Learning				
10. Resilience				
11.				
12.				
13.				
14.				
15.				
16.				
17.				
18.				
19.				
20.				

Copyright 2009 by Douglas B. Reeves. All rights reserved. Reprinted from *Assessing Educational Leaders: Evaluating Performance for Improved Individual and Organizational Results* (2nd ed.), by Douglas B. Reeves. Reproduction authorized only for the local school site that has purchased this book.

LEADERSHIP PERFORMANCE STANDARDS

The Standards Imperative

In Chapter 2, we noted that one of the hallmarks of effective leadership evaluation is that it is standards based—the *s* in the mnemonic *presto*. The term *standards* has suffered from ambiguity, multiple meanings, and outright misuse. For example, I have heard some educators assert that the evidence of high standards is the high failure rate of students in their classes or the rarity with which students receive high grades, when neither of those criteria is related to the successful implementation of educational standards. Opponents of standards frequently use the term *standardized* as the object of their ire, failing to differentiate between standards and standardization. Given the significant potential for ambiguity and misunderstanding surrounding the topic of standards, let us carefully define terms. Whether the context is student academic performance, the evaluation of teaching professionals, the evaluation of leaders, or the evaluation of any performance of any sort in any organization, the essence of a standards-based approach is that the performance is compared to an objective standard, not to the performance of others. We do not care if the restaurant in which we are about to dine has better kitchen hygiene than the café on the corner; we only care if the restaurant meets health standards. We should not be terribly concerned or proud if our child is reading more slowly or quickly than the child next door; we should focus on whether our child meets state reading standards and is prepared to enter the next grade level with success and confidence. When we are evaluating leaders, we should gain scant comfort from a comparison of the leadership effectiveness of one person when compared to leaders in a neighboring district or state. Rather, our focus must be on the extent to which the leaders we are evaluating meet our standards and how our evaluative process can help them progress toward higher levels of performance. By focusing on performance improvement rather than comparisons to others, standards-based leadership evaluation simultaneously will encourage the leader who needs specific coaching for performance improvement and challenge leaders who might be inappropriately complacent simply because they are better than other leaders with whom they are acquainted.

The Competitive Impulse

In the real world, of course, schools and districts are always ranked against one another. Therefore the inevitable challenge is something like this: "Standards-based evaluation may be fine in theory, but our board—and the people who vote for or against its members—will still compare our performance to all the other districts in the state. It won't be good enough for me to say that I met the standards—we must be competitive with other districts!" Principals could make a similar argument, as their schools are compared to other schools in a district or state. I grant that competition is part of the educational landscape, but the essential question for leadership evaluation is *how* to improve competitive success. It is unlikely that the key to improved performance for a school or district is a chorus of critics who annually exhort the leaders with the helpful advice, "Higher!" Rather, evaluators who want to be competitive with other schools and school systems must first seek to have higher standards than their competitors. When the standards are sufficiently high, leaders who appear to be better than their competitors on the latest school rankings will continue to be challenged for continuous improvement. In addition, leaders who suffer from a drop in ranking may nevertheless be encouraged by successful achievement of other high standards.

Case Studies of the Competitive Distortions

Two examples illustrate how a leader can have a change in relative ranking that creates the illusion of success or failure that is greatly distorted without the context of standards. Roger Blackburn, principal of Maple Hill Middle School (while the names of the individuals and schools are disguised, the case studies are based on real events and people), has been under intense pressure to improve the scores on his eighth-grade middle school state assessments. He identified 48 students in the seventh grade who are deficient in reading and who, if allowed to take the state test next year, will have an adverse impact on the test scores. Roger has met with his counselors and found that 12 of these students have been diagnosed as learning disabled. Unfortunately, even the accommodations that have been provided for those students have been insufficient to allow them to perform at the proficient level on the state exam. With Roger's encouragement, the special education teams will arrange to have the appropriate documentation so that those 12 students will be excluded from the assessment next year and take an alternative assessment. Of the remaining 36 students, 30 have had two or more disciplinary incidents in the past year.

The frustrations over low academic performance frequently are reflected in emotional and behavioral problems, so this observation is not particularly striking. What is new is the district's new policy for "safe and secure schools" that gives the principal the authority to involuntarily transfer repeat offenders to the alternative school. With the stroke of a pen, 30 more students are off the list of next year's eighth-grade class. These students—and their low scores— will appear on the roster of a different school that has traditionally expected, and accepted, low scores. That leaves only six more of Roger's underperforming students remaining, and he intends to meet with the parents of each child to explain how the test may not reflect the child's true ability and how the parents can, if they wish, sign a document that will exclude their child from testing or, in the alternative, enroll their child in a different school. With no modifications in curriculum and instruction, the next year's eighth-grade reading scores will be remarkably higher. Shortly after the announcement of those scores, the framed certificate for "Most Improved School" is proudly displayed in Roger's office. The newspapers, school board members, and superintendent are unanimous in applauding Roger's success, and other middle school principals are studying Roger's methods for improving student achievement.

Laurie Golden, the principal of Roosevelt High School, has long enjoyed a reputation for promoting academic excellence. The school has the highest average college admissions examination scores in the state and a rigorous

Advanced Placement program that allows many students each year to graduate from high school with a full year of college credit. Searching for ways to improve her performance continuously, Laurie examines her data. "We do a great job of serving about 30 percent of our student population," she explains. "But we have a lot of kids slip through the cracks. The unsuccessful kids are quickly identified and moved to alternative programs and more than half of the students in this academically rich high school don't even bother to take the college entrance exams! We've got to work on that." Laurie gathers her faculty and counselors and works to develop a program to increase the number of students who have broad choices after high school. "I'm not saying that everybody has to go to college," she told the staff. "But I want more of our students to be able to make that choice for themselves—it should not be predetermined because of mistakes they made in middle school or their first two years of high school. Eventually, I want every student here to take those college entrance exams. Even if they don't use them, they will at least have more choices than they had before." The staff enthusiastically takes up Laurie's challenge.

Concerned that some students cannot afford to take the exams, the staff agrees to divert some professional development dollars to allow every student to take the exams without cost. Another faculty group voluntarily establishes a college entrance examination test preparation program before school, during lunch, and after school. The counselors arrange for a college fair to bring financial aid officials, student loan experts, and admissions counselors from area colleges and universities. They make a special effort to invite the students who had previously not regarded themselves as destined for college. They provide child care for the teen parents and transportation for parents and students who need it. Counselors meet with students to offer tutoring and encourage students to take more rigorous courses. Throughout the entire year, the faculty work exceptionally hard to create more academic opportunities than had ever previously existed for all the students at Roosevelt.

When the percentage of students taking the ACT and SAT almost doubled, Laurie beamed with pride and the faculty celebrated the new spirit of academic opportunity that they had collaboratively created at Roosevelt High School. Two months later, the scores were announced. Although many more students took the test, the vast majority of new students taking it received only average scores—a remarkable accomplishment considering where they had started. But adding these students into the mix of formerly high-achieving students depressed the overall average of test scores. Roosevelt not only lost its former top ranking, it wasn't even in the top 10. Board members called the superintendent within hours of the delivery of the morning paper, and by that afternoon, Laurie was summoned to the superintendent's office to explain why the academic performance of her school had deteriorated so badly in a single year. "I'm sure," the superintendent said through gritted teeth, "we will not have the same problem next year. Can I count on that?"

Resolving Standards and Competition

When evaluation hinges upon competition, and particularly when competitive success is reduced to a single number, abuse and distortion are inevitable.

Corporate America provides the best examples. When stock analysts, the media, and the investing public focused on the stocks with the greatest earnings, corporations systematically accelerated earnings and deferred expenses, creating artificially high profits. In the most egregious cases, such as Enron and WorldCom, the accounting maneuvers were fraudulent. But in thousands of other cases, corporate leaders engaged in the legal use of discretion to engage in the practice euphemistically known as "managed earnings." A more conservative approach that carefully matched income and expenses would have resulted in dismissive reviews from securities analysts and allegations that such stodgy management just didn't get it and should be replaced. Corporate manipulation of earnings, like Roger Blackburn's manipulation of test scores, is rewarded in the short term. A focus on long-term success, particularly when associated with a short-term drop in competitive performance, is mercilessly punished in the corporate and educational worlds alike.

The only way to resolve this dilemma is context. Test scores are important. In many districts, not only is student achievement important, but relative rankings are also part of the political landscape. An effective leadership evaluation system can acknowledge those political realities without succumbing to the dangerous distortions in which manipulation is rewarded and success is punished. Only a multidimensional leadership evaluation system provides the context that would make it clear that Roger's illusory success was purchased at the price of fewer students taking the assessment, and Laurie's apparent failure was associated with dramatic gains in equity and excellence for a broader number of students. If those explanations are offered after test scores are announced, they sound like excuses. If those explanations are an integral part of the leadership evaluation system, then they are part of the context—the story behind the numbers that every good accountability system must have.

MULTIDIMENSIONAL LEADERSHIP ASSESSMENT

One excellent framework for a standards-based approach to leadership evaluation is multidimensional leadership assessment (MLA). The MLA system is a matrix in which each row contains a critical dimension of leadership. Some of these dimensions are universal and applicable to all leaders in every organization. A list of possible dimensions of leadership is contained in Figure 4.2. Examples of universal leadership dimensions include integrity, respect for colleagues, and continuous learning. Other leadership dimensions will be more specifically related to particular leadership responsibilities. For example, a superintendent may have positive board relationships and proactive board communication as essential leadership dimensions, while the technology director's leadership performance matrix may include references to technical proficiency and leadership of complex group processes. A building principal's leadership dimensions would include curriculum analysis, student assessment, and teacher evaluation. This chapter and Resources A–D include sample leadership domains as well as blank forms that can be reproduced and used to create your own multidimensional leadership assessment system.

Although the rows will differ with each leadership position, the column headings should be consistent throughout the organization. The terms we will use to represent various performance levels are precisely the same ones we use to describe student performance (Reeves, 2002b): exemplary, proficient, progressing, and not meeting standards. The following paragraphs briefly elaborate on each level of leadership performance.

Exemplary Performance

Exemplary performance not only meets the requirements for proficiency, but goes far beyond those requirements and thus creates a model to which other leaders can aspire. The identification, nurturing, challenging, development, and retention of exemplary leaders are the most important strategic tasks for any organization. The description of exemplary performance is difficult and eludes many senior leaders. They use vague terms such as *superior* or *outstanding,* but upon further reflection, these turn out to be comparative descriptions rather than a clear standard of achievement. In order to describe exemplary performance successfully, we must envision it with great specificity, while leaving room for the fact that genuinely exemplary leaders will surprise us with their creativity and novel accomplishments. Nevertheless, we need not leave everything to chance. Some exemplary performance is clear and, however rare, can be defined. Consider the case of student assessment for building principals. While the proficient leader understands and regularly uses assessment data in making instructional decisions, the exemplary leader does far more. Some real-world exemplary leaders regularly engage in the following professional practices in the domain of student assessment:

- Monthly posting of student assessment performances based on teacher-created standards-based assessments and use of those data to guide adjustments in teaching, curriculum, and leadership
- Regular training of teachers, support staff, parents, and students in the constructive use of assessment data to improve student learning
- Assessment training led not only by the principal, but by five or more additional staff members who are so proficient in student assessment that they regularly lead professional development for their colleagues at this and other schools
- The principal personally evaluates student work and participates in collaborative scoring sessions in which the percentage agreement by the faculty is measured and posted
- The principal personally reviews faculty-created assessments as part of each teacher evaluation and coaching meetings
- The principal serves as an assessment mentor to at least one other principal in the system and has created objective evidence that the other principal's assessment skills have improved based on that principal's leadership performance matrix

These professional leadership practices in the single domain of assessment are far beyond what we expect of most principals. Yet they represent a clear picture of what extraordinary performance can be. It is not just a little bit better than the performance of colleagues, but dramatically superior in its impact on students, staff members, parents, and the entire district. Indeed, a hallmark of exemplary leaders is not making their schools or departments better than their competitors, but rather regularly helping every other element of the organization become as good as they are. Let me reiterate: Exemplary leaders are not merely successful at their own job. That sort of performance is expected, is proficient, and represents the majority of leadership performance. Given the difficulty of proficient performance, it is a worthy accomplishment. But it is not exemplary. Exemplary leaders have an impact on an entire organization and are a primary source of developing additional leadership in their organizations. These leaders do not covet the staff they have trained, but take great pride in each former colleague who leaves the school to accept leadership challenges elsewhere in the system.

Proficient Performance

Proficient performance meets organizational needs. It is adequate and indeed necessary. The vast majority of leaders in an effective organization are proficient.

The risk in even considering the discussion of exemplary leadership performance is that it renders any discussion of proficient performance as second rate and faintly undesirable. Thus, exemplary performance becomes the expected level of performance (and the expected level of evaluation by leaders) and the word *proficient* is linked to mediocrity. This is not the case. Evaluation systems that are profligate in their use of superior adjectives have no credibility with leaders or policymakers and are merely a reflection of the grade inflation that has rendered the A an entitlement and the B+ an insult, at least in some schools. In such an environment, it is difficult to identify the meaning of the evaluation, since the student's mere presence in the classroom appears to be sufficient justification for a grade. In leadership evaluation, such inflation becomes a self-fulfilling prophesy as the evaluators think, "We wouldn't have hired her if she were not outstanding, so she must be outstanding, right?" If the purpose of leadership evaluation is to massage the egos and assuage the guilt of evaluators and those being evaluated, then perhaps such logic has some merit. But if the purpose of leadership evaluation is the improvement of learning and teaching, then nonspecific and uniformly high feedback is worse than a waste of time—it is counterproductive. It validates performance that is poor, fails to recognize performance that is genuinely exemplary, and ultimately discourages and drives out exemplary leaders, the very people every organization must strive to maintain. Therefore, proficient performance is not at all mediocre or unacceptable. It is challenging and difficult, taking perhaps years to attain. Proficient performance is both necessary and sufficient for leaders to maintain their positions.

Consider the leadership domain of building safety for an assistant principal in a middle school. Proficient performance might include the following leadership practices:

- Compliance with all state, local, and school system hazardous waste policies
- Enforcement of a zero tolerance weapons policy and timely and accurate reporting of weapons incidents
- Staff proficiency in safety procedures, measured by individual and group assessments in emergency procedures, followed by group reflection and specific improvement plans for individuals and groups
- An emergency operations plan that is reviewed by appropriate external officials and posted in every classroom and office
- First aid supplies readily available throughout the building
- Safety procedures that are posted and followed (as noted in spot checks) in all science labs, technology classes, and other places where the use of chemicals, electricity, or equipment poses potential health and safety hazards

These may seem fairly basic, but if they are not clearly articulated, then leaders will not know that it is their responsibility. While the issues may be clear in traditional administrative domains such as building safety, the picture will become much more challenging when we begin to specify what the overused and underdefined phrase *instructional leadership* really means.

For example, here are some basic requirements for the proficient leader in the domain of curriculum:

- The school has a curriculum for every class based on the standards of the state and district.
- Each course has a document (syllabus, course outline, learning objectives, or other appropriate document) that identifies what students are expected to know and be able to do in order to be successful in the class. This document expresses, in language accessible to students and parents, the teacher's expectations. These expectations accurately reflect the standards of the state, along with the student work created in response to those assessments and the teacher's evaluation of the student work. The leader documents the coaching of the teacher for improved assessment and student evaluation, including the identification of superior work and the identification of teacher evaluation that is inconsistent with state and local standards.

That's a lot of work! True, but if we define proficient performance with sufficient clarity and rigor, then leaders at all levels understand what is expected of them. Moreover, when proficient performance is so challenging, it clearly makes a contribution to the organization. The more clearly and rigorously we define proficiency, the more exceptional the work of the genuinely exemplary leader will be. In each case, students, teachers, and leaders are reinforced and challenged. The very word proficiency takes on new power and meaning when it is consistently applied to everyone in the organization, from students to superintendents, to convey a clear description of the challenging requirements for effective performance.

Progressing Performance

The identification of leaders who are progressing, but not yet proficient, allows today's leaders to coach the effective leaders of tomorrow. While progressing leaders are not yet proficient, they have the willingness and ability to learn the skills required for leadership proficiency. There is, in traditional evaluation models, a vast chasm that separates proficient from nonproficient leaders, with the former secure in their jobs and eligible for future promotion while the latter face a series of Kafkaesque hearings, counseling sessions, warnings, admonitions, and other bureaucratic processes until at last, the inept person recognizes the futility of persistence and resigns or is fired. In fact, however, there are two very different types of nonproficient performance, and the organization's reactions to these should be quite different. Many nonproficient performers understand what is required for success, are willing to work toward that goal, and, with coaching and support, can become proficient. These leaders we will call *progressing.* They are not proficient, and we will not lie to them, providing bland and unbelievable assurances that all is well when, in fact, they have a good understanding of the requirements for success and have chosen not to pursue that course of action. Coaching, threats, pleading, and, worst of all, an endless series of reassignments to different leadership positions will not fix this problem. These people need a new job, and the only fair action for the individual and the organization is to provide reasonable assistance for the transition to a new job and get it done quickly. Collins (2001) notes that in virtually every case of a decision for termination or a job change that relieves a person of duties, both the individual and the organization are not meeting standards.

Because leadership time is limited and training resources are finite, it is imperative that leadership coaching is focused on progressing leaders—those with the potential to become proficient. One of their rewards for continued progress is the organization's continued investment in their training and development. This is one reason that leadership training should be invitational and voluntary. The person who continually declines opportunities for leadership development is, by definition, not progressing. When the organization devotes time and resources attempting to fix nonproficient leaders through unilateral action, the result is almost always counterproductive, with the involuntary engagement of disruptive or nonparticipating behavior during the training and passive–aggressive behavior after it. One of the most obvious signs of a dysfunctional school system is the presumption that learning is something that is done primarily by students, occasionally by teachers, and rarely by administrators. When the superintendent introduces a guest speaker and then leaves the room to attend a more important meeting, it sends the unmistakable signal that adult learning is unimportant for leaders. When principals pop in and out of professional development sessions with cell phones blaring, the message is clear that their need for and interest in learning stopped long ago. Effective leadership evaluation programs will challenge these presumptions by explicitly identifying the learning needs of every leader and providing accountability for the continuous development of the knowledge and skills of school leaders.

One of the most challenging elements of dealing with progressing performance is that it is poorly defined in most organizations. Because leadership has been so frequently associated with ethereal qualities that border on the mystical, those who evaluate leaders can easily fall prey to the "I know it when I see it" fallacy. However stellar their judgment and keen their insight, these evaluators render their judgments in a vacuum, with neither the organization nor the leader possessing a clear understanding of the differences between success and failure. The French expression *je ne sais quoi* refers to undefined qualities of a person. Those who employ the phrase, feigning sophistication, should bear in mind the literal meaning that the speaker simply doesn't know.

The problem is particularly acute when progressing leaders do not recognize that they are not proficient. Because progressing leaders are not utterly wretched and defiant, they are tolerated by the organization, and the absence of overtly negative feedback creates the illusion of proficiency. It is as if the leader is driving a car across the desert and sees the engine warning light. But the driver doesn't smell the engine overheating nor does the car appear to be slowing down. From outward appearances, the engine is functioning well. The driver, willing to respond to only the most obvious feedback—a car stranded on the desert with a blown engine—will assiduously ignore the engine warning light and drive ahead. "Yes," the leader says contentedly, "student achievement is down, teacher turnover is up, and we have not implemented any of the recommendations of the last accreditation report, but I don't hear any complaints. Besides, if it were really that bad, somebody would be saying something to me about it." This leader is at the crossroads between progressing and not meeting standards. With clear and unambiguous feedback, the leader can recognize the warning signs, accept the feedback, and make significantly different decisions. This will require a courageous senior leader who will say without equivocation, "Your performance is not proficient. We are not going to fire you because we have confidence that you can improve, learn, and become proficient. But we are telling you that you are not meeting the requirements for proficient performance. We also need to ask you if you are willing to work toward becoming proficient. The first step toward that journey is acknowledging that you are not proficient now and that a continuation of the present level of performance is not acceptable." In today's litigious environment, most senior leaders hesitate to have such conversations. As a result, the leader who is finally terminated offers the defense, "Nobody ever told me that anything was wrong." Successful terminations are possible, even for tenured staff members with long histories of employment, provided that due process has been observed in which leaders are either acceptable or unacceptable, proficient or nonproficient, excellent or awful. The world of leadership requires more subtle distinctions and more strategic differentiations among varying levels of performance.

Consider, for example, the leadership domain of time, project, and task management. While the proficient leader maintains a daily prioritized task list and consistently focuses on tasks in priority order (Reeves, 2002a), the progressing leader's performance might be described as follows:

- The leader maintains a master task list, but it is not updated daily or is not maintained in order of priority.
- The leader frequently is diverted by low-priority tasks that are not on the task list and are not the most important issues requiring the leader's time.
- The leader turns in projects that are late or incomplete, though the projects are always completed and improved eventually.

The essence of these performance descriptions is that the leader knows what to do, but poor time and project management skills prevent the leader from doing the job proficiently. This is quite different from the leader who has no list and fails to complete projects because he does not understand what to do or does not choose to comply with the requirement for the completion of the project. The phrasing of these performance descriptions is sufficiently clear that the leader who receives an evaluation of "progressing" need not wonder about how to proceed from that level to proficient. The criteria for evaluation as well as the requirements for success are transparent. It is not a guessing game, but a decision. Progressing leaders can choose proficiency; they can also choose to remain nonproficient. Their choice will determine their future with the organization as well as their personal effectiveness and satisfaction in their profession.

Not Meeting Standards

Leaders who do not understand what is required for proficiency or who have demonstrated through their action and inaction that they choose not to become proficient do not meet your standards. Identifying the leader who does not meet standards is essential, as it allows the organization the opportunity to diagnose problems before they become crises.

Why do so many organizations appear to tolerate bad performance? It is not, in my judgment, a death wish, a lack of intelligence, or even a lack of will. Rather, the problem is a lack of definition. We have failed to call poor performance what it is—a threat to the organization and the people in it. Leaders who do not meet standards have a terrible impact on staff morale, employee turnover, community communication, and student achievement. John Goodlad (1984) pioneered research into the profound impact, for good or ill, that a single leader can have on the organization. Senior leaders rarely confront these problems until after a full-blown crisis has occurred. The bullying boss is terminated only after the district loses a multimillion-dollar employee lawsuit, even though signs of inappropriate employee interactions had been apparent for years and even the most rudimentary employee feedback system would have provided evidence that something was very wrong. Another leader is terminated after her school loses its accreditation, jeopardizing the credibility of transcripts for several classes of students and the careers of scores of teachers. Years of academic decline, a chaotic curriculum, incoherent academic plans, and the absence of instructional leadership had been clear to senior leaders for years, but until the crisis of the loss of accreditation, no one thought it was bad enough to take action. Besides, they reasoned, who else can we get to take this school? Thus the schools that most need proficient and exemplary leaders become doomed to become those most likely to have leaders who do not meet standards.

We have thus far explored the four levels of leadership performance. To briefly review,

- *Exemplary* leaders provide performance that is far beyond proficient. One of the distinctive characteristics of exemplary leaders is that they have systemwide impact. They routinely share their ideas, mentor other leaders, and see their role not only as the improvement of the part of the system for which they are personally responsible, but as an agent of systemwide improvement.
- *Proficient* leaders meet the requirements for organizational success. Their performance is both necessary and sufficient for their continued employment. Proficiency is a challenging, rigorous, and demanding standard of achievement. Leaders can be proud of achievements. Nevertheless, they are able to understand clearly that their present level of performance is not proficient, but on a path toward proficiency.
- *Progressing* leaders understand what they must do in order to become proficient and have the desire and personal motivation to make the decisions necessary to become proficient. While not yet proficient, the progressing leaders can benefit enormously from coaching, constructive evolution, and clear expectations for improved performance.
- Leaders who *do not meet standards* do not have a future in a leadership role with your organization. The question is not *if* they are counseled out of the profession, but *when.* Ineffective organizations will wait until a crisis to take action, and the impact of their delay will cost the organization and its people dearly. Effective organizations will identify, define, and document inadequate performance and make the necessary changes very quickly.

In the next chapter, we will explore the continuum between each level of leadership performance. Once you have identified leadership domains appropriate to your organization and accurately evaluated each leader, the challenge is how each leader is coached to the next level of performance.

Using Evaluation to Improve Performance 5

If leadership evaluation is to be used constructively, then those conducting the evaluation must never be content merely to render a judgment. Rather, it is their obligation to coach exemplary leaders to extend their influence throughout the organization, and proficient leaders must be shown the path toward exemplary performance. One of the most critical jobs of leadership evaluation is to bridge the gap between the progressing and the proficient leader. Every success in this task is a career-saving opportunity for the leader who is being evaluated and contributes enormously to reducing turnover and improving performance. Finally, the leaders who do not meet standards must be relieved of their duties. Due process is certainly required, and that is one reason comprehensive leadership evaluation systems are essential. But in every case of the removal of a leader who is failing to meet standards, both the organization and the leader will heave a sigh of relief. Leaders who fail to meet standards are not, with rare exceptions, malevolent people or people whose character defects are so enormous that they cannot serve their organization. Rather, their failure to meet leadership standards and to progress toward proficiency indicates that they must serve the organization in a capacity other than leadership. Senior leaders who

Figure 5.1 Coaching Continua for Leadership Evaluation

Multidimensional Impact

Capacity building throughout the organization as exemplary leaders leverage their knowledge and skills

Challenge individual leaders to stretch themselves, mentor others, and share their knowledge

Exemplary Performance

Proficient Performance

Clear short-term performance objectives to become proficient

Remove from leadership duties. Provide other opportunities within organization or take appropriate due process steps to terminate as employee

Progressing Performance

Not Meeting Standards

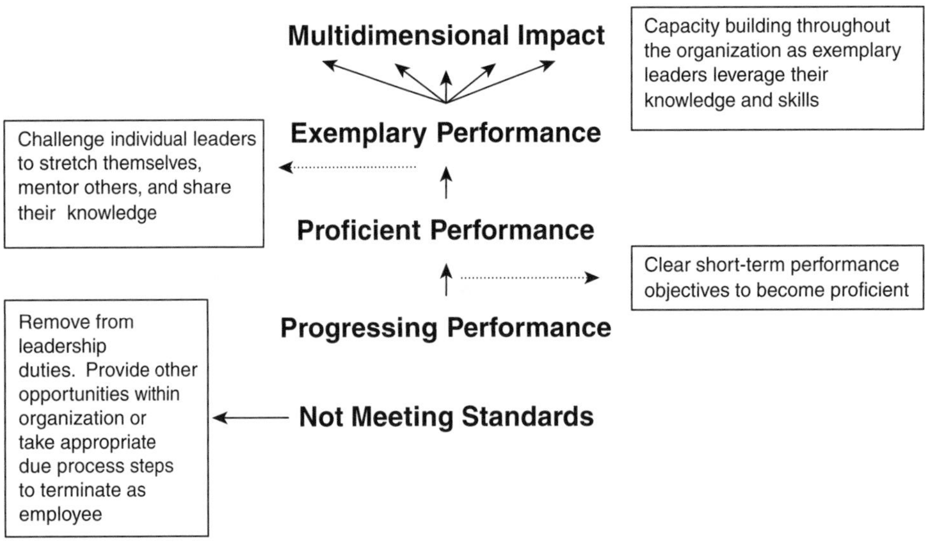

delay making these decisions, perhaps fearing litigation or hurt feelings, do their organizations no favors. In fact, they do the failing leader no favors. The sooner people in your organization find a role in which they can be successful, the happier and more productive they—and the entire organization—will be. The progression of leadership evaluation continua is displayed in Figure 5.1.

As Figure 5.1 illustrates, organizations must do more than evaluate leaders; the organization must act on that information. Each level of evaluation requires a thoughtful response by the organization. For the exemplary leaders, the organization creates maximum leverage by providing opportunities for multidimensional impact, giving these leaders mentorship responsibilities, advanced learning opportunities, and visibility both inside and outside the system. For proficient leaders, the organization fights the possibility of complacency by stretching these leaders to become exemplary. For the progressing leaders, the organization makes it clear that proficiency is the requirement for continued leadership responsibility. For the ineffective leader, the organization avoids a possible leadership crisis and the associated legal, financial, and human costs by relieving such a leader of responsibilities and, where appropriate, reassigning that individual to nonleadership responsibilities or terminating the leader's employment. Figure 5.2 details some of the organizational responses for each continuum.

THE CAPACITY-BUILDING CONTINUUM

What should be done with exemplary leaders? Conventional wisdom might assert that we pay them more money or give them more recognition. Money and recognition are necessary but insufficient for this rare and critically important situation. These motivators are organizational hygiene—doing what is necessary

(Continued on page 59)

Figure 5.2 Organizational Actions in Leadership Evaluation Continua

Continuum	From	To	Organizational Leadership Actions	Results
Capacity Building	Exemplary Performance	Multidimensional Impact	Provide opportunities for impact beyond present position. Provide advanced professional development. Encourage coaching of peers inside and outside the organization.	Mentors for new and veteran leaders throughout the organization. Clearly identified candidates for systemwide leadership.
Challenge	Proficient Performance	Exemplary Performance	Clearly identify the difference between proficient and exemplary performance. Ask the question: Do you want to become an exemplary leader? Provide challenges that allow for a display of exemplary performance. Provide frequent and specific feedback on performance, making clear that proficient performance is acceptable, but it is not the same as exemplary performance.	Clear identification of high-potential leaders. Redefine organizational requirements for leadership success. Link organizational strategic needs to leadership actions.
Coaching	Progressing Performance	Proficient Performance	One-to-one peer coaching by exemplary leader. Frequent feedback—at least every three months. Clear identification of tasks, actions, behaviors, and achievements that move the leader from progressing to proficient. Clear statement that proficient performance is required for continued assignment in a leadership position.	Focus coaching resources on leaders with potential for success. Immediate and measurable performance in leadership.

(Continued)

Figure 5.2 Continued

Continuum	From	To	Organizational Leadership Actions	Results
Counseling	Ineffective Performance	Avoiding Leadership Crises	Gather evidence of ineffective performance, consistent with human resources guidelines, negotiated agreements, district policy, and legal requirements for due process. Relieve the ineffective leader of duties immediately, while continuing employment in another position. If positions are available where the former leader can be successful, offer a probationary opportunity in an alternative position. If there are no positions where success is likely, terminate the employee.	Avoid crises that expose the organization to legal liability, that result in the loss of employees who are demoralized by the ineffective leader, and that cause the deterioration of the performance of the part of the organization that is under the control of the ineffective leader.

to maintain employee satisfaction. Exemplary leaders have, in most cases, their material needs met and have a wall full of plaques as well as a drawer full of letters testifying to exemplary performance. What now?

The Churchill Impasse

For the exemplary leader, the only thing worse than not achieving a goal is achieving it and then settling into a let-down that is close to depression. Having achieved the objective after Herculean effort, Sisyphean persistence, and the determination of Odysseus, the leader asks, "Is that all there is? What now?" The people around the leader have worked hard, sacrificed much, and wish to enjoy the fruits of their labor. The leader is ready to seek another challenge. This is what we shall call the *Churchill impasse.* Sir Winston Churchill, arguably one of the greatest leaders of the 20th century and perhaps many other centuries as well, is remembered for his fierce oratory during the darkest times of the Second World War: "We shall fight them in the air. We shall fight them on the sea. We shall fight them on the land." He promised a beleaguered Britain that when the history books were written, that nation, then shaken by Nazi bombardment, would engage in heroic determination so great that in future generations it would be said that "This was their finest hour." He endured nighttime missile attacks, made heart-breaking decisions to sacrifice troops and towns, and kept his island nation together and, with the United States and (lest history forget) Russia, saved Europe and defeated Hitler. After this stunning military victory, Winston Churchill was defeated at the polls and sent to ignominious retirement by an ungrateful nation. Is the analogy between a wartime leader of the past century and educational leaders of today inappropriate? The crises are real, including unprecedented financial strains, threats to personal safety, an uncertain future, unrelenting personal stress, and a personal responsibility for the lives and livelihoods of children, families, and colleagues. Among the Churchills of our day are the profoundly successful educational leaders who leave their organizations after great accomplishments. One leader in particular, who prefers to remain anonymous, led her school system from failure to success, setting a state record for schools moving from academic probation to accreditation. Her reforms were popular with parents and students and respected by most teachers and administrators. A small minority of teachers, administrators, and parents, however, were so successful in transforming their disaffection and anger into a campaign against the superintendent, that board meetings soon became a relentless assault on the character and daily tasks of the district leader. The attack worked in that a neighboring district recognized the value of exceptional leadership, snatched the superintendent, and left the district in the hands of a fractious and eternally discontented board.

Effective leadership assessment must identify and recognize the leader who not only is distinguished in achieving local results, but has the capacity to improve education throughout the world. This is not hyperbole. Ask the most effective leaders what they want to do and, initially, you will hear, "I want to make an impact." In less guarded moments, you will hear, "I want to change the world. Certainly not alone, but I believe that with my terrific staff and the generations of students we will serve, we can really have an impact that will allow us to say some day that we made a significant difference not only within the walls of this school and the borders of this district, but wherever in the world our students and employees happen to be." This much is certain: If organizations that are fortunate enough to have exemplary leaders fail to provide world-changing opportunities for them, then these leaders will find ways to make an impact. They will volunteer for other activities, present at national and international conventions, be recruited by competing districts, or perhaps find fulfillment outside of education in the world of business, nonprofit organizations, or government service. Successful organizations identify, nurture, and keep their exemplary leaders.

THE CHALLENGE CONTINUUM

This continuum, the land of the proficient but not yet exemplary leader, could also become the *complacency continuum* if organizations fail to provide opportunities to stretch and challenge their proficient leaders. These are leaders who may not have received an evaluation for a while. They are, after all, successful veterans, secure in their positions, and politically well connected and have fallen into a satisfying routine. They are doing their jobs well and, though they are hardly setting the world on fire, they get the paperwork done, maintain discipline, have a reasonable schedule, and are, well, proficient. Because they are neither exemplary nor remarkably ineffective, the proficient leader attracts little attention. Unfortunately, the ranks of today's proficient leaders constitute the source of tomorrow's exemplary leaders or, in the alternative, tomorrow's cynical, disengaged, and ineffective leaders. These are the leaders who, without attention from the organization, are prime candidates for what the military calls ROAD status—retired on active duty. Organizations ignore the proficient leader at their peril.

The first and most important step in challenging proficient leaders is the recognition that their potential extends beyond their present level of performance. Rather than accept the philosophy of, "If it ain't broke, don't fix it," we must embrace Tom Peter's admonition that such an attitude embraces mediocrity and stultifying obsolescence. Peters and Austin (1986) reject conventional wisdom and say provocatively that the organizational structures that are not broken should be occasionally broken, suggesting not mindless destruction, but continued innovation, challenge, and constructive dissatisfaction with existing levels of performance. In most organizations, there will be some proficient leaders who are satisfied and are not interested in becoming exemplary. My strong conviction, however, is that human beings love to succeed. While they can conceal enthusiasm—think of the disengaged algebra student, the 32-year classroom veteran of too many fads, or the principal weary of political infighting—each of these people can be energized by a vision that moves them from complacency to challenge to success. Effective organizations have a clear and definitive answer to the question, "Is that all there is?" The answer, unequivocally, is "No." The challenge to move from proficiency to exemplary leadership provides a lifelong motivation that allows us to anticipate each day with the confidence that our organization and our leadership can be better than they were the previous day.

THE COACHING CONTINUUM

The coaching continuum must be an important focus of organizational efforts. This continuum specifically identifies nonproficient leaders who have the potential to become proficient. This definition includes new leaders, probationary leaders, and leaders in training who need intensive coaching and mentoring to cross the bridge from progressing to proficient performance. This definition of progressing may also include veteran leaders who, despite their experience, are not performing at a proficient level. These are the leaders who have slipped through the system for years without any meaningful leadership evaluation or who have received satisfactory ratings in a system in which almost everyone is outstanding or superior. The label of satisfactory was misleading—somewhat like the grade of C in the classroom. Ask any teacher what students who meet their expectations will receive on the report card, and the typical answer is an A, or in some cases a B. Teachers regard a grade of C as a clear signal that all is not well, that the student is failing to master the material, is not turning in homework, is not participating in class, and may have trouble in the future. But the grade of C appears, to the parents and students who view them on report cards, to be "average" and thus perfectly acceptable. In the context of leadership evaluation, the senior administrator who assigned the rating of satisfactory may have regarded it as a clear signal of inadequate performance, but this inadequacy is tolerated and encouraged by the misuse of language. If the leader is not performing at an acceptable level, then the organization has one of two choices: either the leader is regarded as progressing, in which case the actions required in the coaching continuum are appropriate, or the leader is regarded as ineffective, in which case the leader must be reassigned, offered alternative positions in the system, or terminated.

There is an important synergy between the different leadership evaluation continua. The progressing leaders need coaches, one-on-one relationships with successful mentors who are not their evaluators, but who can give them practical advice on specific daily decisions that will move them from performance that is progressing to performance that is proficient. The source of these mentors and coaches should be leaders who are exemplary and who must be given the opportunity for multidimensional impact throughout the system. The progressing leaders need mentors; the exemplary leaders need the opportunity to have an impact.

THE COUNSELING CONTINUUM

Perhaps the most disturbing conclusion of our national leadership study was hardly a finding at all. Anyone who spends much time in schools knows that it does not require extensive empirical research to know that many organizations tolerate leaders that are ineffective. While there are frequent complaints that unions and legislated job protections prevent school leaders from terminating the employment of ineffective teachers, there are rarely such obstacles to the reassignment or termination of school leaders. Nevertheless, a combination of community politics and, more frequently, the unwillingness of senior leaders to admit a mistake, allows the persistent assignment of ineffective leaders to critical positions in schools and central offices.

The counseling continuum provides three levels of action by the organization. First and most important, the organization must define clearly the difference between leadership performance that is progressing and thus potentially worthy of an investment in coaching for improved performance and leadership performance that is ineffective. The latter is marked by willful defiance, casual indifference, or repeated failure to meet expectations for proficiency. Great organizations and coaches provide multiple opportunities for success, but they do not provide infinite opportunities for the floundering leader who is not successful in the present assignment. This performance must be identified, documented in detail, and confronted. In most cases, people want to be successful and can recognize that they will have a greater opportunity for success in another assignment and, perhaps, another field.

If the recognition of ineffective performance does not happen on the part of the failing leader, then the organization must take the second step, alternative assignments. This is the humane and necessary thing to do. The failing leader is relieved of leadership responsibilities and given an opportunity to succeed in an assignment that is a better fit for this person's abilities. In this case, frequent monitoring and feedback will be necessary to validate the assumptions made when the assignment decision was made. A person who is not a good project manager or who is unskilled in delegation—two critical leadership failings—might be very successful in an independent assignment with clear boundaries. A person who is not successful in an assignment requiring political skills and complex organizational skills can nevertheless be successful in a position that does not impose such requirements. But a person who, for example, lacks integrity, communications skills, or a commitment to equity probably will be unable to find any position in an educational system in which these failings will be acceptable. Thus we proceed to the third decision, termination of employment. While this is never a pleasant task, it is absolutely necessary. Ask colleagues who have been through the process of terminating an ineffective employee about their regrets. The single most frequent regret I hear is, "I wish I would have done it much sooner. It would have been better for the employee, the organization, and me. I wasted way too many hours trying to make this work, when we both knew that it was heading nowhere. It was frankly a relief for everyone concerned when the matter was completed. All the time I spent engaged in combat, in lawyer's offices, and personnel discussions could have been devoted to instructional leadership if only I would have documented the performance, made a reassignment, or started the termination process much earlier."

DEFINING PERFORMANCE: THE KEY TO USING THE LEADERSHIP EVALUATION CONTINUA

The use of performance continua will be ineffective if your organization does not define with precision the difference between each level of performance. Senior leaders, new leaders, and prospective leaders must all know what proficient really means and how it is different from progressing. This must be clearly distinguished from performance that is exemplary or inadequate. Whatever terms you use, each level of performance requires definitions that are absolutely clear. The continued use of ambiguous terms such as *exceeds standards* or *outstanding* is a prescription for failure. While the continuum analysis in this chapter can be a powerful leadership tool, it will only be effective if you first take the time to define leadership performance at each level. Resource A provides a useful guideline for consideration. While each organization must define its own leadership domains and reach a consensus on the description of each performance level, one thing is clear: Ambiguity will undermine even the most well-intentioned and expertly constructed leadership evaluation system. Those who oppose specificity in performance definition sometimes complain that leadership evaluation is an art, not a science, and that human performance is, in the end, an esoteric judgment call. Such excuses make plaintiff's attorneys salivate, as the excuses provide clear evidence that the system cannot or will not define performance and is unable to grant due process to any employee it wishes to terminate. The need for specificity is more than a legal maneuver, however. Fairness demands specificity. Organizational success requires specificity. Clarity of vision demands specificity. The emphasis on visionary leaders has allowed some people to conclude that the visionaries dream great dreams, while the details can be left to mere mortals in the leadership food chain. In fact, visions are pipe dreams without a leader who can not only articulate the vision, but also make clear in specific terms how the vision will be achieved. Finally, specificity is a matter of the personal credibility of the senior leaders in the system. If senior leaders cannot articulate the specific performance that they require, then how will new or prospective leaders divine the intention of their leaders?

Of course, it is possible to be too specific, to the point that individual judgment is utterly removed. Thus in a system composed of human beings, you have two imperfect choices—too much specificity or not enough of it. The risk of the former choice is one that undermines your entire evaluation system and the effectiveness of the organization along with it. The risk of the latter choice is one in which, over time, individuals can be coached to exercise discretion, and the language that is excessively specific can be modified. This risk is by far the lesser of the two, and thus confronted with the choice of too little or too much specificity in leadership performance, organizations should opt for the latter.

You now have the components of an effective leadership evaluation system. The domains of leadership identify your expectations for leaders. For each of these domains, you will specify performance levels that can be used to challenge your most effective leaders, encourage and coach those who aspire to become proficient leaders, and counsel those who are not successful and fail to meet your standards. Most important, you have the capacity to transform leadership evaluation from a destructive and demoralizing process into a mechanism that will have a constructive impact not only on the leaders being evaluated, but on the entire educational system. In the next chapter, we turn our attention to the specific steps necessary to assemble your new leadership evaluation system.

Developing a 6
Multidimensional
Leadership
Assessment System

This chapter provides step-by-step guidelines for creating your own multidimensional leadership assessment (MLA) system and then provides guidelines for the practical implementation of the system in your schools. Although there are abundant sources of guidance for potential leadership domains, it is imperative that your organization identify those domains that are most appropriate. Similarly, there are examples of descriptions of a continuum of performance for leadership, such as Resource A of this book. These resources are, however, merely examples, not prescriptions. The acid test of the utility of your multidimensional leadership assessment system is the degree to which you can use it as a research goldmine, linking specific leadership profiles to organizational results.

LEADERSHIP DOMAINS

A domain of knowledge is a logical grouping of characteristics, traits, and performance indicators. In most complex human endeavors, multiple domains are required for a good understanding of performance. For example, a marathon runner might be evaluated in the domains of speed, endurance, resilience, and training discipline. A cellist might be evaluated in the domains of intonation, accuracy, dynamics, interpretation, bow technique, and practice discipline. Both expert marathon runners and cellists will recognize that I have only scratched the surface of potential domains. They know from experience that the simultaneous interaction of many complex variables forms the basis of their success or failure and that omission of a critical variable is a critical training error. They also know that they can fall victim to "analysis paralysis" in which they fail to focus on the most essential domains of performance. They also know that neither the applause of the audience nor the abrupt critique of a reviewer is as useful as a thoughtful analysis of their performance, including specific areas of exemplary performance as well as the identification of parts of the performance that can be improved in the future. At the same time, an exhaustive critique into every conceivable nuance of the performance becomes tedious, repetitive, and unhelpful. Thus effective performance assessment is neither superficial nor exhaustive, but rather focuses on the most important domains of performance that can be used to improve future results.

We previously considered potential domains of leadership performance (Figure 4.2) in a list containing such leadership essentials as resilience, decision making, and time, task, and project management. For each leadership position, you will want to consider the extent to which those domains are most related to leadership success. There are many other domains of leadership provided in other documents, such as the Interstate School Leaders Licensure Consortium's *Standards for School Leaders,* published by the Council of Chief State School Officers (1996). Every week you can count on some publisher to announce with breathless enthusiasm that there is another breakthrough leadership book with secrets of leadership, sometimes associated with a historical hero extending from Moses to Queen Elizabeth I to General Patton and sometimes associated with a presumptive contemporary hero, taken from the world of sports, business, or politics. At the end of such a book, we have learned such insights as the importance of people, the value of integrity, and the essential nature of exercising power wisely. None of those blinding flashes of the obvious, however, will instruct the reader how to develop those characteristics in emerging leaders or how to assess those characteristics in incumbent leaders. In other words, the description of leadership domains without an accompanying description of performance levels is a vacuous exercise. In our national study of leadership evaluation, the best assessment instruments included domains that were postulated to be relevant to the position. Only a handful of them included explicit descriptions of a range of performance or included a systematic method for relating each leadership trait to organizational performance. Those challenges are the subjects of the remainder of this chapter.

LEADERSHIP PERFORMANCE

For each leadership domain, the organization must describe in detail a continuum of performance. What precisely does proficient performance mean? How is this different from exemplary performance? In this book, I suggest that one of the key differences between proficient and exemplary performance is that the proficient leader has a satisfactory impact on the local environment—the school, department, or district. The exemplary leader, by contrast, has an impact well beyond the expectations of the job description and thus provides a positive impact throughout the entire system. The exemplary principal, for example, not only provides effective leadership within the school, but routinely shares ideas and techniques with other principals, mentors colleagues, and recruits the next generation of leadership. The exemplary department head is not only proficient in the leadership of direct reports, but also helps them grow to assume new responsibilities elsewhere in the system, cooperates with colleagues to add value to their efforts, and generally improves the results of the entire organization by selfless assistance well beyond the borders of a single department. Note well that both the proficient and the exemplary leaders are successful in their positions, but an effective leadership assessment system draws a clear distinction between the leader who has an impact on a single part of the organization and the leader who has an impact on the entire system.

Just as there are two levels of acceptable leadership performance—the proficient and exemplary—there are also two levels of unacceptable leadership performance. The first level of unacceptable performance is the progressing leader. We all begin our careers in this mode. Armed merely with a graduate school education and administratively required leadership credentials, we don't know enough to run an organization. But we do know enough to learn, listen, and eventually become proficient. Our leaders allow us to remain in this zone for a limited period of time, cognizant of the fact that no one begins a career in leadership with all the knowledge and skills that are necessary for success. Progressing leaders actively seek and benefit from coaching and professional development. These leaders understand their limitations, set clear goals for themselves and the organization, and can be ruthlessly clear about their own weaknesses and strengths. The bridge from progressing to proficient is not easy to cross, but with sufficient clarity with regard to the boundaries, the leader knows when the transition has been made. A cardinal principle of leadership assessment is that the organization invests its resources in those leaders in whom it will have the maximum impact. Thus it is absolutely essential that the progressing leaders are afforded the opportunity to learn, grow, reflect, and progress through the introspective steps required to become proficient.

Some of the nonproficient leaders have potential for success, growth, and learning. They are, as the name implies, progressing. But other nonproficient leaders are simply ineffective, with the wrong person in the wrong position. These people can be offered training that consumes thousands of dollars and weeks of time, but they are unable or unwilling to react to it. The difference between progressing and ineffective can be elusive, as neither of these leaders possesses the characteristics and performance that the organization requires. But the difference is a crucial one in order to direct leadership development efforts with precision. Consider this example of a question that will differentiate the progressing from the ineffective leader: How does the leader respond to data? The progressing leader will ask, "What can I do to make a difference?" The ineffective leader blames the victim. In the context of student achievement, the leader with potential for development will examine data about inadequate student achievement and ask about curriculum, teaching, and leadership. The essence of these questions will be, "What can I do to make a difference to improve this situation?" The ineffective leader will look at the same set of data and ask, "What can I do? If the kids and parents aren't willing to help, then these kids are just doomed—there's nothing that curriculum, teaching, and leadership can influence here." This attitude can best be described as chosen impotence—the leader is unable or unwilling to assume responsibility for results. The key phrases that you will hear from these leaders include the following:

> We've only got six hours a day—what happens at home is a lot more important than anything we can do during the school day.

> What did you expect? They came here two grades below grade level— once they are that far behind, there's nothing we can do.

> We'd like to change the schedule to give students more time for literacy and math, but the last time we tried to make a change it was resisted by parents and teachers, so we're really just stuck with what we have.

> I know that we have standards, but I just don't know if it's appropriate for me to tell teachers what to teach or how to assess—after all, they are the experts, not me. Besides, I never wanted anyone telling me what to do when I was in the classroom.

> I just took over this department and don't want to make waves—after all, we've got a lot of buy-in for the way we have been doing things, and I need to respect that.

> I'd like to change things, but if I do, I'm sure that there will be some complaints, and I don't want to have my subordinates lose confidence in me before I start.

These leaders are not malevolent. Indeed, they are frequently appreciated and supported by their faculties. But they are ineffective, indifferent, impotent, and ultimately destructive to the cause of improved student achievement. They are not instructional leaders, but merely landlords, opening and closing the building or department. They are caretakers, not leaders.

Consider the example from Resource A on Domain 3.0, Student Achievement. The exemplary leader "routinely shares examples of specific leadership, teaching, and curriculum strategies that are associated with improved student achievement. Other leaders in the system credit this leader with sharing ideas, coaching teachers and leaders, and providing technical assistance to implement successful new initiatives." The proficient leader has "goals and strategies [that] reflect a clear relationship between the actions of teachers and leaders and the impact on student achievement. Results show steady improvements based on these leadership initiatives." The progressing leader "has established goals related to student achievement that are specific and measurable, but these efforts have yet to result in improved student achievement." The ineffective leader is remarkably different, because the "goals are neither measurable nor specific. The leader focuses more on student characteristics than on the actions of the teachers and leaders in the system."

Specification of performance is essential to the creation of an effective multidimensional performance assessment system. The traditional use of descriptions such as *outstanding, above average,* or *needs improvement* are unacceptable substitutes for the clarity and rigor of performance specification.

LEADERSHIP ASSESSMENT AS A RESEARCH GOLDMINE

When multidimensional leadership assessment is used effectively, it becomes a research goldmine that helps students, teachers, and leaders throughout the system. It is possible to evaluate system, building, and department results and ask this central question: Which leadership performance indicators were most clearly associated with our most important results? Systematic analysis of leadership behaviors and organizational results are rare, but they do exist. Collins (2001) provided some counterintuitive examples in which charisma, for example, was not related to improved organizational performance. The most important impact of multidimensional leadership assessment, however, is not resorting to external research literature, but rather a systematic set of observations about the degree of relationship between leadership performance and organizational performance. Each selection of a leadership dimension represents a hypothesis about the relationship between leadership practices and organizational results. Hypotheses are "if, then" statements. For example,

- If the leader provides exemplary performance in data analysis, then the organization will respond to data in such an effective manner that it will make appropriate mid-course corrections and improve performance.
- If the leader creates common performance assessments based on state standards, then the degree of reliability (agreement among teachers in scoring student work) will increase and the percentage of students who are proficient will increase.
- If the leader increases the number of faculty meetings and professional development sessions devoted to case studies of effective teaching practice, then the replication of best practices will increase and student achievement will improve.

- If the leader dresses in a manner that the district has traditionally approved, with men wearing coats and ties and women wearing dresses, then leadership performance will be more effective.

Whether these hypotheses are supported by the evidence is an open question. Although there is a substantial amount of national evidence to support some of these hypotheses, the only question relevant to your teachers and leaders is, "Does it work for me?" Multidimensional leadership assessment provides a systematic answer to that question. Because leadership performance is evaluated along a continuum of performance, the hypothesis can be tested. One example of data that supports the hypothesis is provided in Figure 6.1. An example of data that fails to support the hypothesis is provided in Figure 6.2.

At first glance, Figure 6.1 is a success while Figure 6.2 is a failure. In fact, we must respond to Figure 6.2 with the researcher's maxim that "we learn more from error than from uncertainty." Every mistaken measurement or unsupported hypothesis is an opportunity to learn more and to refine leadership practice. The accumulation of these hypotheses—both those supported by local evidence and those that are unsupported—provides the basis for focused leadership decisions in the future. The research goldmine provided by multidimensional leadership assessment is more than a guide for contemporary leaders. It will also provide a guide for the next generation of leaders and for those who select and train them.

Once you have created a multidimensional leadership assessment system, the challenge is to implement it within the unique culture of your system. This requires a respect for the goals, values, and priorities of your system as well as the systematic application of the leadership dimensions and performance specifications that you have developed. Although MLA provides the opportunity for quantitative analysis—the systematic measurement of the relationship between leadership practices and desired results—there is also an opportunity for qualitative analysis. With a combination of rich description and narrative analysis, qualitative research provides the lens through which quantitative analysis can be better understood.

ORGANIZATIONAL GOALS, VALUES, AND PRIORITIES

Fair and effective leadership evaluation is a mirror image of the organization's goals, values, and priorities. If the organization values integrity and teamwork, for example, then it does not reward leaders who achieve objectives at the cost of dishonesty or who elevate themselves at the expense of a team. When the leadership evaluation is not aligned with goals, values, and priorities, it is worse than no evaluation at all. In the absence of evaluation, leaders and other employees can wonder about whether the organization lives its values. When evaluation is misaligned, there is no doubt—the organization is hypocritical and the resulting loss of trust has a devastating impact on morale and productivity (Goleman et al., 2002). A brief review of Resource B reveals examples from the National Leadership Survey of respondents who might have been effective leaders, but whose evaluation experiences were so destructive that the organization lost credibility. The three greatest concerns of the respondents were the following:

Figure 6.1 Hypothesis Confirmed

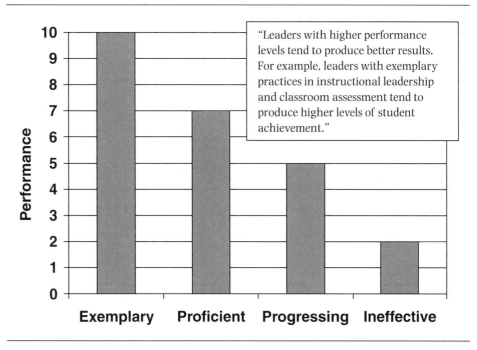

"Leaders with higher performance levels tend to produce better results. For example, leaders with exemplary practices in instructional leadership and classroom assessment tend to produce higher levels of student achievement."

Figure 6.2 Hypothesis Not Confirmed

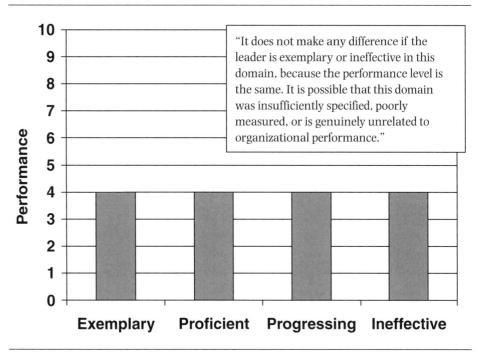

"It does not make any difference if the leader is exemplary or ineffective in this domain, because the performance level is the same. It is possible that this domain was insufficiently specified, poorly measured, or is genuinely unrelated to organizational performance."

1. No evaluation at all. Some respondents reported the utter absence of evaluation for years—in one case for 15 years. They regarded this as the ultimate in disrespect—that no one cared about their performance or took the time to acknowledge good work or help improve effectiveness.

2. Vague evaluation. Interestingly, the respondents to the leadership survey said that they could handle negative feedback, provided it was constructive. Among their comments were a dissatisfaction with "vague, broad compliments" and the statement that "everything's great—but no suggestions of what to do to help." Another respondent spoke for many saying, "Generally I have felt rather empty when no suggestions were given to me for improvement. Whenever evaluations are all positive and contain no suggestions for improvement, it leaves no motivation for growth and improvement."

3. Evaluation that reflected a personal agenda of the evaluator rather than of the organization's priorities. In the strongest possible terms, leaders accused their evaluators of lying to them when they had been told that the organization held one set of priorities, but their evaluations revealed a different set of priorities. Some evaluators collected complaints from parents, students, and colleagues and used the evaluation as an opportunity to review those anonymous complaints, with little regard to the leader's point of view. Other evaluators composed evaluations without any regard to the teaching, curriculum, and educational mission of the school. As one cynical respondent said, "I learned how to get a good evaluation—it's a dog and pony show." This is consistent with my observations of senior-level district officials who give the greatest weight in evaluating principals to attendance at district administrator meetings and far less consideration to leadership effectiveness in living the values, goals, and priorities of the school system.

Figure 6.3 provides a starting point for the alignment of leadership evaluation with the values of the organization. Begin by identifying the values, goals, and priorities of the district. Ideally, these are matters that the board and superintendent have articulated and supported over the course of years. Then for each area of organizational priority, identify a leadership domain. Examples of leadership domains are in Resource A, but each system will want to identify its own domains, using language that is most appropriate for the cultural context of that organization.

The senior leadership team must challenge itself to avoid the "kitchen sink" syndrome in which every desirable trait finds its way into the leadership evaluation system. Some of these evaluation systems become so cumbersome that they are used infrequently and ineffectively. While these systems may represent the accumulation of many stakeholders, they provide the discernment of none of them. Discernment requires focus and the making of difficult choices. Not every ideal leadership characteristic belongs in your leadership evaluation system. Rather, it is essential that only those leadership domains that are fundamental, linked to your mission and values, and subject to rigorous measurement should be included. If your leadership evaluation is too cumbersome, then it will not be used. That leads to the worst evaluation of all—no evaluation. Therefore, this alignment exercise must be used not only to add leadership domains that are absent from the system, but also to eliminate those parts of the current leadership evaluation system that are not linked to the values, goals, and priorities of the organization. In crafting the leadership domains for your organization, there is a delicate balancing act that is similar to that

Figure 6.3   Aligning Leadership Domains With Organizational Values, Goals, and Priorities

Values	Leadership Domains
Goals	Leadership Domains
Priorities	Leadership Domains

Copyright 2009 by Douglas B. Reeves. All rights reserved. Reprinted from *Assessing Educational Leaders: Evaluating Performance for Improved Individual and Organizational Results* (2nd ed.), by Douglas B. Reeves. Reproduction authorized only for the local school site that has purchased this book.

surrounding the establishment of an effective accountability system. When accountability is limited only to a consideration of test scores, it omits exceedingly important elements of the organization, such as teaching practice, curriculum, and leadership practices. However, when the accountability system attempts to reflect everything that every school and department is doing, it becomes a laundry list of initiatives and programs, offering little insight into how individual activities are related to student results and other system priorities. A balanced view of accountability includes not only test scores, but other priorities (safety, financial stability, continuous improvement, and student success beyond test scores) and links those priorities to specific actions by teachers, leaders, parents, and community members. This holistic view of accountability suggests a model for the selection of leadership domains in multidimensional leadership assessment. The domains should be more than instructional leadership, but less than a list of every personal and professional characteristic that a committee can imagine. Many of the national models of leadership evaluation suffer from this committee approach, and thus the leader, scrambling to be proficient at everything, focuses on nothing.

THE PERFORMANCE CONTINUUM

Even in those organizations that have articulated leadership domains and successfully aligned their domains with their values, goals, and priorities, the job of leadership evaluation is not complete without a consideration of the leader's performance in each domain. This is where the vast majority of the leadership evaluations we studied failed. While many educational systems have meticulously listed leadership domains and developed exhaustive evaluation programs of which they are very proud, they undermine the quality of their work by lapsing into ambiguity by allowing evaluators to describe each domain with terms such as *meets standards, average,* or *excellent* without ever describing in specific and objective terms what those descriptions mean.

The Specificity Imperative

How specific should performance descriptions be? The direct answer is "as specific as necessary to gain agreement by 80 percent of evaluators who consider the same leader in the same domain." Because perfection is not an option in this enterprise, evaluators have two choices of errors they might commit. The first error is that they are insufficiently specific and that error carries with it the risk of rampant unfairness, destructive evaluation practices, and demoralization of the leaders who are being evaluated. The second error is that the evaluators are too specific, and that carries with it the risk of failing to recognize creative and positive divergence from leadership domains and perhaps some legalistic hairsplitting on the degree to which certain criteria are met. Neither error is particularly appealing, but the second error—overspecificity— carries much less risk for the organization than the first error of insufficient specificity. If the performance criteria are described with too great a level of precision, then an open-ended qualitative description can be permitted so that the evaluator recognizes those leadership activities that took place outside of the described leadership domains. But if the performance criteria are imprecise, then the leader lacks a clear idea of how to move to the next level of performance.

Leadership Performance Levels

The terms used in multidimensional leadership assessment are the same as those used in assessing any other performance, whether by a student, teacher, or superintendent. Those terms are *exemplary, proficient, progressing,* and *not meeting standards.* Exemplary leaders not only meet all of the criteria for being proficient, but also have an impact beyond the walls of their organization. These leaders share information, serve as models and mentors for others, and regularly share their successes and failures in order to help the entire organization learn and grow. Examples of exemplary performance are contained in Resource A. The proficient leader meets the requirements for success in the organization. Proficiency is a required performance level for continued employment. The progressing leader is, as the label implies, making progress, but not yet proficient. This leader, however, has the potential to become proficient and represents an ideal candidate for the organization to invest time in professional development, mentoring, and coaching. The leader who does not meet standards is not making progress, shows little evidence of improvement, and is a poor candidate for the investment of time and resources in professional development. Organizations will not fix these leaders, but must reassign them to a role that is better suited to their talents.

QUALITATIVE INFORMATION: THE LENS FOR UNDERSTANDING QUANTITATIVE DATA

No matter how specific leadership assessment becomes and regardless of how much we attempt to quantify human behavior, there is inherently a qualitative element to leadership performance that must be the lens through which we better understand quantitative data. Qualitative information can include rich descriptions of organizational climate, detailed observations about the leader's personal characteristics and impact on others within the organization, and perhaps most important, notes and reflections by the leader, such as those discussed in the next section. The evaluator's qualitative information should be required to support with details any performance that is described as exemplary or not meeting standards. In fact, however, every rating should be supported by details, examples, and direct observations. While the qualitative dimension to leadership evaluation can become too voluminous to manage without some limitation on length, the exclusive reliance on numerical ratings and labels is inherently superficial. It is possible to have two leaders who are rated as proficient, but the qualitative information in the leadership narrative provides rich detail that illuminates significant differences between the two apparently identical leaders.

The need for the qualitative element in leadership performance evaluation has never been as important as it is now, when test scores dominate the landscape of educational evaluation. Only with qualitative descriptions can we learn the story behind the numbers. Inevitably, there will be an educational Enron in which the numbers look great and attract much favorable attention. After all, Enron was, not long ago, voted one of the most admired corporations in the United States, and observers ranging from stock analysts to business school professors were fawning over its innovative approach to business. With the loss of tens of thousands of jobs and tens of billions of dollars in personal savings and untold destruction to the personal lives of employees, it is fair to speculate that the admiration based on short-term stock price and illusory earnings was misplaced. There was, of course, a story behind the numbers, but the numbers looked so great that few people bothered to look deeper. The educational Enron will be the school that has apparently high test scores, but did so by accelerating the dropout rate, misusing special education labels and exclusions, and delaying admissions of students who might adversely affect test scores. Devastated students and demoralized faculty do not appear anywhere on a list of test scores, but they will be readily apparent in the qualitative information of an effective leadership evaluation system.

REFLECTION AND SELF-REGULATION

The most effective student assessments are used not merely to evaluate student work, but to improve student learning. Similarly, the most effective leadership assessments do far more than meet a requirement for the human resources department, but become a constructive force for personal improvement by every leader in the system. Leaders need not write an autobiography, but they should engage in some serious reflection as part of the evaluative process. Too frequently, the leader's participation in the evaluation devolves into a point–counterpoint, with an attempt to refute any implication by the evaluator that the leader is less than stellar. These arguments almost always appear defensive and petulant, and rarely have the positive impact the leader had expected. Rather than a reactive contribution, the leader should provide a proactive contribution to the evaluation. Before the evaluator has begun the process of evaluation, the leader should contribute to the process by responding to these questions and perhaps others that the evaluator and leader regard as important:

- What has the leader learned since the last evaluation?
- What does the leader regard as an important strength that should receive greater focus and attention?
- Who has the leader identified as people with additional leadership potential?
- What examples can the leader provide in which decisive leadership decisions have had an impact on other individuals and on the organization as a whole?
- How can the organization better support the leader to become more effective?
- What are the leader's personal goals to improve personal leadership performance?

The answers to such probing questions can range from detailed descriptions to "I honestly do not know." Whatever the response, leaders cannot expect students and teachers to be reflective learners if the leader does not model such a challenging discipline of thoughtful and rigorous self-analysis.

In many cases, leadership evaluation casts a backward glance, focusing on the previous performance of educational leaders. When it reaches its greatest potential, however, leadership evaluation is forward looking. Using the tool of multidimensional leadership assessment, we can not only consider the past actions of leaders, but use what we have learned to build the next generation of school leaders. That is the subject of the next chapter.

Building the 7
Next Generation of
Educational Leaders

THE LEADERSHIP DEVELOPMENT IMPERATIVE

At a recent Leadership and Policy Forum at Harvard University, the general issue of the crisis in education quickly became the issue of the crisis in educational leadership. Participants bemoaned the fact that a growing number of schools were opening without principals and an increasing number of districts had superintendents who were serving in an interim status. Indeed, there is a growing market for retired superintendents who are willing to serve in that capacity while the board of education continues its futile search to find the perfect candidate who has all of the qualifications of a Fortune 500 CEO and who will work for 1/100th of the pay. To some extent the crisis in leadership is a self-inflicted wound. As districts have improved the pay of teachers, the equation is not difficult to figure out: "I can make $75,000 at the top of the teacher pay scale on a nine-month contract and make in the neighborhood of $52 an hour. Or I can take a promotion to become an administrator for $80,000 a year, so I can work a 12-month year of 50-hour weeks—far more if I am successful and become a principal or superintendent—and then my hourly rate declines to about $32. Now tell me again how this is a promotion?

As a teacher I had seniority and tenure, but as an administrator I have a daily diet of threats, intimidation, humiliation, and zero job security." When the phenomenon of principal shortages is combined with that of early retirements, there is an imminent crisis in leadership development. There is a name for people who can successfully manage hundreds or thousands of people and who can balance multimillion-dollar budgets. We call them presidents and chief executive officers, and we pay them hundreds of thousands of dollars, along with stock options and munificent benefits. To be blunt, money matters.

In the nation's most challenging schools, teachers and principals leave in droves (*Quality Counts,* 2003). These professionals are regarded as the cause of school success or failure and are weary of the accusations that seem never to prevail in a wealthy suburban setting. Thus, the principals and educators leaving high-poverty urban schools in particular are not enticed by money alone. They require safety, time, and respect, as a good start, to remain in their positions. For a limited period of time, school systems can raid neighboring districts for leadership talent, but over the long haul, each school system must develop its own leadership talent base. Moreover, if the organization is ever to have congruity between its values and the daily decisions of leadership, then the people assigned to leadership positions must largely share the values, history, culture, and traditions of that organization. This requires internal leadership development.

PROTOTYPE FOR A LEADERSHIP DEVELOPMENT SYSTEM

It starts with the custodian. In a remarkable Ohio school system, the superintendent decided to meet the challenge of a teaching and leadership shortage with the people he or she knew best—their own employees. These people loved kids, devoted their careers to being around them, and cared deeply about their success. For whatever reason, they had not achieved a college degree and the opportunities associated with it. But they had the bone-deep belief in children. Thus they recruited custodians, paraprofessionals, secretaries, recreation aides, food service workers, and others to join in an effort to finish their degrees, to become student teachers, and eventually to assume teaching positions in the schools. When a 50-year-old man can address his new class of fourth-grade students, who only a year before knew him as the custodian, he is a walking example of the impact of high expectations. Before this gentleman retires, he will be a principal. There is leadership potential under our noses if only we will acknowledge that talent emerges in the most unusual places. Thus the first step to prototypical leadership development is this: enlarge the talent pool. Quantity precedes quality. Rather than raiding neighboring districts or, more tragically, taking a wonderful teacher from the classroom—a teacher who does not have interest or ability in leadership—find the leaders who are all around you.

AUTHENTIC ASSESSMENT FOR FUTURE LEADERS

Step 1: Use Leadership Domains to Create Vignettes of Exemplary Performance

The time to consider the relationship between leadership evaluation and organizational performance is before the leader's first day on the job. Excellent teachers do not delay assessment until the end of the school year, but start each year with assessment so that they can better understand the needs of students and develop educational strategies that are related to those changing needs. Similarly, great organizations do not assess leaders only when it is time for the official evaluation, but rather begin the assessment process before the leader is hired. Thus it is impossible to create a leadership assessment system unless you have first identified leadership domains as described earlier in this book. Further, it is impossible to create meaningful leadership domains if the organization does not have clear vision, mission, goals, and priorities. Without explicit and widely understood vision, it is impossible for the leadership domains to be aligned with the organization's priorities.

After you create leadership domains for your organization, create scenarios in which each domain might be lived out. Write vignettes—realistic stories with rich descriptions of human behavior and decision-making processes— that portray exemplary performance for each domain. These vignettes serve to create a theoretical view of leadership competencies. For example, Leadership Domain 1.4 is "Constructively handles dissent from subordinates." The description of performance for that domain appears in Figure 7.1.

Figure 7.1 Performance Levels for Leadership Domain 1.4, Constructively Handles Dissent From Subordinates

Exemplary	Proficient	Progressing	Not Meeting Standards
Creates constructive contention, assigning roles if necessary to deliberately generate multiple perspectives and considers different sides of important issues. Recognizes and rewards thoughtful dissent. Uses dissenting voices to learn, grow, and where appropriate, acknowledge the leader's error. Encourage constructive dissent, in which multiple voices are encourage and heard, and the final decision is made better and is more broadly supportedas a result.	Leader uses dissent to inform final decisions, improve the quality of decision making, and broaden support for final decisions.	Leader tolerates dissent, but there is very little of it in public because subordinates do not understand the leader's philosophy about the usefulness of dissent.	Dissent is absent due to a climate of fear and intimidation.

Based on the description of exemplary performance in this leadership domain, we might create a vignette such as this:

James Sackett was in his third year as principal at Madison Middle School, and precisely 30 seconds into the faculty meeting, the taciturn seventh-grade math teacher, Mr. Bruce, was at it again. "Administrators have had some bone-headed ideas around here in my 32 years of teaching, but this takes the bloody cake!" And that was just the start. James came to this school after the brief tenure of an autocratic bully who never permitted dissent and kept Mr. Bruce, and everyone else for that matter, under his thumb. Dissent happened, of course, but it occurred in secret, out of the earshot of the principal. Student performance and faculty morale were awful, and James was brought in with the mandate of either turning the building around or facing mandatory reconstitution, with the faculty and administrators facing reassignment or job loss. James has, so far, been successful. Achievement is up, though still in need of improvement. Faculty morale is far better, with laughter heard in faculty meetings for the first time in years. But James' open and welcoming style of leadership has a downside—it liberated the cynics like Mr. Bruce to revel in their long-lost freedom to express themselves at every opportunity. The challenge was not how to stifle Mr. Bruce and repeat the mistakes of the past, but rather to channel his energy in a more constructive way.

"That's precisely what we need!" James said enthusiastically to Mr. Bruce's caustic remark. Perplexed, Mr. Bruce was quiet for the first time in anyone's memory. "You see," explained James, "we can't build great ideas with only one point of view, and we need Mr. Bruce and others to participate in what I'm going to call *constructive contention.*"

Regaining his familiar ground, Bruce countered, "I don't care what you call it, this idea for every math teacher using the same exam every quarter is still dumb."

"OK," said James, "I assume that means you will volunteer to be on the team to critique that idea. That's exactly what we need. Will anyone else join Mr. Bruce? Great."

"What do you mean constructive contention?" Ms. Boomer, a first-year math teacher quietly asked.

"Whenever we make important decisions, we need to consider all the pros and cons, advantages and disadvantages. So Mr. Bruce has offered to help make this common assessment program better by contributing ideas about why it might fail. We need to anticipate all of these ideas as well as the possible advantages of the proposal, in order to make the best decision possible. We'll devote some time in the next two faculty meetings to identifying these issues and then reframe the decision so that we minimize the disadvantages and maximize the advantages."

"Why bother?" interrupted Mr. Bruce. "The central office is going to do what it wants to anyway."

"There are some things we can't control, and you're right that the superintendent is going to require common assessments every quarter, but by taking into account your point of view, we can anticipate all the things that can go wrong and avoid a great deal of difficulty in the future. I understand that you don't like the decision and I respect that, but your ideas are actually very valuable in helping all of us to make this work. So, Mr. Bruce, let's start the process. Please identify what can go wrong here—I'll be happy to take notes. . . ."

Because the discussion required Mr. Bruce to be specific rather than general, he had only a few things to add to the discussion, but he felt validated by the respect granted by the principal. Mr. Bruce is still unhappy and cynical, but the rest of the faculty noted that this conversation opened the door for dialogue rather than argument, for reasoned disagreement rather than angry confrontation. Moreover, Mr. Bruce did have some good ideas, such as accommodations for the needs of developmentally delayed students, that the central office had not taken into account. For the first time, he heard an administrator accept his concerns, validate them, and agree with them. While Mr. Bruce did not succeed in scuttling plans for the common assessments, he left the meeting feeling that he made a contribution to the decision-making process. More important, the faculty observed in James Sackett's skillful handling of the matter a combination of leadership, respect, sensitivity, and listening that they had rarely seen in a school leader.

Is James Sackett a principal of mythic proportions? As exceptional as he was in the handling of dissent, perhaps Mr. Sackett is not so great in other leadership dimensions. Neither he nor any leader represents perfection, but he does perform in an exemplary manner in this particular leadership domain. The story of James Sackett is a far more compelling way to describe leadership performance than the words of an evaluation form. Moreover, the thought required to create the vignette requires the organization's senior leaders to put muscle, sinew, and flesh on the skeleton of leadership domains. With vignettes full of rich description, the leadership domains become living documents.

Step 2: Use Exemplary Leaders to Add Realism to the Vignettes

The next step is to identify leaders who are exceptional—far beyond proficient and by consensus opinion the prototype of exemplary performance for each domain. Do not select the "generally excellent" leader, but rather identify the leader who is superior for each individual trait. It is entirely possible that the leader who excels in technology may not excel in instructional leadership, and the leader who is superior in personal relationships may not excel in data analysis. By focusing on each individual leadership domain, you will build the composite picture of leadership excellence to which all candidates for leadership positions should aspire. Ask the exemplary leaders to describe, with as much detail and authentic description as possible, examples of their performance in the domain in which they have been identified as exemplary. These descriptions may be less elegant than a contrived scenario, but they will contribute authentic details. By combining the vignette with the realistic examples of exemplary performance from real leaders, you will be able to refine the vignettes and increase their authenticity and value to the leadership evaluation process.

Step 3: Create Realistic Leadership Scenarios

In the vignette above, we saw a realistic scenario—a negative and cynical staff member challenging the leader about a new policy. This is something virtually every leader must face. Prospective leaders will react in different ways to this scenario: Precisely 30 seconds into the faculty meeting, the taciturn seventh-grade math teacher, Mr. Bruce, announces, "Administrators have had some bone-headed ideas around here in my 32 years of teaching, but this takes the bloody cake!" Mr. Bruce is referring to the new district policy of requiring common end-of-quarter math assessments. How would you handle this situation?

This challenge can be presented in writing or, better yet, in a performance assessment in which one of the interviewers is playing the role of Mr. Bruce. The leadership candidate's actual words and responses will be far more revealing than the abstract descriptions that are the stuff of unproductive interviews. In the safety of an interview, the candidate might mouth the words, "Of course I respect different points of view" or the candidate might wish to exude authority by saying, "I'll consider dissent, but once the district has made the decision, it's my job to execute it," thinking that the district official interviewing him wants to hear such obedience. In the context of a performance assessment, however, the otherwise gentle and articulate candidate can melt under the pressure. Some will wilt, attempting to agree with Mr. Bruce in an attempt to mollify him. Others will metamorphose into Attila the Hun, pounding the table and snapping, "That's enough of your bull. This isn't your decision, so just do what you're told." Other leaders will retreat into obsequious submission to the organization and say (as I heard a supervisor once say), "We're just cogs in the machine here, so you do your job and I'll do mine." When interviewing leadership candidates, their reactions to scenarios are always more revealing than their reactions to questions. Attila might say, "I like people!" but would show his barbarian side when confronted with a scenario. Casper Milquetoast will exude authority in the abstract, but will melt under the pressure of a confrontation of a dissident faculty member. In fact, the interviewer is not looking for the right answer, but rather the behavior that is most similar to the successful actions of the leader in the vignette and the successes described by real leaders within the organization.

Step 4: Ensure Fairness in Leadership Evaluation

If we were assessing students, the key requirements would be validity and reliability. In lay terms, the requirement for validity is that we test what we think we are testing. In the context of the classroom, it means that if we claim to assess something called "mathematics" then we really are assessing math, rather than some combination of English literacy, personal behavior, time management, and parental attention. In the context of leadership evaluation, validity means that if we claim to assess a leadership domain, we are assessing that domain rather than some combination of personal eloquence, appearance, grooming, and style. The requirement for reliability is also key to fairness. Reliability is all about consistency—the same performance must yield the same score in a reliable evaluation, whether that performance has to do with behavior in the classroom, writing a history exam, or performance on a leadership assessment. If five different teachers evaluated behavior and history performance in five different ways, we would complain that the evaluative process is unfair. If five different senior leaders would evaluate a leadership candidate in five different ways, then such a process is also decidedly unfair—it is not consistent and therefore it is not reliable.

How can leadership evaluation achieve the goal of fairness? First, there must be a crystal-clear relationship between the questions and scenarios of the evaluative process and the priorities of the district. It sounds obvious, but it is not. We must consider whether we are asking the questions that are most relevant to leadership success. That is why the leadership vignettes and scenarios from the most successful leaders are so important. Second, we must ensure that each evaluation is consistent. Candidates must be asked the same questions in the same way. They must be offered the opportunity to react to the same scenario in the same way. If some leadership candidates respond in writing while others respond orally, it is neither a consistent nor a reliable system of evaluation. If some leadership candidates have a time limit and others do not, it is neither reliable nor fair.

Real Time Feedback for Improved Leadership Performance

Here is a radical idea: Use leadership evaluation to improve the performance of leaders who do not yet work for you. Traditionally, job interviews are one-sided. They are designed for the exclusive benefit of the employer, not the prospective employee who is, after all, the supplicant at the table. This equation would change dramatically if we used job interviews to improve the performance of each candidate, even those we did not hire. The only way this can happen is if we provide real time feedback. That is the antithesis of, "We'll let you know in a few weeks." One person receives a call of congratulations, while all the other candidates receive a form letter saying that they were not selected. No one in the process learns what the interviewers really thought, but only received binary feedback—yes–no, hire–reject, wonderful–wretched. This system would change dramatically if the senior leaders conducting the leadership interviews would only consider devoting a few minutes to real time evaluation. This might be as simple as sharing with the candidates the vignettes and descriptions of exemplary performance from the district's own best leaders. The conversation might sound something like this:

"We have not made any decisions yet about hiring the candidate for this position, but we would like to offer you some information about how your responses to our questions and scenarios compared to those of the ideal candidate. . . ." When candidates are hired, they know what is expected. For those candidates who are not selected, they received more than a job interview—they received exceptional professional development in effective leadership. The risk in such a procedure is that the expectations of the district will be leaked to other candidates in the future. This would be the adult equivalent of teaching to the test. So the worst case scenario is that prospective leaders in your system learn what you want, change their leadership style, and deliver what you wish in order to meet your expectations. That is not cheating; that is learning.

Leading Leaders 8

THE COACHING CONUNDRUM: RESULTS OR ANTECEDENTS?

If multidimensional leadership assessment (MLA) were only used for evaluating leaders, it would fall far short of its potential. Moreover, the time required for MLA would not be justified if this system only provided information to leaders and policymakers. The ultimate value in any information, and particularly in the information generated by MLA, is the application of that information to improve performance by both the leader and the entire organization.

It is tempting to oversimplify the equation. The clarion call of "We want results!" rings from boardrooms and executive suites throughout the world. Cartoonists have lampooned bureaucratic processes with justification, as they highlight the antics of leaders who provide terrible results but nevertheless take great pride in their skill with meetings or their enthusiastic flogging of the latest management fads. To be sure, results are important. The leader who possesses integrity, empathy, technology savvy, and a host of other desirable characteristics is of little value to an organization that is threatened with disintegration. While bankruptcy used to be a fear only in the business world, a growing number of school leaders face legislatively mandated takeovers by state officials if the results they produce are insufficient. There is no doubt about it: Results matter, but results are not enough. Senior leaders—the leaders of leaders—must continuously monitor their systems to identify a combination of results and antecedents.

In education in particular, there is a common dichotomy between processes and results. In the classroom, I have heard teachers say with some pride that

"We focus on process, not product," as if the final product were irrelevant to the students' ultimate success. Other educators and leaders take equal pride with their focus on the educational bottom line, saying in essence, "Use whatever processes you want to, the only thing that matters is your next set of test scores." As Goleman et al. (2002) have pointed out, there are times for leaders to assume a variety of different roles, including that of visionary, relationship builder, and taskmaster focused on immediate results. Their analysis makes clear, however, that the taskmaster approach can be effective only in the short term, typically in a time of crisis. Ultimately, a balanced approach of leadership styles is required, either by the senior leader developing the capacity to adopt multiple leadership styles or, more commonly, by the senior leadership team explicitly sharing different essential leadership roles. As the pool of educational leaders continues to erode, the identification, development, and nurturing of leaders is one of the highest priorities of every senior leader. Superintendents and board members who are not devoting extensive time, attention, and resources to leadership development are building a house of straw that, in the next few years, will fail to withstand the winds of challenge and change.

The Futility of Impatience

Senior leaders (and the boards to which they report) are notoriously impatient. Indeed, impatience is often regarded as a strength. Psychologists refer to *achievement orientation* and *drive* as terms that characterize successful leaders. These leaders excuse their impatience by saying, "I never ask more out of my subordinates than I expect of myself." True to their word, these driven leaders lead by example, arriving early, staying late, making sacrifices to advance the interests of the organization that they serve. Rather than develop leaders, they seem to attract similarly driven people who share the ambition, relentlessness, drive, and willingness to sacrifice that their leader exemplifies. In the short term, this personal commitment driven by a charismatic leader may suffice to develop a leadership cadre. But over time, charisma is ephemeral. Leaders move, subordinates become burned out, and competing demands, including family, health, and personal development, compete with the leader's latest emergency project. Thus the impatience that we so frequently associate with leadership drive is not sustainable as a long-term leadership development strategy.

Patience is essential because leadership development takes time. Few leaders would wish to replicate their performance on their first day on any job, from classroom educator to superintendent. Although the length of the learning curve may vary among people and positions, it is almost always longer than we initially assume. We learn to give ourselves multiple opportunities for success, just as the best teachers routinely give students many opportunities. These great teachers use feedback to improve performance and insist that students continue to learn and grow through numerous attempts at difficult and challenging tasks. Similarly, the leader is far better in conducting the 20th interview, evaluation, or performance review than in the first such encounters. Nevertheless, multiple opportunities for success cannot become infinite opportunities for success. Time limits, for leaders, their subordinates, and entire organizations, are appropriate. But time limits only have value if the leader is willing to state what the limit means. "Do this by January 31st or I will be disappointed," is much less meaningful than, "If the project is not completed by January 31st, I will reassign it to another leader. Please tell me now if you are willing to make a commitment to finish it by January 31st." When it comes to leadership development, the choices are not between the patient and impatient senior leaders. A more nuanced approach is necessary, requiring explicit deadlines and clear consequences where appropriate and the patience required for multiple—perhaps dozens—of attempts to become proficient in a particular leadership domain.

INQUIRY AND HYPOTHESIS TESTING

The mythology of leadership suggests that instinct and intuition are the primary tools in the arsenal of the successful senior leader. Much of the popular press nurtures this myth, as secrecy and legend are more easily marketed than a more mundane, systematic, and logical approach. In practice, I hear few successful leaders advocate a practice because "I feel it in my gut," and a growing number of successful leaders say, "What information do we have to guide this decision? Let's look at the data." Multidimensional leadership assessment gives the senior leader a wealth of information, the power of which extends far beyond personnel evaluations. Specifically, MLA allows the senior leader to ask questions and test hypotheses. Questions that leaders may wish to consider include the following:

- Of our highest-performing leaders, what were the leadership domains where those leaders exhibited exemplary performance?
- Where else in our system can I find exemplary performers in these same leadership domains?
- Of our highest-performing leaders, what were the leadership domains where those leaders exhibited less than proficient performance?
- What would a map of our strengths look like? Where can I find exemplary practice in each of our leadership domains?
- Of our newest leadership recruits, in which leadership domains do they exhibit the greatest and least strength?
- How does our professional development and leadership development curriculum correspond to our leadership domains? How does it correspond to the leadership domains where we lack exemplary performers?
- How does the training provided by our outside vendors of leadership training correspond to our leadership domains? How does it correspond to the leadership domains where we lack exemplary performers?

Hypotheses are "if, then" statements that are subject to empirical testing. Hypotheses that senior leaders may wish to test include those that are frequently implicit, but rarely tested. The following three hypotheses are almost always untested because their truth has been widely accepted, as if faith in the unseen is a substitute for evidence:

- If we send a leader who is less than proficient to a one-day time management training program (or coaching, or project management, or fill in the name of any of the popular management training programs here), then the leader's performance in this domain will improve to a proficient or exemplary level.
- If I hold a performance coaching session with a leader whose performance is unsatisfactory, then the leader will use that feedback to become proficient.
- If a prospective leader has a doctorate, then that person will perform at a higher level according to our leadership domains than a leader who holds a master's degree.

Unless these hypotheses and many others like them are rigorously tested, we are unable to give senior leaders the focus that they need to be effective. One useful device for developing senior leadership focus is the leadership and learning matrix (Reeves, 2002a), displayed in Figure 8.1.

On the vertical axis, we plot the results—student achievement, parent involvement, attendance rate, school safety, staff morale, or any number of other important factors that the senior leadership regards as essential for organizational success. The senior leader focused only on results would stop there, but as the matrix indicates, such a superficial approach fails to distinguish

Figure 8.1   The Leadership and Learning Matrix

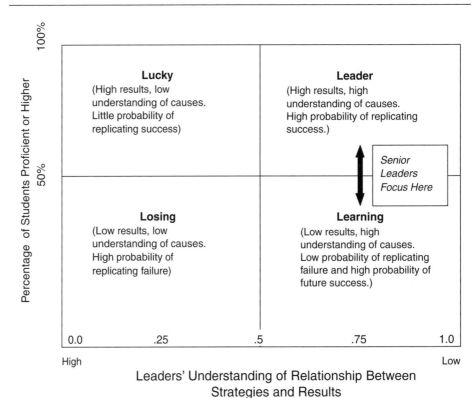

between the leader who is merely lucky (high results with a low understanding of causes) and the leader who is likely to have long-term success. Similarly, a focus on results alone will smear both the "loser" who replicates poor decisions for failure to understand them and the "learner" who, despite poor results, has conducted deep inquiry and achieved a comprehensive understanding of the antecedents of excellence. The value of the leadership and learning matrix is this: Senior leaders focus their energy on the continuum between the leader and the learner. They maximize the strengths of their strongest leaders and apply those strengths to the leaders with lower results who have the deepest understanding of how to improve. Senior leaders are not enamored of the superficiality of the "lucky" leader, and the only time they devote to the "loser" is the arrangement of a change in job assignment.

APPLYING MLA THROUGHOUT THE ORGANIZATION

Clearly the use of MLA has application for more than leadership evaluation. It can be an integral part of the daily development of today's leaders as well as the identification and recruitment of the next generation of leadership. But MLA has application beyond those identified as leaders. When we think of the imperative for leadership in complex organizations, the definition of the leader must extend far beyond those who have the title. In some school systems, bus drivers participate in professional development programs on student psychology and discipline, and proudly display their certificates of completion in their buses, right next to their awards for improved bus behavior. In a growing number of schools, teachers are running faculty meetings and professional development seminars, as principals dispense with their traditional practice of reading announcements and sit literally on the same side of the table with teachers, modeling the need to learn even as they lead. When accountability and evaluation become constructive forces in an organization, all stakeholders, including employees, vendors, parents, and students, know the importance of their role and how they are as surely a part of the antecedents of excellence as are the senior leaders. When used publicly and widely, multidimensional leadership assessment sounds the clarion call that "what you do matters."

The history of evaluation as a negative and destructive force has had another unfortunate consequence—secrecy. Thus, not only do traditional leadership evaluations fail to help the leader improve performance, their secrecy prevents any potential use to improve organizational performance. MLA, by contrast, can be used to improve the results for the individual and the organization if it is a transparent process and the cumulative results are shared widely and used as the basis for leadership development and decision making. Because the MLA process is constructive, transparent, and fair, leaders can post their evaluation publicly. Rather than react to evaluation with inappropriate defensiveness or misplaced pride, leaders can use MLA to acknowledge their limitations and seek the collaboration of their colleagues and subordinates.

Imagine for a moment the educational leader who returns from an evaluation session, posts the evaluation on the wall of the faculty lounge, and then says the following words with conviction:

> There isn't a leader in the world who is exemplary in every category, and I know that I am not either. But I intend to work every day to become better, and I need your help to do it. You can help improve academic achievement by sharing your best practices. I have so much I need to learn, and some of the best teachers are in this room, if only you will share your best practices and let me publicize them. You can help me improve resilience by encouraging me when I'm down just as I will seek to do for you. You can help me to improve the way that I handle dissent by reminding me of the value of constructive contention and helping to separate issues from personalities. You can help me improve the way we use data analysis by sharing classroom data and thoughtfully linking it to other data sources. No one knows your classroom assessment results better than you, and we both know that accountability must be more than a listing of state test scores.
>
> Finally, you can help me identify future leaders. I know that some of them are in this room. Some of them are your student teachers, and some of them are students in your classrooms. We are in an honorable profession, and we need great teachers and leaders. I haven't done a good enough job of telling you how much I love my job, how personally satisfying it is, and why those of you with leadership aspirations should consider a future in educational leadership. Of course I'm not exemplary in every area, but I know that with your help I can become better. That's why I'm posting my own multidimensional leadership assessment on the board in this room. I want you to know my weaknesses as well as my strengths, and I want you to know that I believe that you can help me become a more effective leader. If we are to build a climate of trust and mutual collaboration in this organization, then the leader must be trusting. So I am. Could this be embarrassing? Sure, but I have a feeling that you already know most of the areas where I need more work. Whatever embarrassment I feel by sharing this assessment will be more than compensated for by the improvements we will all make together. I'm counting on you.

Improving Leadership Evaluation With Multidimensional Leadership Assessment 9

Topics Presented in Chapter 9 Include

- ✓ Analyze the Present Evaluation System
- ✓ Create Dimensions of Leadership
- ✓ Specify Performance Levels
- ✓ Field Test the Instrument at Multiple Levels
- ✓ Implement Throughout the Organization
- ✓ Share Results With Universities and Research Institutions
- ✓ Use MLA for Training, Recruiting, and Developing Leaders

This chapter presents a summary of multidimensional leadership assessment (MLA) and describes the steps to move this system from conception to reality. Because MLA provides a continuous stream of data on leadership effectiveness within your system, it invites unending improvement and refinement. Some dimensions will prove more powerfully related to your organizational objectives than others. Some dimensions will require greater specificity, while others will require more flexibility. New challenges will arise for educational leaders, and new dimensions of leadership will be required to assess performance in those areas. Thus MLA is not a package to be neatly wrapped in a bow and delivered to a school system. Rather, it is an ongoing process that will help the most experienced leaders become more effective and help them identify, train, and develop the leaders of tomorrow.

ANALYZE THE PRESENT EVALUATION SYSTEM

Change never occurs without dissatisfaction. Senior leaders search in vain for a painless way to get buy-in from their staff for a new initiative. If the term *buy-in* connotes a sense of joyful acquiescence to the abandonment of practices to which the staff has been emotionally attached for decades, then it is a fruitless quest. Losses are painful, even when a rational examination of the evidence suggests that those losses will be replaced by new practices that are more productive. For every leader who has been frustrated with the reluctance of a staff to change, the prospect of replacing the old leadership evaluation system will create a striking degree of empathy for the resisters of change. After all, the old leadership evaluation system has treated many leaders very well. While it may not have been related to the leader's daily tasks or the organization's mission, the annual evaluations did provide some affirmation and tangible evidence of recognition. For leaders who receive an unrelenting barrage of criticism and few financial rewards compared to their counterparts in the private sector, these traditional evaluations have been among the most important pieces of compensation that they receive. These systems will not be changed unless there is a rigorous examination of their frailties and sufficient discontent with their weaknesses.

One good exercise would be for a task force to review a sample of 30 or more evaluations (with no names, of course) from your system over the past 2 or 3 years. Look for comments that range from constructive to destructive, from specific to ambiguous, from direct relationship to the organization's mission to a reflection of personal agendas. After this examination, see if some of the narrative comments we received in the National Study of Leadership Evaluation resonate with you:

> Generally I have felt rather empty when no suggestions were given to me for improvement. Whenever evaluations are all positive and contain no suggestions for improvement, it leaves no motivation for growth and improvement.

> As a new principal, I would have appreciated and grown professionally if I valued the evaluation process. . . . The process was just a task that had to be completed. No standards or performance goals [were] communicated.

> While I was an assistant principal, I did not receive an evaluation for 3 years. I was never sure what the principal wanted.

> My worst experience being evaluated as a leader is my current year—my first as an elementary school principal. The person supervising me is an assistant superintendent, a person with whom I have few contacts. I feel that I do not have frequent access to this person for clarifying questions and for feedback. I feel as though I am expected to know exactly what to do in every situation. There is no scaffolding of

learning and I am required to seek out knowledge and information on my own from many sources. In this environment, I do not feel that the final evaluation that I will be receiving will be at all meaningful or helpful.

Most evaluations have been very generic. Administrators simply check "Professionally Competent" in each category. This does not give me specific feedback. It doesn't inspire me or help me set goals. Evaluation in its formal sense seems only to be an isolated process completely disconnected and unrelated to my instructional practice. Furthermore, I've not yet had an administrator whom I consider to be an instructional leader. They are so disconnected from the classroom reality that they can't properly advise me.

These are not the comments of people who fear evaluation or object to requirements for improved performance. But they find their evaluation systems are ill-equipped to help them achieve their potential. There are a number of newly developed leadership evaluation systems that started down the right path, identifying characteristics of leadership that were more closely linked to student achievement and other systemwide objectives than had previously been the case. A growing number of states have created leadership standards or adopted the leadership standards suggested by national organizations. But even evaluation systems based on these standards are of little value if the performance specification for each standard lapses into the ambiguous language of "sometimes, always, never" or "some evidence, much evidence" or "outstanding, average, poor." Finally, even if a system similar to MLA has been adopted in your district, it must be continuously examined for improvement. Are the results of leadership evaluations used as a research goldmine? Are the hypotheses suggested by each dimension of leadership rigorously tested with real data? Is the system open to the creation of new dimensions of leadership, the refinement of others, and the elimination of those dimensions that no longer serve a useful purpose?

Because the authors of your leadership evaluation system are probably still employed in your organization, it is essential that they are part of the solution. The recognition of the need for MLA or any other systemic improvement does not convey malice or incompetence for the creators of previous systems, any more than the development of improved student assessments conveys an intentional insult to the designers of tests in the past. But none of these improvements will happen without a candid analysis of the present system and an open and frank discussion of its weaknesses. Change will not happen without dissatisfaction.

CREATE DIMENSIONS OF LEADERSHIP

The dimensions of leadership suggested in Resource A are merely suggestions, not prescriptions. They are at best a first draft for a consideration by your task force as it seeks to create dimensions of leadership that reflect the unique needs and specific culture of your system. Whenever a group is processing ideas, however, it tends to be much better at the accumulation of ideas than the refinement of them. That is the reason that initiatives, strategic plans, and board goals tend to grow into ever-expanding monsters that consume time, energy, and money but lack the focus required for effectiveness. Each participant affirms everyone else's ideas because the participants wish their own ideas to be similarly affirmed. Thus the list grows without boundaries and, with each subsequent addition, there are fewer minutes, dollars, and quantities of leadership attention available to be devoted to any individual item on the list. The process of accumulation is fine for brainstorming, but it will ruin the utility of your leadership evaluation system if the process of accumulation is not followed by a process of refinement. While there is no magic number of leadership dimensions, it is fair to say that the more qualities of leadership you identify, the less able the individual leader will be to focus on each of those qualities. This book identifies 10 dimensions of leadership, and while that number may not be ideal, it is certainly better than the lists we observed in other evaluation instruments that extended into 20 or 30 different areas. While each of those areas may have been important, the inability of the authors of those instruments to refine them prevented leaders in those systems from focusing on the areas that might have been most important for leadership success.

SPECIFY PERFORMANCE LEVELS

The most glaring omission in most leadership evaluation systems is the failure to specify performance levels. We know that if feedback is to be effective for students, it must be specific, accurate, and timely. The need for specificity is essential in every area of human performance. Moreover, those who are evaluating leaders have a moral obligation to be fair and consistent in their expectations. If they cannot specify what a quality such as instructional leadership or communication skills really means, then they cannot evaluate these qualities with any degree of fairness.

Evaluation is frequently regarded as something designed only for those new in the profession. For teachers, for example, evaluations have the greatest impact during the early years when tenure is far from certain. But for the 20- or 30-year veteran of the profession, evaluation—if it happens at all—tends to be infrequent and superficial. After all, the reasoning goes, if it does not have an impact on hiring and firing, what value does evaluation really have? In MLA, the value can be extraordinary. Because performance is specified at all levels, the veteran leader who is proficient can nevertheless be challenged to become exemplary. The exemplary leader can be challenged to share her gifts throughout the system in order to have a multidimensional impact. The progressing leader who has been tolerated for years but is not really proficient can be challenged with very specific guidance to attain proficiency. None of these challenges happen with earnest exhortation. Effective challenges occur only with specificity. If I wish to lower my blood pressure, it is of little help for my physician to vigorously shout the word "lower" during my physical examination. I need specific guidance with regard to the regimen of exercise, diet, and other health practices that the physician regards as proficient and exemplary performance. My health depends on this degree of specificity. Your organizational health similarly depends upon the level of specificity that you provide for each leadership dimension.

FIELD TEST THE INSTRUMENT AT MULTIPLE LEVELS

Once the dimensions of leadership have been established and performance has been specified for each dimension, then the new instrument must be field-tested. A field test should include the voluntary application of the new evaluation tool with leaders in the central office and in schools. Ideally, the field test should include a broad spectrum of leaders, including those who are new to their positions as well as veterans with decades of service. During the field test, at least two evaluators should be assigned to each leader, and their evaluations must be conducted independently. The reason for this is that two thoughtful and intelligent people can look at the same performance and apply the same evaluation instrument and come to different conclusions. When this occurs, it is not a reflection on the perceptive abilities of the evaluators, but rather on the ambiguity of the instrument. This is a sure sign that the dimensions of leadership and, more particularly, the performance descriptions for each dimension require more specificity. During the field test, all leaders receiving the evaluation should also complete an evaluation of themselves, and this evaluation should be compared to those of the two evaluators. When there is consistent agreement about a performance level, then there is a high degree of probability that the dimensions of leadership and performance specifications you have developed are reliable.

In addition to a consideration of the reliability and accuracy of the instrument, the field test should provide insight about the value of the process. The leaders and evaluators participating in the field test should be able to provide candid and anonymous feedback about the instrument and the impact it had on their present and future performance. Their feedback and their comparison of the proposed new evaluation system to its predecessor will help the task force to make the final refinements to your leadership evaluation process before it is implemented throughout your organization.

IMPLEMENT THROUGHOUT THE ORGANIZATION

Implementation of MLA throughout your organization requires time, coordination, and extensive professional development. Before leaders can be held responsible for performance in a new evaluation scheme, they must be thoroughly familiar with the new expectations associated with the system. The timeline for implementation should include ample opportunity for each leader to read and become familiar with the new dimensions of leadership and the performance levels for each dimension. Professional development sessions should allow opportunities for each leader and evaluator to use the new system in realistic scenarios that clearly differentiate among various performance levels for each dimension of leadership. Finally, the earliest phases of implementation must include regular communication between leaders and evaluators so that no evaluation ever comes as a surprise. One promising technique is the use of a free evaluation, one that is not disclosed to the human resources department but used only as a coaching vehicle for discussion between the leaders and evaluator. Because this free evaluation is explicitly low stakes and confidential, it encourages candor and coaching.

For maximum impact, every leader in the organization should participate in the new evaluation system. The expectations of the superintendent must be clear and public. Ideally, the members of the board are equally clear about their expectations of themselves. Leading by example, board members and superintendents can demonstrate that evaluation can be a constructive and positive process that is directly related to the mission and values of the organization.

SHARE RESULTS WITH UNIVERSITIES AND RESEARCH INSTITUTIONS

MLA can result in a treasure trove of research, but most school systems do not have the research and analysis resources to take maximum advantage of the data. Partnerships with universities and other research institutions can reveal the relationships (and lack of relationships) between leadership practices and organizational results. Moreover, a comprehensive approach to the research questions surrounding leadership evaluation allows an investigation into multiple variables at the same time. The basic questions are "Which leadership practices are most effective?" and "Do leaders with higher ratings in our system really have higher performance?" Comprehensive research, however, will ask additional questions:

- Which dimensions of leadership are most associated with high performance in high-poverty schools? Are these dimensions the same as or different from those dimensions of leadership associated in other schools?
- Which dimensions of leadership are most associated with high performance in schools with inexperienced staffs? With veteran staffs?
- Which dimensions of leadership are most associated with high performance in departmental leadership in the central office? How are these qualities similar to or different from the characteristics of effective leadership in schools?
- Which dimensions of leadership are most influenced by leadership professional development? Which professional development programs have the greatest and least impact on leadership performance?
- Which dimensions of leadership are most affected by changes in financial resources?

Each of these research questions requires a holistic view of the educational system, with information on student achievement, demographic characteristics, professional development, staff qualifications and background, financial resources, and other variables that may be related to leadership performance. By sharing leadership assessment data with research partners, organizations will gain insight into which dimensions have the greatest impact on effectiveness of the entire organization.

USE MLA FOR TRAINING, RECRUITING, AND DEVELOPING LEADERS

Multidimensional leadership assessment is more than an evaluation system. It is a means by which an organization can develop and sustain leaders for the future. Many leadership training programs, both in universities and within school systems, are fragmented. Give the leader a three-hour course in school finance and she is expected to manage a multimillion-dollar budget. Give the leader a course in curriculum and assessment, and he is to become an instructional leader. Send a group of leaders to a seminar in data analysis and they will become experts in statistics, assessment, and educational measurement. Surely we can do better. Once MLA has been implemented, it should form the basis of the curriculum for leadership training. Because the definitions of proficient and exemplary performance are explicit, professional development for leaders will require, in many cases, a significant improvement in rigor. Many leadership training seminars that provide mere awareness and exposure to ideas will be replaced by more extensive educational programs that provide the skills and knowledge leaders will require in order to perform at an exemplary level on each dimension. This will inevitably lead to fewer inspiration speeches, fewer workshops in which personal anecdotes supplant solid research, and reduced support for graduate school curricula that fail to address the needs of today's leaders.

Consider this thought experiment. Take the total amount of money devoted to leadership professional development programs in your district over the past five years. Divide into that quantity the number of leaders in your system. Compare this dollars-per-leader figure to the cost of acquiring a master's degree or doctorate at an area university. This brief analysis will reveal, in most cases, that school systems are investing an amount equivalent to an advanced degree for every leader in their district. Frequently, the rationalization for the fragmented and ineffective leadership development programs in districts is that, "after all, we're just a school system, not a university." But when professional development programs are viewed over a five-year period and their investment is compared to that required of a comprehensive doctoral program, then school systems must regard staff development leaders not as purveyors of an array of different programs, but as the dean of education of your own university. In creating the curriculum for leadership development, the dean of education will focus on the knowledge and skills that leaders will require. The curriculum will focus on each dimension of leadership, and the program of instruction will recognize that leadership participants bring different levels of background, knowledge, and experience to their courses. Thus, rather than asking every leader in the system to attend the same seminar, the dean of education will recognize that some leaders will require extensive support and multiple courses, while other leaders may successfully achieve the course requirements through independent study. Finally, the dean will recognize that some of the prospective students are, in fact, qualified to be professors in this leadership institute.

CONCLUSION: FINDING ANSWERS INSIDE

After a significant amount of formal research, informal observation, and casual conversations with leaders throughout the world in education, business, government, health care, military, and nonprofit organizations, I cannot provide the reader with any secrets that make effective leadership easy or without risk. In fact, with each additional inquiry, I become more convinced that many organizations hold the keys to their own leadership effectiveness. When I ask leaders in a school system to share with me on a confidential basis their greatest success and their greatest challenge, an interesting thing happens. For almost all of the challenges that are listed by these leaders, there is another leader in the same system who has been remarkably successful in addressing that same issue. The culture of the organization required that they seek solutions to their challenges from the outside, but the solutions of outsiders were then rejected because they failed to be sufficiently tailored to the needs of that particular area. Thus the cycle of frustration continued, with challenges identified, solutions sought, and solutions rejected. The reality is that the solutions are within districts if only there is a mechanism for recognizing them. While leaders, educators, and education advocates decry the way that school systems are treated in the media, we bear some of the responsibility for this state of affairs if we fail to tell our own success stories. If we expect education reporting to be more than a litany of test scores, we must consistently, vigorously, accurately, and relentlessly tell our success stories. If we expect school administrators to be respected, then we must document their exemplary performance and share the evidence of their effectiveness with stakeholders inside and outside of the district. Multidimensional leadership assessment is just one tool, but it can be a powerful one that will allow you to know your strengths, both on an individual and on a collective basis. It will allow you to identify and confront weaknesses, knowing that ineffectiveness is rarely the result of a personal defect, but rather the failure of the leader to acquire the necessary knowledge and skills to become effective. Failures persist not because of the ignorance of the individual or ineptitude of the organization, but because we fail to recognize that the development of the knowledge and skills required for exemplary leadership performance takes time, practice, feedback, coaching, and evaluation. By identifying, documenting, and replicating the strengths of our most effective leaders, organizations will build confidence, improve morale, and lay the foundation for generations of successful performance.

Senior Leadership Assessment 10

The Hallmarks of Excellence Leadership Research

Perhaps the most important development in educational leadership assessment is the distinction between evaluation and coaching. It is directly analogous to the distinction in the classroom that Rick Stiggins has thoughtfully offered: that is the distinction between assessment *of* learning and assessment *for* learning. In the context of leadership assessment, we might suggest the comparable distinction between assessment *of* leadership performance and assessment *for* leadership performance. As the research presented earlier in this volume makes clear, assessment of leadership performance has been problematic. Some assessments are superficial and unrelated to key objectives while others—perhaps including the Leadership Performance Matrix in this book—will be too long and burdensome for some school systems. Of course, the biggest leadership assessment challenge is not a quibble about form or length, but rather the complete absence of leadership assessment, a problem most likely to affect veteran leaders.

CHALLENGES OF SENIOR LEADERSHIP ASSESSMENT

At the most senior levels of leadership, there is another set of assessment challenges. Initially there is the loss of confidentiality, particularly for superintendent evaluation. Though most personnel matters are exempt from open meeting laws and public record requirements, the evaluations of superintendents frequently become public because those evaluations are linked to public discussions of superintendent compensation. Thus, what might be a reasonable attempt to

SOURCE: The research and commentary in this chapter is used with the kind permission of CHORUS, Inc., developer and owner of the Hallmarks of Excellence in Educational Leadership model and assessment system. Hallmarks and Hallmarks of Excellence is a copyright and mark of CHORUS, Inc., Indianapolis, IN.

improve performance, when expressed privately, can become a personal indictment of the leader's competence and a headline in the local newspaper when the same attempt to improve performance enters the public record. Moreover, senior leaders achieved their present positions because they had years, perhaps decades, of superior ratings. Any rating less than superior can, for a senior leader, be seen as a sign of immense dissatisfaction and a personal insult. This combination of public scrutiny and the presumption of superior marks dooms most senior leadership evaluations to ineffectiveness.

ASSESSMENT *FOR* LEADERSHIP: THE HALLMARKS OF EXCELLENCE IN EDUCATIONAL LEADERSHIP

The Hallmarks of Excellence is a sophisticated assessment model with a strong research base that includes multiple disciplines. The results provided to leaders are entirely confidential—indeed, school systems execute a legally binding agreement that prevents the use of Hallmarks for evaluation or the release of the assessment to third parties, including the news media. Of equal importance, the feedback from Hallmarks is invariably challenging. The "forced-choice" nature of the Hallmarks assessment requires senior leaders to acknowledge that they are stronger in some areas than others. Every senior leader I have interviewed who has taken the Hallmarks assessment has the same reaction: "This is the first time in my career I've received this sort of candid feedback that suggested improvement." The perfect score—so common in senior leadership evaluation that perfection becomes little more than average—is impossible in Hallmarks. Leaders are challenged to capitalize on their strengths, confront their challenges, and most important, build a leadership team with complementary talents, characteristics, and strengths.

THE FUNDAMENTALS OF HALLMARKS

The leadership model of the Hallmarks of Excellence in Educational Leadership is founded on three fundamentals of leadership; all of the leadership characteristics, attributes, attitudes, intuitions, and behaviors discussed and delineated will point back to and be a part of these basics. The three fundamentals that all extraordinary leaders continually focus on are these:

1. Mastering Your Core

2. Forging the Path

3. Ensuring Extraordinary Execution

Mastering Your Core

To be more personal, it's about Mastering *Your* Core. For the superior leader, *Mastering Your Core* means that the launch of all endeavors starts first with deep, candid, and honest personal self-awareness. Superior leaders then take that self-awareness and intentionally work to increase their leadership effectiveness by creating an executable path for personal improvement. Mastering Your Core includes honing your character with regards to all aspects of leadership integrity. It means being willing to understand and manage your own emotions while respecting and acknowledging the feelings, emotions, and attitudes of others. Mastering Your Core carries a steadfast commitment to being a lifelong learner, assuming personal responsibility for growth, keeping on the cutting edge of best practices, and always maintaining a willingness to share knowledge and skills with others. Leaders who strive for unmatched achievement and impact always begin with Mastering Your Core.

Forging the Path

To put leadership into action, great leaders must consciously be *Forging the Path* for those they lead. There is an old, blunt adage that tells others to "Lead, follow, or get out of the way." In plain language, leaders need to lead; leaders must lead. And in the words of Captain Kirk of the Starship Enterprise, they *must* be willing to "boldly go where no man has gone before." And they must be willing to go first.

People are captivated by strong leaders who know where they are going and where they want the group they lead to go. By "strong leaders," we don't mean strong people who simply dominate or "bark orders" and get their people to follow by coercion. The extraordinary leader is a type of individual who wins the minds *and* hearts of people; such leaders inspire passion and stir excitement over what *could be* if the path were followed—the path the leader is already creating. Leaders who are Forging the Path use concepts and big ideas to create a stirring vision and plan that provide clear direction for their organizations. They are not driven by money, but rather by service of their people; they are not driven by power, but rather an understanding of how their leadership can improve the lives of others.

Leaders who are Forging the Path live life with a compelling vision at the center of their core; they are motivated to create a better world, and they are excited to lead others down that road.

Ensuring Extraordinary Execution

Larry Bossidy, chairman and former CEO of Honeywell International, states, "Execution is the leader's most important job." In the book, *Execution: The Discipline of Getting Things Done,* Bossidy and Ram Charan (2002) give example after example of company leaders who do *not* take execution seriously and do *not* oversee the task of execution very well. Our experience at CHORUS underscores Bossidy's observation on the large number of leaders who either think they can delegate execution to someone else in their organization, or, worse, believe that after they lay out the strategy, execution will take care of itself. Extraordinary leaders are committed to *Ensuring Extraordinary Execution.*

It may not sound like the most glamorous job on the planet, but if you truly desire to be a great leader, execution is something that must not be ignored. Superior leaders do not just understand their own strengths and gaps; they do not stop at creating a vision and forming a path for others; superior leaders make sure the plan gets executed. Superior leaders "get it done." In committing to do the work of extraordinary leaders, there is something very important to remember: Mastering Your Core, Forging the Path, and Ensuring Extraordinary Execution are *not* prerequisites to becoming a superior leader—*they are* what extraordinary leaders do. They do these things now, and they'll do them tomorrow. And they did them when they started. The path *to* superior leadership is also the path *of* superior leadership.

FROM ASSESSMENT TO IMPROVEMENT: LEADERSHIP PERFORMANCE COACHING

If the objective of effective senior leadership assessment is improved performance, then even a superior assessment instrument such as Hallmarks is insufficient unless it is accompanied by a commitment for follow-up and coaching. The Leadership Performance Coaching model linked to Hallmarks is a research-based process (Boyatzis & McKee, 2005; Reeves, 2007) that provides continuous learning and introspection by the leader. Specifically, long-term personal and organizational change depends not only upon accurate, confidential, and constructive feedback, but also upon clarity about the difference between the present and what Boyatzis refers to as the *ideal state*—a level of performance significantly different from the present, no matter how successful the leader may be. The Leadership Performance Coaching model places into operational terms the notion popularized by coaching pioneer Marshall Goldsmith (2007), whose book title makes the point: *What Got You Here Won't Get You There.* The activities, disciplines, and characteristics that defined a career from a first-year teacher to a top-rated assistant superintendent are not necessarily the same activities, disciplines, and characteristics that will sustain the career of a successful superintendent.

The Leadership Performance Coaching cycle is continuous. As the Hallmarks assessment suggests, superior leaders find learning a continuous source of challenge, renewal, and enjoyment. Once leaders have distinguished the ideal state from the present, they must develop a learning agenda and then experiment with different leadership behaviors. Learning without application in the context of leadership is like reading a dictionary in another language but never assembling the words into sentences. On the heels of experimentation is feedback and correction. Perhaps most important, senior leaders must develop a network of support for continuous improvement. This almost never happens within the organization they are leading, because the essence of a successful support network is a combination of challenge and candor that subordinates rarely provide to bosses.

CONCLUSION

Senior leaders in education (and in any organization) face challenges that can be overwhelming. They are held responsible for results that, in many schools, are influenced by factors beyond the control of the leader. Even when leaders are successful, their job security can be undermined by prevailing political winds. Indeed, the very decisions that lead to success—particularly decisions that lead to improved student achievement—are the same decisions that irritate powerful stakeholders. Therefore, senior leaders need a consistent and objective source of feedback. Objective feedback depends not on popularity but effectiveness, and that distinction is the hallmark of successful senior leadership.

Leadership Responsibilities for Planning, Implementation, and Monitoring

11

The development of school improvement plans, strategic plans, building plans, and other planning documents can occupy an extraordinary amount of time for school leaders. Each time state and district policymakers add an element to a school or district plan, there is the expectation of a relationship between the contents of the plan and the performance of the district. This is the heart of the presumption of planning in general and strategic plans for schools in particular. That presumption is a testable hypothesis. Although there are partisans on both sides of the planning debate (Cook, 2004; Reeves, December 2007–January 2008; Schmoker, 2004), the issue is not whether planning "works," but rather which elements of school planning are most effective. Moreover, our research suggests that planning cannot be evaluated in a vacuum, but instead must be considered in the broader context of the monitoring and implementation activities of school leaders. It is, we have learned, the monitoring and implementation—not the format of the plans—that give plans their relevance and power. Research from The Leadership and Learning Center suggests that some of these efforts are particularly related to improved student achievement. This chapter summarizes this ongoing research.

THE PIM RESEARCH

The PIM (Planning, Implementation, and Monitoring) process has now been applied to more than 2,000 schools representing more than 1.5 million students throughout North America. Although this research is, at this writing, a work in progress, the sample size and diversity is sufficient that we can draw some conclusions that may be useful for school leaders and policymakers. The essence of the PIM process is the double-blind review in which two separate evaluators consider the details of the planning, implementation, and monitoring processes for each school and central office department. Each element of the process is evaluated on a scale of zero to three, with zero representing no indication of success and three representing the highest level of expertise. If there is not a very high level of agreement (at least 80 percent) between the independent evaluators, then the plan evaluation process is terminated and started again. The reasoning behind such a rigorous consistency in requirement is that too many school evaluations are based on subjective and variable opinions of individual school inspectors and other external authority. The thesis of PIM is that the evaluation of planning, implementation, and monitoring processes must be objective, consistent, and fair.

The PIM rubric was created (and regularly revised) based on the requirements imposed by state and district educational authorities. The underlying hypothesis for each requirement is the following proposition: If a school or central office department fulfills this requirement at an expert level, then student achievement will improve. In the present analysis, we have used external assessments from state departments of education and Canadian provinces to represent student achievement variables. Clearly, any standardized test has limitations which include

- The tests may not reflect the taught curriculum.
- Test results can be influenced by many additional variables, including student demographic characteristics, teacher quality, leadership quality, and factors unique to the school environment.
- Scoring of tests may be inaccurate.
- Tests administered within a narrow period of time—typically less than 1 week out of a 36-week school year—do not reflect many other accomplishments of students, teachers, and leaders.

We acknowledge all of these indictments—and many more—when it comes to the weaknesses of standardized tests (Reeves, 2002b). Nevertheless, for large-scale research, these tests represent one method of understanding student achievement. At the very least, it is fair to say that the governing bodies that create detailed planning requirements do so with the expectation that those requirements will help schools improve performance on the tests required by the same governing bodies. After all, when a state health department establishes hygiene requirements for food establishments, it does so not to inflict burdensome-but-irrelevant requirements on restaurants, but rather to assure the health of the citizenry. Similarly, when state education departments establish education requirements for school and district plans, they do so with the expectation that compliance with these requirements will lead to improvements in student achievement.

HOW LEADERSHIP PLANS IMPROVE ACHIEVEMENT

The PIM analysis so far has been surprisingly robust, with the findings after examination of 2,000 school plans remarkably similar to the findings after 300 schools were reviewed. In particular, the following characteristics of school plans are strongly related to improved student achievement:

1. Monitoring

Schools earn the highest scores in monitoring by developing the following four monitoring characteristics:

- *Frequency:* The more frequently that plan goals are monitored, the more likely it is that those goals will be achieved. This finding is directly analogous to the findings of Marzano (2007) that the frequency of assessment is directly related to higher student achievement. The PIM research suggests that this stands true whether the monitoring is of student achievement or of teaching and leadership practices.
- *Specificity:* Monitoring that is most effective is specific, providing feedback to teachers and leaders in a manner that allows them to make midcourse corrections and improve professional practices. The models here are teachers in music and coaches in athletics, neither of whom advise their students to "play better" or "work harder." Rather, they give specific feedback on intonation, timing, or athletic movement. PIM processes that score well in the domain of specificity allow school leaders to use the plan as a living document throughout the year, noticing the differences between ideal instruction and leadership and the daily reality of instruction and leadership.
- *Measurability:* The plans with the strongest relationship to student achievement gains had measurable goals. The difference between "improve student achievement" and "improve reading proficiency from 54 percent of students reading at grade level to 90 percent of students reading at grade level" is directly and consistently related to better academic performance. For all that has been written about "SMART" goals (Ainsworth, 2003a, 2003b; White, 2005a, 2005b), the PIM research suggests that the first two elements of SMART goals—specificity and measurability—have a disproportionate influence on student achievement.
- *Comprehensiveness:* Effective monitoring is never a simple recitation of test scores. School systems around the world claim to be "data driven" and yet their monitoring practices are limited to the results of their work—typically annual test scores. It is as if they were monitoring the health of their students by having an annual weigh-in and then placing on a chart the average weight of students, not caring whether weight loss was due to a regime of diet and exercise or the result of devastating eating disorders and drug abuse.

The PIM research so far suggests that schools with the highest monitoring scores have more than five times the gains in student achievement than schools with the lowest monitoring scores.

2. Inquiry

The "inquiry" variable is based on an analysis of the response of the leadership team to the following question: What are the primary causes of student achievement? School plans offer a revealing insight into the answer to this question. At one extreme, the explanations within the plan attribute the causes of student achievement to external variables—typically student demographic characteristics—and include broad statements associating student performance with the economic status, language, and ethnicity of the students. In this context, the word "diversity" is not an attribute to be celebrated, but a condition that leads to an explanation for lower achievement. Phrases such as "Because we are a very diverse school. . ." or "Because of increasing diversity. . ." are sometimes followed by statements about declining achievement scores. The other end of the inquiry scale is occupied by schools that attribute the causes of student achievement not to student characteristics, but to teachers and school leaders. This view of student achievement is not only a matter of research (Darling-Hammond, 2000; Marzano, 2003; Reeves, 2006) but also personal conviction. Essentially, it is a repetition of the Pygmalion Effect: When school leaders believe that they can influence student achievement, it becomes a self-fulfilling prophecy (Rosenthal & Jacobson, 2003). When leaders believe that they are impotent and unable to influence achievement, that too becomes a self-fulfilling prophecy. Specifically, the PIM research so far suggests that schools with the highest inquiry scores have more than three times the gains in student achievement when compared with schools with the lowest inquiry scores.

3. Focus

Among the counterintuitive findings of the PIM research is the inverse relationship between the number of goals set and gains in student achievement. This conclusion stands in striking contrast to the well-intentioned demands by advocates for many different leadership and teaching strategies, each of whom demand that a goal reflecting their point of view is reflected in a "complete" school improvement plan. Our research revealed schools that suffered from "goal proliferation"—plans with more than 50 (the record so far is 77) strategic goals, each one of which was listed to meet the requirement of some external accreditation or policy-making authority. But however well-intentioned goal proliferation may be, it is counterproductive. When considering the powerful impact of monitoring—schools with the best monitoring scores had five times the achievement gains as schools with low scores in that domain—this makes sense. It is not possible to have a high score on monitoring—particularly with the requirement for frequent and specific monitoring—on more than a few goals. Although it is premature to specify an optimal number of goals, some leadership literature has suggested the "rule of six." It is not coincidental that high-performing systems consistently have between three and nine areas of focus, each of which receives frequent and specific monitoring, and low-performing systems are weighed down by hundreds of pages of "strategies" that evaporate as soon as the document is printed.

4. Format

Although the neatness and elegance of format may provide a degree of convenience for those who review school plans, the research so far does not suggest that there is a positive correlation between high scores on compliance with format requirements and improved student achievement. Indeed, the PIM research is consistent with other findings (Prichard Committee for Academic Excellence, 2005) that note an inverse relationship. That is, schools with lower scores on format have higher achievement. This finding does not suggest that school leaders should create plans that are deliberately messy. Rather, it suggests that some of the effort presently devoted to format compliance might be more appropriately directed to leadership activities that have a clear and demonstrable impact on achievement: monitoring, inquiry, and focus.

CONCLUSION

When school leaders consider their "top 10" list on a daily basis, it is unlikely that school improvement plans will find a place among the exigencies of the moment. Nevertheless, school improvement plans can have a significant and positive effect on student achievement if—and only if—they are focused on the right areas. Voluminous plans can be replaced with plans that are brief and focused. Analyses of demographic characteristics of students can be interesting but dangerous, particularly if those analyses lead to the presumption that teaching and leadership practices are no longer significant causes of student achievement. Most important, policymakers and accreditation officials who bear responsibility for the creation of school planning requirements must regard each of those requirements as a hypothesis to be tested. If superior compliance with a requirement is significantly and consistently associated with improved student achievement, then policymakers have a strong rationale for the continuation of the requirement. If, on the other hand, requirements for school plans—however well-intentioned those requirements may be—are either unrelated or inversely related to student achievement gains, then policymakers have a duty to remove those requirements. The best news from this research is that some senior leaders and policymakers will announce to school and district leaders, "I've examined the research and our planning document requirements, and would like to announce the following items that you do *not* have to do this year. . ." The author of such an announcement will be a hero to principals and superintendents everywhere.

Resource A

The Leadership Performance Matrix

Leadership Dimension	Exemplary (Systemwide Impact)	Proficient (Local Impact)	Progressing (Leadership Potential)	Not Meeting Standards
1.0 Resilience				
1.1 Constructive reaction to disappointment and failure	Public reports, including accountability documents, plans, and oral presentations, include frank acknowledgment of prior personal and organizational failures, and clear suggestions for systemwide learning resulting from those lessons.	Readily acknowledges personal and organizational failures.	Acknowledges personal and organizational failure when confronted with evidence.	Defensive and resistant to the acknowledgment of error.
1.2 Willingness to admit error and learn from it	Shares case studies of personal and organizational errors in a way that is used to guide, inspire, and teach colleagues throughout the organization. Builds resilience in colleagues and throughout the organization by habitually highlighting and praising "good mistakes" where risks were taken, mistakes were made, lessons were learned, and both the individual and the organization learned for the future.	Admits failures quickly, honestly, and openly with direct supervisor and immediate colleagues. Evidence of learning from past errors. Nondefensive attitude in accepting feedback and discussing errors and failures.	Able to accept evidence of mistakes when offered by others. Some evidence of learning from mistakes.	Unwilling to acknowledge errors. When confronted with evidence of mistakes, is defensive and resistant to learning from mistakes.

NOTE: Both the Leadership Dimensions and the performance descriptions that follow are only models. It is essential that each organization establish its own leadership domains and describe in explicit terms a continuum of leadership performance.

Leadership Dimension	Exemplary (Systemwide Impact)	Proficient (Local Impact)	Progressing (Leadership Potential)	Not Meeting Standards
1.3 Constructively handles disagreement with leadership and policy decisions	In disagreements with policy and leadership decisions, is able to articulate the disagreement and advocate for a point of view based on the best interests of the organization and is willing to challenge executive authority and policy leaders appropriately with evidence and constructive criticism, but once the decision is made, fully supports and enthusiastically implements organizational policy and leadership decisions.	Accepts and implements leadership and policy decisions.	Sometimes challenges executive and policy leadership without bringing those concerns to appropriate executive and policy authorities. Sometimes implements unpopular policies unenthusiastically or because "I'm just following orders, but I don't like it."	Ignores or subverts executive and policy decisions that are unpopular or distasteful.
1.4 Constructively handles dissent from subordinates	Creates constructive contention, assigning roles if necessary to deliberately generate multiple perspectives and consider different sides of important issues. Recognizes and rewards thoughtful dissent. Uses dissenting voices to learn, grow, and, where appropriate, acknowledge the leader's error. Encourages constructive dissent, in which multiple voices are encouraged and heard, and the final decision is made better and more broadly supported as a result.	Leader uses dissent to inform final decisions, improve the quality of decision making, and broaden support for final decisions.	Leader tolerates dissent, but there is very little of it in public because subordinates do not understand the leader's philosophy about the usefulness of dissent.	Dissent is absent due to a climate of fear and intimidation.

Leadership Dimension	Exemplary (Systemwide Impact)	Proficient (Local Impact)	Progressing (Leadership Potential)	Not Meeting Standards
1.5 Explicit improvement of specific performance areas based on the previous leadership evaluation	Previous evaluations are combined with personal reflection and 360-degree feedback to formulate an action plan that is reflected in the leader's daily choices of priorities as well as in the organization's priorities. The influence of previous evaluations has an impact not only on the leader, but on the entire organization.	Previous evaluations are explicitly reflected into projects, tasks, and priorities. Performance on each evaluation reflects specific and measurable improvements along the performance continuum from ineffective, to progressing, to proficient, to exemplary.	Leader is aware of previous evaluations, but has not translated them into an action plan.	No evidence of reference to previous leadership evaluations in the leader's choices of tasks and priorities.
2.0 Personal Behavior				
2.1 Integrity	This leader meets commitments—verbal, written, and implied—without exception. Commitments to individuals, students, community members, and subordinates have the same weight as commitments to superiors, board members, or other people with visibility and authority. The leader's commitment to integrity is clear throughout the organization, as any commitment from anyone who reports to this leader is as good as a commitment from the leader.	The leader meets commitments or negotiates exceptions where the commitment cannot be met. Verbal commitments have the same weight as written commitments.	The leader meets explicit written commitments. The need to "get it in writing" does not allow subordinates or superiors to make assumption that verbal statements have the weight of a commitment.	The words "I'm working on it" or "I'm doing the best I can" are regarded as acceptable substitutes for commitments. This leader cannot be trusted to follow through with tasks, budgets, priorities, or performance.

Leadership Dimension	Exemplary (Systemwide Impact)	Proficient (Local Impact)	Progressing (Leadership Potential)	Not Meeting Standards
2.2 Emotional self-control	The leader possesses complete self-control, even in the most difficult and confrontational situation, but also provides assistance to colleagues on the techniques of emotional intelligence. Not only is the leader an exemplar of emotional intelligence, but the entire organization reflects this commitment to self-control, empathy, and respect.	The leader can deal with sensitive subjects and personal attacks with dignity and self-control. The leader never meets anger with anger, but defuses confrontational situation with emotional intelligence, empathy, and respect.	Occasional raised voice when angry or threatened, leading to a climate in which people are reluctant to raise sensitive issues.	Loses temper and emotionally unstable. Conversations on any sensitive topic are brief or nonexistent.
2.3 Compliance with legal and ethical requirements in relationships with employees	Meets the letter and spirit of the law, avoiding both the fact and appearance of impropriety. Inculcates the foundations of mutual respect for colleagues and for the law throughout the organization.	No instances of illegal or unethical conduct with employees, prospective employees, or other conduct that crosses the line of policy or law.	There is no "progressing" in this category—one strike and you're out. Failing to be proficient is the same as being ineffective.	Violates—even just one time—the legal and policy requirements for the relationship between leaders and employees.
2.4 Compliance with legal and ethical requirements in relationships with students	Uses leadership as an opportunity to teach faculty and students respect for one another, creating a climate for mutual trust and respect. Builds in all employees and faculty members an environment in which student safety is paramount, and inappropriate contact with students never occurs.	Meets all legal requirements for student contact and takes swift and appropriate actions when inappropriate contact between employees and students has been detected.	There is no progressing in this category. A single violation is a career killer.	Failure to protect student safety by permitting or engaging in inappropriate contact with students.

Leadership Dimension	Exemplary (Systemwide Impact)	Proficient (Local Impact)	Progressing (Leadership Potential)	Not Meeting Standards
2.5 Tolerance of different points of view within the boundaries of the values and mission of the organization	Actively seeks differences in perspective, encouraging difference scenarios and curricula in the context of academic standards. Explicitly differentiates divergent thinking when it is constructive and facilitates a transition to convergent thinking to support organizational goals.	Focuses evaluation on the achievement of mission and adherence to values, without penalizing differences in points of view that are within the framework of organizational requirements.	No punishment of alternative points of view, but little or no development or encouragement of those views.	Suppresses other points of view and discourages disagreement or divergent thinking.
2.6 Organization, including calendar, desk, office, and building(s)	Maintains a daily prioritized task list that can be spontaneously produced at any time. Clean desk, with highest priority work on the desk and other work in pending files. Calendar is openly available, free of conflicts, focused on the priorities of the leader and the organization. The building is spotless and reflects the leader's commitment to a personal sense of pride. Every administrator's and teacher's desk is clean, calendars are consistent, task lists are visible and in priority order. Grounds, buildings, restrooms, lounges, public areas, and especially classrooms reflect the leader's sense of dignity, order, and decorum.	Personal work space is flawlessly organized, with a daily prioritized task list and up-to-date calendar always available.	Calendar and task list can be available with warning. Work space is tolerable, but imperfectly organized. The rest of the building does not reflect a commitment to organization and discipline.	Messy desk, no task list, outdated calendar. The building, public areas, classrooms, and other physical facilities are a mess.

Leadership Dimension	Exemplary (Systemwide Impact)	Proficient (Local Impact)	Progressing (Leadership Potential)	Not Meeting Standards
3.0 Student Achievement				
3.1 Planning and goal setting for student achievement	Routinely shares examples of specific leadership, teaching, and curriculum strategies that are associated with improved student achievement. Other leaders in the system credit this leader with sharing ideas, coaching teachers and leaders, and providing technical assistance to implement successful new initiatives.	Goals and strategies reflect a clear relationship between the actions of teachers and leaders and the impact on student achievement. Results show steady improvements based on these leadership initiatives.	The leader has established goals related to student achievement that are specific and measurable, but these efforts have yet to result in improved student achievement.	The goals are neither measurable nor specific. The leader focuses more on student characteristics than on the actions of the teachers and leaders in the system.
3.2 Student achievement results	Consistent record of improved student achievement on multiple indicators of student success. Student success occurs not only on the overall averages, but in each group of historically disadvantaged students. Explicit use of previous data indicates that the leader has focused on improving performance. In areas of previous success, the leader aggressively identifies new challenges, moving proficient performance to the exemplary level. Where new challenges emerge, the leader highlights the need, creates effective intervention, and reports improved results.	The leader hits the numbers, meeting performance goals for student achievement. The average of the student population improves as does the achievement of each group of students who have previously been identified as needing improvement.	There is some evidence of improvement, but insufficient evidence of changes in leadership, teaching, and curriculum that will create the improvements necessary to achieve student performance goals.	Indifferent to the data, this leader blames students, families, and external characteristics. This leader does not believe that student achievement can improve. This leader has not taken decisive action to change time, teacher assignment, curriculum, leadership practices, or other variables in order to improve student achievement.

Leadership Dimension	Exemplary (Systemwide Impact)	Proficient (Local Impact)	Progressing (Leadership Potential)	Not Meeting Standards
3.3 Student achievement reporting to students, parents, teachers, and other leaders	Reports at all levels extend far beyond the report card, but include standards achievement reports, detailing student performance on the most important standards including "power standards" identified by teachers as those most related to student performance at the next instructional level. Faculty meetings and professional development meetings are focused on the locally produced academic reports, and there is clear evidence of changes in leadership, teaching, and curriculum as a response to these analyses. Reports of academic achievement can be produced at any time, and for students who require particular assistance, the frequency of academic achievement reporting is increased.	Student achievement reports include not only traditional report cards and grades, but also standards achievement reports, detailing student performance on standards, as a part of each reporting period.	Required report cards are delivered in a timely and accurate manner. Faculty members and administrators can explain the relationship of grades to standards where required.	Standard report cards with letter grades are provided. Any relationship between grades and standards is a matter of the teacher's individual discretion.

Leadership Dimension	Exemplary (Systemwide Impact)	Proficient (Local Impact)	Progressing (Leadership Potential)	Not Meeting Standards
3.4 Use of student achievement data to make instructional leadership decisions	There is clear evidence of the use of data from state, district, building, and classroom data to make specific and observable changes in teaching, curriculum, and leadership decisions. The leader regularly shares with other leaders and teachers both successes and failures based on local data analysis. The data wall is the focal point of both formal and informal leadership and faculty discussions.	Clear evidence of changes in curriculum, teaching, and leadership based on data. Data wall in evidence and both leader and teachers refer to it in order to inform instructional decisions.	Participation in data-driven decision-making workshops, and limited evidence of changes based on data.	Indifference to data, no changes in schedule, instruction, curriculum, or leadership compared to the previous year. The data screams "Change!" and the leader's actions say, "Everything is just fine."
3.5 Understanding of student requirements and academic standards	The power standards are used and shared with other buildings. Every faculty meeting and staff development forum is focused on student achievement, including reviews of individual student work compared to standards.	Each academic standard has been analyzed and translated into student-accessible language. Power standards are widely shared by faculty members and visible throughout the building. The link between standards and student performance is in evidence from the posting of proficient student work throughout the building.	Standards are posted and required training has been conducted.	Classroom curriculum is a matter of individual discretion, and the leader is hesitant to intrude or indifferent to decisions in the classroom that are at variance from the requirements of academic standards.

Leadership Dimension	Exemplary (Systemwide Impact)	Proficient	Progressing (Leadership Potential)	Not Meeting Standards
3.6 Understanding of present levels of student performance based on consistent assessments that reflect local and state academic standards	There is evidence of decisive changes in teacher assignments and curriculum based on student performance data. Case studies of effective and ineffective decisions are shared widely with other leaders and throughout the district.	Evidence of specific changes based on student performance data.	Leader is aware of need to change, but changes have not yet been implemented.	Leader is indifferent to the need for change—unable or unwilling to make difficult decisions.
3.7 Decisions in teacher assignment, course content, schedule, and student curriculum based on specific needs for improved student achievement	The leader uses multiple data sources, including state, district, school, and classroom assessments, and has at least 3 years of data. The leader systematically examines data at the subscale level to find strengths and challenges. The leader empowers teaching and administrative staff to draw inferences from data. Data insights are regularly the subject of faculty meetings and professional development sessions. The leader can specifically document examples of decisions in teaching, assignment, curriculum, assessment, and intervention that have been made on the basis of data analysis. The leader has coached other school leaders in other schools to improve their data analysis skills.	The leader uses multiple data sources, including state and district assessments, and has at least 2 years of data. The leader systematically examines data at the subscale level to find strengths and challenges. The leader can specifically document examples of decisions in teaching, assignment, curriculum, assessment, and intervention that have been made on the basis of data analysis.	The leader is aware of state and district results and has discussed those results with staff, but has not linked specific decisions to the data.	The leader is unaware of or indifferent to the data.

Leadership Dimension	Exemplary (Systemwide Impact)	Proficient (Local Impact)	Progressing (Leadership Potential)	Not Meeting Standards
4.0 Decision Making				
4.1 Factual basis for decisions, including specific reference to internal and external data on student achievement and objective data on curriculum, teaching practices, and leadership practices	Decision making is neither by consensus nor by leadership mandate, but consistently based on the data. This adherence to the rule of data is reflected in all decisions, ranging from course and classroom assignments to the discontinuation of programs. The leader can cite specific examples of practices that have been changed, discontinued, and initiated based on data analysis. A variety of data sources, including qualitative and quantitative, are used. Data sources include state, district, school, and classroom. Inferences from data are shared widely outside the school community in order to share the analysis and replicate the success of this school leader.	The records of decision making reflect a clear reliance on state and district student achievement data.	Some decisions are based on data, but others are the result of personal preference and tradition.	Data are rarely used for decisions and the predominant decision-making methodology is either a popularity contest or an imperial mandate from the leader.

Leadership Dimension	Exemplary (Systemwide Impact)	Proficient (Local Impact)	Progressing (Leadership Potential)	Not Meeting Standards
4.2 Clear identification of decision-making structure, including which decisions are made by consensus or by the staff independently, which decisions are made by the leader after getting input from the staff, and which decisions are made by the leader alone	All stakeholders understand the difference between decision-making levels, where Level I represents a staff decision by consensus or majority, Level II represents a staff input that will significantly influence leadership decisions, and Level III represents a unilateral leadership decision. The leader uses data in such a compelling way that the vast majority of decisions are Level I decisions. Staff surveys reflect a staff feeling of empowerment and personal responsibility for organizational success.	The leader clarifies the decision-making method for major decisions and shares decisions with the staff, using data to the greatest extent possible to support those decisions.	The leader uses both consensus and unilateral decision making, but the reason for changing decision-making structures is not consistently clear.	The leader lurches from autocracy to democracy with no clear method, demoralizing and bewildering the staff.
4.3 Decisions linked to vision, mission, and strategic priorities	The vision, mission, and strategic priorities of the leader and the organization are visible, ingrained in the culture of the organization, and routinely used as a reference point for decisions. The use of strategic guidelines for decision-making filters makes many decisions self-evident and avoids time wasted on unproductive arguments.	The decisions of the leader are consistent with the vision, mission, and strategic priorities of the organization.	While the vision, mission, and priorities may be visible, they are not consistently linked to the leader's decisions.	The leader is unaware of or disconnected from the organization's vision, mission, and strategic priorities. There is little or no evidence of the relationship of leadership decisions to these organizational guideposts.

Leadership Dimension	Exemplary (Systemwide Impact)	Proficient (Local Impact)	Progressing (Leadership Potential)	Not Meeting Standards
4.4 Decisions evaluated for effectiveness and revised where necessary	The leader can provide clear and consistent evidence of decisions that have been changed based on new data. The leader has a regular pattern of decision reviews and "sun setting" in which previous decisions are reevaluated in light of the most current data. There is a culture of "honest bad news" in which the leader and everyone in the organization can discuss what is not working without fear of embarrassment or reprisal.	The leader has a record of evaluating and revising decisions based on new information.	The leader has new information and appears to be willing to reconsider previous decisions, but does not have a clear record of making changes.	The leader is mired in old decisions, accumulating each one as if decisions were etched in stone. There is little or no evidence of reflection and reevaluation of previous decisions.
5.0 Communication				
5.1 Two-way communication with students	In addition to all of the "proficient" characteristics, the leader goes to exceptional lengths to listen to students. The listening strategies may include focus groups, surveys, student advisory committees, and numerous one-to-one student conversations. Discussions with students reveal that they know that the leader will listen to them and treat them with respect.	The leader knows student names, regularly greets students by name, and is proactive in talking with and listening to students. The leader is particularly visible at the beginning and end of the school day and during all other times when students are present.	The leader knows most student names, is visible and often greets students by name, and talks with students frequently.	The leader does not know student names, avoids student contact except where leadership presence is required, and retreats to the office during most occasions when students are likely to be present. Many students do not know the leader's name or recognize the leader on sight.

Leadership Dimension	Exemplary (Systemwide Impact)	Proficient (Local Impact)	Progressing (Leadership Potential)	Not Meeting Standards
5.2 Two-way communication with faculty and staff	In addition to all of the "proficient" behaviors, the leader actively engages in active listening to the faculty and staff. The leader's calendar reflects numerous individual and small group meetings with staff at every level, not just with the direct reports. Bus drivers, cafeteria workers, first-year teachers all report confidence in their ability to gain a respectful hearing from the leader.	Faculty meetings include open discussions with two-way discussions. Faculty members regularly have the opportunity for one-to-one meetings with the leader. The leader knows all staff members and makes an effort to recognize the personal and individual contribution each one makes.	Typically limits listening to questions during faculty meetings.	Faculty meetings consist of the reading of announcements with little or no interaction.
5.3 Two-way communication with parents and community	Clear evidence of parent and community-centered communication, including open forums, focus groups, surveys, personal visits, and extensive use of technology. Decisions in curriculum, leadership, staffing, assessment, and school appearance reflect parent and community involvement. Survey data suggest that parents and community members feel empowered and supportive of educational objectives.	Conducts frequent interactions with parents and community members, including newsletters, personal briefings, personal visits and calls, and the use of technology (voice mail, hot lines, e-mail, Web sites) where appropriate. Clear evidence of decisions based on input from parent and community members.	Parents and community members receive a respectful hearing when they initiate the conversation.	Parents and community members have little or no role to play in leadership decision making.

Leadership Dimension	Exemplary (Systemwide Impact)	Proficient (Local Impact)	Progressing (Leadership Potential)	Not Meeting Standards
6.0 Faculty Development				
6.1 Understanding of faculty proficiencies and needs for further development	In addition to the "proficient" criteria, the leader has also demonstrated a record of tailor-made professional development opportunities linked to the needs of each staff member, including certified and noncertified staff. The leader personally participates in professional development to demonstrate a commitment to lifelong learning. The leader routinely shares professional development opportunities with other schools, departments, districts, and organizations in order to build the professional knowledge opportunities of the entire community.	The leader has created individualized learning plans for each faculty and staff member, and professional development activities reflect the prioritized needs of these plans.	The leader is aware of differentiated needs of faculty and staff members, and there are a few instances of differentiated professional development.	Professional development is typically "one size fits all" and there is little or no evidence of recognition of individual faculty needs.

Leadership Dimension	Exemplary (Systemwide Impact)	Proficient (Local Impact)	Progressing (Leadership Potential)	Not Meeting Standards
6.2 Personal participation in leading professional development	In addition to meeting the criteria for "proficient," the leader is also an active participant in teacher-led professional development, demonstrating with a commitment of time and intellect that the leader is a learner and is willing to learn from colleagues on a regular basis. The leader routinely shares learning experiences with other leaders and colleagues throughout the system.	The leader devotes faculty meetings to professional development, not announcements. The leader personally leads professional development several times each year.	The leader sometimes devotes faculty meetings to professional development and occasionally shares personal learning experiences with colleagues.	The leader generally stopped acquiring new information after completing graduate school and displays little or no evidence of new learning or sharing that learning with colleagues.
6.3 Formal and informal feedback to colleagues with the exclusive purpose of improving individual and organizational performance	The leader possesses all the attributes of "proficient" performance and also uses creative ways of feedback. Examples are consistent nomination of employees for recognition and awards, letters of commendation, and personal messages of admiration. The entire organization reflects the leader's relentlessly positive reinforcement, and performance by individuals and the organization reflects the leader's focus on recognition that is accurate, timely, and specific. The leader balances individual recognition with team and organization-wide recognition.	The leader provides formal feedback consistent with the district personnel policies and provides informal feedback to reinforce good performance and highlight the strengths of colleagues. Feedback is explicitly linked to organizational goals and both the leader and employees can cite examples of where feedback is used to improve individual and organizational performance.	The leader adheres to the personnel policies in providing formal feedback, although the feedback is only occasionally used to improve organizational performance.	Formal feedback is formulaic and unspecific. Informal feedback is rare and more likely to be associated with negative than positive behavior.

Leadership Dimension	Exemplary (Systemwide Impact)	Proficient (Local Impact)	Progressing (Leadership Potential)	Not Meeting Standards
7.0 Leadership Development				
7.1 Strong assistant administrators who are capable of immediately assuming leadership responsibility in this school or other buildings	The leader has multiple assistant administrators who are ready to assume leadership responsibilities, and the leader has already established a track record of placing former mentees in positions of leadership. The leader continues to provide guidance and mentorship to new, developing, and emerging leaders even when they are outside of the leader's personal span of leadership. Multiple leaders throughout the system cite this leader as a mentor and reason for their success.	The leader has personally trained at least one assistant administrator who is capable of replacing the leader today.	The leader provides some training to an assistant administrator who may, in time, be capable of independently assuming a leadership role.	The other administrators under the leader's direction are not capable of assuming additional responsibilities and there does not appear to be a coherent and consistent leadership training program in place.

Leadership Dimension	Exemplary (Systemwide Impact)	Proficient (Local Impact)	Progressing (Leadership Potential)	Not Meeting Standards
7.2 Consistent identification of potential future leaders	The leader routinely identifies and recruits new leaders. The leader has specifically identified at least two new leaders in the past year and entered them into the ranks of leadership training. The leader is remarkable for identifying leaders from unexpected sources, including helping potential leaders find their own leadership strengths even when they had not initially considered a leadership career. The leader helps other leaders to identify and recruit potential leadership candidates.	The leader has specifically identified and recruited a new leader within the past 12 months.	The leader follows personnel guidelines for accepting applications for new leaders.	The leader appears to be indifferent to the need for leadership in the system.
7.3 Evidence of delegation and trust in subordinate leaders	People throughout the organization are empowered in formal and informal ways. Faculty members participate in the facilitation of meetings and exercise leadership in committees and task forces; other employees, including noncertified staff, exercise appropriate authority and assume leadership roles where appropriate. The climate of trust and delegation in this organization contributes directly to the identification and empowerment of the next generation of leadership.	There is a clear pattern of delegated decisions, with authority to match responsibility at every level in the organization. There is a relationship of authority and responsibility, and delegation of authority is clear in personnel documents, such as evaluations, and also in the daily conduct of meetings and organizational business.	The leader sometimes delegates, but also maintains decision-making authority that could be delegated to others.	The leader reserves almost all decision-making authority, even on immaterial matters. Subordinates are unwilling or unable to exercise independent judgment.

Leadership Dimension	Exemplary (Systemwide Impact)	Proficient (Local Impact)	Progressing (Leadership Potential)	Not Meeting Standards
8.0 Time/Task/Project Management				
8.1 Consistently maintains daily prioritized task list	The leader's prioritized daily task list is a living document, updated at the beginning of every day and throughout the day as tasks are added and completed, and as priorities change. The leader regularly shares the task list with colleagues in order to model what great time management and personal organization looks like, and also to convey an appropriate sense of how organizational priorities are translated into individual action plans and tasks.	The leader can produce, without revision, an accurate and up-to-date prioritized task list that reflects the priorities of the organization and that includes tasks (not projects) that are appropriate for that leader.	The leader maintains a task list, but it is not updated daily and sometimes does not reflect the actual work done by the leader during the day.	The leader's task list is haphazard and not prioritized. Even when the list is created, it is unlikely to bear a clear relationship to the actual tasks accomplished by the leader during the day.
8.2 Choices for time management reflect a focus on the most important priorities	The priorities of the organization and this leader's task list create a mirror image. By looking at this leader's calendar and prioritized task list, one would know and understand the priorities of the organization. The leader not only removes diversions and obstacles from his or her own task list, but also helps to focus the entire organization in the right way by carefully matching tasks to priorities.	The priorities of the organization and the priorities on the task list are closely matched. The leader regularly removes tasks, or delegates tasks, where there is an insufficient link between the task and the leader's and organization's priorities.	The leader is aware of organizational priorities, but the daily emergencies frequently seem to intrude into a focus on the priorities.	The leader is unaware of or indifferent to organizational priorities. The task list, if it exists, is more about putting out fires than about implementing organizational priorities.

Leadership Dimension	Exemplary (Systemwide Impact)	Proficient (Local Impact)	Progressing (Leadership Potential)	Not Meeting Standards
8.3 Complex projects have clear objectives and coherent plans	In addition to meeting all of the criteria for "proficient" project management, the leader also uses project management as a teaching device, helping others in the organization understand the interrelationship of complex project milestones throughout the organization. The leader uses complex project management to build systems thinking throughout the organization. Project plans are visible in heavily trafficked areas so that accomplishments are publicly celebrated and project challenges are open for input from a wide variety of sources.	Projects are managed using clear and written lists of milestones, deadlines, and persons responsible. Project management documents are revised and updated as milestones are achieved or deadlines are changed. The leader understands the impact of a change in a milestone or deadline on the entire project, and communicates those changes to the appropriate people in the organization. The leader's task list carefully differentiates between a task and a project.	Projects are managed using lists of milestones and deadlines, but are infrequently updated. The impacts of changes in one task are not clear and are rarely documented. The leader's prioritized task list includes tasks that are, in actuality, projects composed of multiple tasks.	Project management is haphazard or nonexistent. There is little or no evidence of lists of milestones and deadlines.
8.4 History of completion of projects on schedule and within budget	In addition to meeting the criteria for "proficient" performance, this leader regularly saves resources of time and money for the organization and proactively redeploys those resources to help the organization achieve its strategic priorities.	The leader has a documented history of managing complex projects, meets deadlines, and keeps budget commitments.	The leader sometimes meets deadlines, but only at the expense of breaking the budget, or meets budgets, but fails to meet deadlines.	The leader has little or no record of keeping commitments for schedules and budgets.

Leadership Dimension	Exemplary (Systemwide Impact)	Proficient (Local Impact)	Progressing (Leadership Potential)	Not Meeting Standards
9.0 Technology				
9.1 Demonstrated use of technology to improve teaching and learning	In addition to meeting the criteria for "proficient" performance, the leader serves as a model for technology implementation to other organizations. The links between technology implementation and learning success are clear and public. The leader coaches the entire staff on the results of the linkage between technology and organizational success, creating new ways to save resources and improve organizational effectiveness.	The leader uses technology personally in a competent manner and links technology initiatives of the organization to specific teaching and learning objectives.	The leader is personally proficient in technology and appears to be an advocate for the use of instructional technology, but does not always differentiate between technology implementation and a clear impact on teaching and learning.	The leader does not display personal competence in technology applications. The leader does not link the installation of technology to specific teaching and learning objectives.
9.2 Personal proficiency in electronic communication	In addition to the skills required of the "proficient" leader, the leader creates new opportunities for learning and uses the organization as an example of effective technology implementation. Leading by example, the leader provides a model of new learning.	Personally uses e-mail, word processing, spreadsheets, presentation software, databases, and district software. Personal study and professional development reflect a commitment to continued learning.	Mastered some, but not all of the software required for "proficient" performance. Takes initiative to learn new technology.	Not technologically literate. Little or no evidence of taking personal initiative to learn new technology.

133

Leadership Dimension	Exemplary (Systemwide Impact)	Proficient (Local Impact)	Progressing (Leadership Potential)	Not Meeting Standards
10.0 Learning				
10.1 Personal understanding of research trends in education and leadership	In addition to personal reading that is wide and deep in the field of educational research, the leader contributes directly to research, providing case studies, experimental results, and research questions to serve the interests of other leaders and educational organizations.	Personal reading, learning, and teaching of educational research trends.	Occasional educational research reading and some interest in personal reading and learning.	Little or no evidence of personal learning and research.
10.2 Personal Professional Development Plan	In addition to meeting the requirements for "proficient" performance, this leader approaches every professional development opportunity with a view toward multidimensional impact. Knowledge and skills are shared throughout the organization and with other departments, schools, and districts. Rather than merely adopting the tools of external professional development, this leader creates specific adaptations so that learning tools become part of the culture of the organization and are "home-grown" rather than externally generated.	Engages in professional development that is directly linked to organizational needs. The priority is given to building on personal leadership strengths. The leader personally attends and actively participates in the professional development that is required of other leaders in the organization. In the case of building principals, the leader personally attends and actively participates in the professional development required of teachers.	The leader actively participates in professional development, but it is reflective of a personal agenda rather than the strategic needs of the organization. The leader attends professional development for colleagues, but does not fully engage in it and set an example of active participation.	This leader might introduce a professional development program, but quickly leaves the room, sending the signal to colleagues that "This really is not worth my time." When the leader does engage in personal professional development, it is likely to be a national conference selected for its location rather than its content or the strategic relationship to organizational needs.

Leadership Dimension	Exemplary (Systemwide Impact)	Proficient (Local Impact)	Progressing (Leadership Potential)	Not Meeting Standards
10.3 Professional Development Focus	Can identify specific professional development offerings of past years that have been systematically reviewed and terminated because they failed to support organizational goals. Has a process for prior review of new professional development programs and rigorously applies its applications for time and funding. Can provide examples of having disapproved applications for professional development that failed to meet these criteria. Chooses one or two focus areas for professional development, with extensive time in faculty meetings, grade-level meetings, department meetings, and staff development meetings all focused on intensive implementation of a few areas of learning.	Professional development plan has no more than six areas of emphasis and each of those areas is linked to the organization's strategic objectives.	Professional development opportunities are somewhat related to the organizational objectives, but there is no way of systematically assessing their impact. Participant evaluations are the primary criteria for selection, so programs that are popular but ineffective tend to be the norm.	By personal example, this leader endorses the butterfly approach to professional development. Once a subject has been superficially addressed, then a new fad is chased. Faculty requests are routinely approved whether or not they are related to student achievement. Similarly, the leader's personal professional development agenda is based on whim and preference, not organizational needs.

Leadership Dimension	Exemplary (Systemwide Impact)	Proficient	Progressing (Leadership Potential)	Not Meeting Standards
10.4 Application of Learning	In addition to meeting all the criteria for "proficient" performance, this leader provides evidence of the principle of leverage, taking each learning opportunity and applying it throughout the organization. This leader creates forms, checklists, self-assessments, and other learning tools so that concepts learned in professional development are applied in the daily lives of teachers and leaders throughout the organization. In addition, this leader regularly shares these application tools with other schools, departments, or districts in order to maximize the impact of the leader's personal learning experience.	There is clear evidence of the actual application of personal learning in the organization. Where learning has not been applied within the organization, this leader rigorously analyzes the cause for this and does not continue investing time and money in professional development programs that lack clear evidence of success when applied in the organization.	The leader has given intellectual assent to some important learning experiences, but can give only a few specific examples of application to the organization.	Even on those rare occasions when this leader engages in professional development, the purpose appears to be merely collecting information rather than reflecting on it and applying it to the organization. Professional development is an expense, not an investment in constructive improvements.

Resource B

National Leadership Survey Results

RESPONDENT CHARACTERISTICS

The National Leadership Survey was conducted from March to September 2002 with a nonrandom sample of 510 leaders from 21 states. The average respondent had 11.4 years of total leadership experience and an average of 4.9 years in their present position. While 18 percent of leaders had never been evaluated, the remaining respondents had been evaluated, on average, within the past six months.

LEADERSHIP PERCEPTIONS

Leadership Perception	*Agree or Strongly Agree*
1. The leadership evaluations I have received helped me to improve my performance.	58 percent
2. The leadership evaluations I have received improved my personal motivation.	60 percent
3. The leadership evaluations I have received were directly related to the mission and vision of our school system.	65 percent
4. The leadership evaluations I have received were related to student achievement results.	47 percent
5. The leadership evaluations I have received are generally positive.	89 percent
6. The leadership evaluations I have received were consistent with my original expectations for my job.	76 percent
7. The leadership evaluations I have received were accurate.	79 percent

(Continued)

(Continued)

Leadership Perception	*Agree or Strongly Agree*
8. The leadership evaluations I have received were specific— I knew exactly how to improve performance and exactly what performance I should continue.	47 percent
9. The leadership evaluations I have received were based on clear standards that I knew would be the focus of my evaluation.	54 percent
10. During my last leadership evaluation, I had the opportunity to make suggestions to improve organizational support for me and my colleagues.	46 percent

NARRATIVE EXPLANATIONS: BEST EVALUATION EXPERIENCES

- In a previous school district, the principal had 10+ years experience in my subject field. This principal came to class 5 times for 15 minutes, unexpectedly, sat through an entire class, and then made his evaluation. His comments were more real and helpful than any other evaluation and I learned to be a better teacher.
- Engaged in a point by point discussion of evaluation criteria.
- I had very positive written evaluation as an assistant principal in another district. Receiving the Ohio Hall of Fame Award for my school from the Ohio Elementary Principal Association was a great successful experience. Personal comments from parents and teachers.
- Evaluator was familiar with my work in the field, which allowed for a true understanding of my abilities and performance with district personnel.
- Setting goals and action plans. Use continuous improvement process.
- Our district uses Charlotte Danielson's evaluation program. By focusing on each domain I have greatly improved.
- A collaborative approach based on my goals and clear expectations for the performance responsibilities of the position. We used data from my experience and job performance and data from my supervisory experience and system perspective to cocreate the evaluation document. As such the written document and the experience were more valuable than if they had been entirely by myself or entirely by my evaluation.
- I can remember some experiences as a teacher that helped my self-esteem but were not specific and therefore NOT helpful for improving my teaching.
- I was well prepared for my evaluation. I knew that my evaluation was going to be based on the goals that were written over the summer. I had created a binder organized by goals. The evaluation went very smoothly.
- Last year I had my staff fill out a leadership evaluation form on my performance. I used their recommendations to formulate some of my goals.
- My evaluation is a way that I can affirm that I am doing my best for students, and I feel I am best at being with students while they are at school.

- Discuss with superintendent my goals for the year related to our strategic plan, the board goals, the superintendent's goals and our leadership team goals—these are all related to Baldridge Initiative criteria. I'm looking forward to our exit evaluation at the end of the year.
- I have an extremely supportive superintendent. I value the one-on-one time with him during the evaluation process.
- As a principal, my former superintendent not only adequately and consistently evaluated performance but also gave one a feeling of personal value, warmth, and success. In other words, not only were there data to indicate completion of goals but also a narrative regarding overall participation and importance to the organization.
- Evaluation was constant interaction and was not necessarily formal.
- Specific references to strengths, things to work on. Also specific, reasonable ideas of how to improve—offers to provide resources, mentors to help with a problem. Assurances that it is okay to "let some things go. . . ."
- We are a small organization. We do not have a lot of formal evaluations but we discuss strengths and weaknesses openly and correct or rethink processes all year long. Our communication is very open and honest. I can say "I screwed up" and know that we can all learn from this.
- The superintendent worked with me on a monthly basis in the school setting. We evaluated monthly newsletters, staff evaluation forms, and the building environment. Staff input was sought, along with these monthly evaluation sessions, to formulate a final evaluation.
- Having to list all my goals for the year and being reviewed by my supervisor. These same goals were reviewed at mid-year and finally at the end of the year. Keeping these goals in front of me and focused I feel was valuable.
- My most successful evaluation experience was my last evaluation. My administrator complimented my strengths, while giving constructive criticism. She offered suggestions as well.
- My superintendent focused on my talents and strengths. Although I have areas to improve, he clearly wanted me to focus on my talents and strengths to make improvements and manage my weaknesses.
- A comprehensive narrative evaluation was given in March of a year in which the superintendent (because of special projects, programs, etc.) had spent a great deal of time in my building. He was able to be much more specific (and positive) than usual.
- Very first evaluation as a supervisor: When we interviewed you and hired—who is she, where did she come from—by the end of the year same questions except where have you been. . . . Not well written but conveyed we couldn't believe our luck in finding you and seeing progress this year.
- When I was a teacher and allowed to choose a project to work on (portfolio), I actually did research that was helpful in my job.
- My first year as an administrator, my secretary gave the superintendent specific examples of my daily work. She was trying to be helpful because I had only been visited twice. The secretary's notes were references to my positive attributes.

- Informal statements (written/verbal) shared with me by staff, community members, students, parents, and supporters that have been both critical and positive.
- My last evaluation was more narrative and included district and personal goals.
- Good positive feedback for strengths and solid concrete examples for improvement.
- In my current position, my supervisor is very collaborative. Our division has a plan and my evaluation was based on that.
- First evaluation in present position helped to establish clear expectations and area of future focus. Present evaluator (Superintendent) knows what she wants and is not shy about expressing expectations.
- I was allowed to build on the positives, meaning I listed projects that I was in charge of and the steps I took to accomplish the goal (end product).
- I have been lucky with having a director that is accessible to me and my school and who supports decisions and out of the box activities that I have tried. When she needs to advise me of something I need to do or haven't done, she does it in a nonthreatening way and provides the guidance and help that we need to make the change. It motivates me to follow the district's lead when I can still have the freedom to lead my staff on the journey in a way that we are all engaged in the learning that leads us on that road. My evaluator helps me do that.
- The feedback I received—specific—has helped me to understand the district culture and enabled me to modify my behavior and expectations to fit the organizational culture and be more productive.
- My most successful experience being evaluated as a leader was my first year as our assistant principal. The person supervising me was the principal of the school, a person with whom I had contact on a daily basis. This contact allowed me to ask frequent clarifying questions and to receive timely feedback. I felt that the principal scaffolded my learning for me across the entire year, as she worked to make sure that I gained the required knowledge to be successful at this particular school.
- Two hour meeting—me and the superintendent to discuss progress on measured district progress—what worked, what plans do I have to improve for next year.
- Allowing me to fit my yearly objectives (only after the first year when I knew the job responsibility) and then a year-end follow-up with my reflections. These were used as the basis for the supervisor's final evaluation.
- When I had an opportunity to self-evaluate as part of the process.
- Balanced evaluation between what I do well and what needs are for growth—my self-evaluation as part of evaluation—examples related to comments.
- In a previous district in Illinois, we developed goals based on the goals and vision of the district. This was useful, positive, and kept me focused on what was important. My current district has a checklist that doesn't match anything.

- The ability to actually see that I have made a difference in process or a person. Giving back and mentoring a team of people. I am new to the teaching profession, but have been in leadership training and development positions.
- I participated in drawing up the guidelines for my own evaluation, which was merged with district guidelines as well. Evaluation was clearly based on job description so I knew exactly what was expected of me and whether or not I fulfilled the guidelines.
- I facilitated a group of social science teachers who came to monthly meetings and went back to their campuses and shared their experiences. The end of the year reflection piece was very complimentary toward my work with them.
- Conversationally oriented evaluation.
- Feedback, encouragement, support.
- My principal and I defined daily, which gives immediate positive feedback and areas for focus.
- I worked at a particular school where the principal operated as a dictator. He single-handedly made all of the decisions and instilled fear in all of us. He chose not to interact with staff or students, so we only saw him where there was a problem . . . or when it was time for your evaluation. This man was extremely impressed with my teaching and was very complimentary. Although I did not consider him to be an instructional leader, I was comforted by the fact that he issued me a compliment. It boosted my confidence . . . and I pushed myself to continue to learn, grow, and improve in my instructional practice.
- I was given my evaluation sheet (blank) in advance. I filled out my own evaluation and submitted it to my evaluator. Ideally, my supervisor would have used her form and mine to lead a discussion and then after the discussion fill out the final evaluation meshing the two documents. In reality, my supervisor merely copied my own words, signed her name, and submitted it.
- My past evaluation outlined our division's accomplishments for the year and my involvement in these accomplishments. What made this successful to me was that my evaluator was aware of and appreciated our accomplishments. She also put the accomplishments in context, which gave them extra value. We then discussed our next steps together in a very positive environment.
- Specific feedback . . . constructive criticism is helpful . . . honest assessment from all stakeholders, students, parents, administration, district . . . ongoing assessment . . .
- Assistant Principal . . . (2) attended four sessions, (3) power standards, importance of writing, celebrating success, (4) fewer announcements and reports at meetings—more time for staff development.
- The most successful experience has been when I've set the goals for which I would be evaluated and received feedback on these.
- Using the portfolio when I had to identify my visions and goals. The goals had to be based on student and teacher needs identified by data analysis.

- For the most part, all evaluations have focused on positive aspects of my performance as it related to the integration of technology.
- Currently I experience weekly coaching in which I am able to ask questions, set goals, etc. The annual evaluation is then written with my input.
- Discussions of the evaluation and areas of concentration for the next year.
- Completing the process of evaluation in meeting the district's requirements for evaluation.
- Reinforcing what was positively accomplished and not just suggestions.
- My most successful experience was being promoted from [assistant] principal to principal. Being promoted for doing a good job as a leader was a great experience.
- My most successful experience involved clear descriptions of my strengths and areas to improve as a leader. It was very informative. However, the reason I feel it was successful was because I respected the person who was completing my evaluation!
- The person evaluating me was able to cite specific examples of what he had observed me do or not do. The person evaluating me was honest. I was able to ask questions and ask for feedback about specific actions or decisions I had taken, and my evaluator gave me practical suggestions and feedback.
- To reinforce the goals and objectives of my position.
- I had a close working relationship with my evaluator. The day-to-day suggestions, interactions, and comments were more valuable than the formal evaluation.
- I only received a narrative evaluation. My experience was rather neutral. There were no specific checklists or portfolios requested or used. My superior told me I was doing a good job but not formally.
- As an assistant principal, I was never evaluated! I begged for it because I learn from good effective feedback!
- I am told that I am very approachable and have a calming nature.
- I felt confident that I was doing a good job in my role as a leader when I was given the current position. Until that happened I really didn't know if others thought I was doing a good job prior to that.
- The establishment of goals.
- I appreciate the annual conference with the building principal to review my performance and set goals for the following school year.
- Genuine, sincere criticism.
- I have never had a successful evaluation experience. From the time I was a teacher, to guidance counselor, to principal, to superintendent, my evaluations have indicated my performance was exemplary. Never in 28 years have I received constructive feedback specific to an area where my performance was inadequate or ineffective. I am not perfect. I could benefit from constructive criticism and/or direction.
- A conference was held early in the school year at which goals were formulated and discussed with the superintendent. A formal written evaluation followed.
- Very positive comments on evaluation. Positive comments from students, parents, staff.

- My experiences have been very similar. They have been rather general in nature based upon vague guidelines. All of my experiences have been positive to date.
- Years ago—meeting with the superintendent. To discuss focus, goals, and improvement. Goals were established and work toward the success of goals—improvement of my skills was focus.
- Feedback on a situation where the evaluator felt improvement could be made. It focused my attention to the area, and I feel I became a better administrator.
- Relating the corporation and school goals to accomplishments made during the year.
- When all the various aspects of my job were addressed.
- Creating a portfolio to be presented during my evaluation.
- Direct, practical feedback—no ambiguity.
- Informal process was MUCH better.
- Rich discussions and true focus on achievement.
- [My best evaluation experiences are] when I have been in an evaluation meeting. Where my supervisor shared with me areas that he saw a need for growth and then discussed strategies with me. We also spent time discussing areas in which I have grown professionally over the last year.
- Seat evaluation that was based upon quality criteria. Subordinate evaluation—if truly confidential it can be brutally honest and enlightening, particularly patterns that emerge.
- Increase in students' achievement as demonstrated by test scores or successful demonstration of learning.
- I really have had good evaluations but none have helped me think about areas that I could explore for my own personal growth. I have had to seek my own growth decisions from my own view, which might not be as effective in real growth.
- Being uninformed of my leadership skills that I brought to the table.
- When my evaluator was someone I respected.
- When I set an ambitious goal and met it—and I could share the efforts and successes.
- Monthly "feedback sessions" with supervisor; weekly communication (verbal, written, email) between staff members.
- It was a self-evaluation based on goals I set myself related to students' outcomes.
- When I had input as to the direction the school system was going.
- Evaluation was based on the goals that I had submitted. These goals had been edited by the principal.
- My principal selected me to take a leadership position in our elementary school as the Literacy First Educator. This was very complimentary of my professionalism and effectiveness.
- My first evaluation I was rated "exemplary" in "Learning for Excellence" because of raised test scores. However, while I appreciated the rating, the original "assigned focus" of my position wasn't in that area.

- (1) Setting goals collaboratively with the board in the summer/fall. (2) Review throughout the year with updates and continuous communication. (3) Summative analysis collaboratively accomplished with the board.
- Our school system's evaluation process is on a goal setting basis and is not geared toward growth.
- Positive reinforcement of success.
- I was asked to evaluate myself and state short and long term goals for my positions.
- These were taken to the evaluation conference where my evaluation was compared to that of my supervisor. From there, we discussed my goals with questions and input from my supervisor. The tone of the conference was professional, positive and supportive.
- The evaluation form included a narrative outlining strengths.
- Having specific goals and then being evaluated is always positive because measurable growth can be easily determined.
- Writing professional goals, documentation and self-reflection.
- Was asked if there was an area that surprised me, where there was any discrepancy . . . gave me a chance to say "I didn't perceive myself in that light, so what were you noticing that made you rate me at that level" (my self-expectation was higher than evaluator).
- Personalized to my school, position, and goals for performance, A sharing of what I do well, as well as those items needing attention.
- Moving forward with technology and library–media center philosophy in their goal setting. Library media specialists can profoundly influence school climate, collaboration and literacy.
- The significance and usefulness is dependent on the effectiveness of my evaluator.
- Working collaboratively with my superior to achieve academic and effective school goals tied to district goals. Together, we were a success.
- When given specific feedback on strengths and weaknesses.
- Leadership evaluations are based on meeting goals determined by myself. Several years ago my evaluator worked with me in a negative way to choose these goals. Time was taken at the end of the process for both of us to reflect on how goals were met, what was learned, etc.
- When reflection and self-evaluation, aligned with goals for my performance, were a major part of my evaluation.
- The Agency that I worked for used Personal Growth Plans that were linked to Agency and personal goals. These plans were reviewed 3x a year with a peer. At the end of the year they became a part of my professional portfolio. This was a wonderful way to motivate and perpetuate professional growth. The Agency used the work of W. Edward Deming as the basis for the evaluation system.
- Through the cognitive coaching process I was afforded a preobservation conference where outstanding questions were asked of me and influenced my desire to grow.

NARRATIVE EXPLANATIONS:
NEGATIVE EVALUATION EXPERIENCES

- I currently have a principal who is a former band teacher (I teach physics) doing my evaluations. He has been to one of my classes. Though his evaluation was positive, it doesn't mean much to me for personal improvement. Learned how to get a good evaluation (dog and pony show).

- To appease a few anonymous letter writers, the superintendent and Union official invited everyone to come to my office and a schoolwide award was presented to the teachers in my absence.

- Using "perceptions" only as a measurement of effectiveness.

- My beginning teaching—1970—the principal did not like my bulletin boards and my students' posture!! No word about my teaching/curriculum.

- The worst experience in a sense was to receive no evaluation at all. This message was, "You are not important enough to take my time to give you an evaluation." The second worst experience was an evaluation never getting any input from me, never scheduling a progress or evaluation conference. He just wrote a minimum document, sent it to me, told me to sign it and return it by a certain date.

- I received satisfactory and higher evaluations (4 out of 5). I was asked to resign and told that these "good" evaluations really didn't mean anything—even though they were written and signed, I was told they weren't truthful. The 5th evaluation was satisfactory and at the bottom the principal wrote "please don't share this with her."

- Being evaluated as an assistant principal by a principal that was very vague and uninspiring!

- Little discussion—no evaluation of goals, accepted my report with little review.

- Most have been positive.

- Simply accounting of data as it related to goals created by me and the evaluator.

- Checklist and certain positives and negatives "picked" out as strengths and weaknesses.

- 1. Vague broad compliments—"Everything's great." 2. No suggestions of what to do to help: "Gee, that's a tough one. I don't know what to do either."

- Criticized for asking for placement in a particular building. Notations of insubordination were placed in the final evaluation because I did not agree with the superintendent's decision . . . And years of not being evaluated at all!

- Nothing in particular. Generally I have felt rather empty when no suggestions were given to me for improvement. Whenever evaluations are all positive and no suggestions for improvement, it leaves no motivation for growth and improvement.

- Administrator evaluations are all the same with 1 sentence specifically related to my building leadership.
- Evaluations were not based on frequent observations and dialogue—it was based on asking other personnel in the administration office their input—then wrote it based on mostly that. This entire process was not done with my awareness.
- The superintendent explained that every administrator this year is receiving an "unsatisfactory" mark in a certain area because he felt that area was a weakness district-wide.
- Checklist—three levels, everything marked down the middle. Narrative that was generic, so it included things wanted everyone to do—but as an individual already doing them—but not acknowledged!
- No formal evaluation for 7 years.
- As a new principal, I would have appreciated and grown professionally if I valued the evaluation process. My evaluator knew little failures or successes. Process was just that—a task that had to be completed. No standards/performance goals communicated.
- Most of my evaluations were based on a friendly conversation—"Everything appears OK in your classroom, therefore keep it up." There was little to no goal setting, professional dialogue, etc. . . .
- No feedback.
- While I was an assistant principal, I did not receive an evaluation for 3 years. I was never sure what the principal wanted.
- An evaluation which was a "pat on the back" but not related to expectations or results.
- Some circumstances and acknowledging the blunder on personnel areas.
- Last year wasn't the worst; however, one notation on the evaluation was bothersome. In essence, I was told not to talk to other directors regarding school site issues.
- I worked with a very ineffective principal. As the coordinator, then assistant principal, I had a lot of responsibilities. I was in charge of Categorical Budgets and some others.
- Professional Director, new teachers, etc. The only time the principal gave me feedback was when she felt threatened that the staff came to me for decisions or that I knew more about programs, budget, etc. than she did. Although I learned much and had tons of responsibilities—it wasn't because of her guidance but lack of it that gave me the experience.
- Really none—only when the process of evaluation has "felt" not real—only done to satisfy an organization's request.
- My worst experience being evaluated as a leader is my current year—my first as an elementary school principal. The person supervising me is an assistant superintendent, a person with whom I have few contacts. I feel that I do not have frequent access to this person for clarifying questions and for feedback. I feel as though I am expected to know exactly what to do in every situation. There is no scaffolding of learning and I am required to seek out knowledge and information on my own from many

sources. In this environment, I do not feel that the final evaluation that I will be receiving will be at all meaningful or helpful.

- No evaluation at all—no feedback given to assist my performance.
- Only occurred once—but following the end of year evaluation which was positive, and then an abrupt change of perception . . . within a 30-day period (driven by 2 specific incidents).
- Changing jobs mid-year and having objective for my job no longer apply—not knowing what to work for.
- Generally, when I knew what was being said was not truthful from evaluator—really just done as an "exercise" and not trying to give me honest feedback.
- Currently, a checklist is used and it doesn't correlate to anything. Since I was used to setting goals in a previous district, I still do that for myself! All my evaluations have been very positive—just not useful or growth producing.
- Working with a project team who was not on the same page—didn't have the same objectives from the beginning of the project. The team had not been brought together as a team—too many separate agendas—I wasn't able to bring them together as an effective team.
- I've been in this position for 10 months without any kind of a quality evaluation of my performance.
- During a goal setting process I was asked to modify my goals. In essence, my supervisor's goals were imposed upon me. I cannot remember them—they were set 8 months ago.
- Student teaching—I was evaluated on my wardrobe not my teaching!
- "This doesn't apply to you, but I have to do it anyway" stated by more than one principal.
- No formal evaluation.
- Most evaluations have been very generic. Administrators simply check "Professionally Competent" in each category. This does not give me specific feedback. It doesn't inspire me or help me set goals. Evaluation in its formal sense seems only to be an isolated process completely disconnected and unrelated to my instructional practice. Furthermore, I've not yet had an administrator whom I consider to be an instructional leader. They are so disconnected from the classroom reality that they can't properly advise me. . . .
- I was called in to a cold office, sitting across the large desk from a stern principal. She handed me an evaluation with the areas (which I had never seen) already filled in. When I could give proof that the evaluations were not accurate, the supervisor (principal) agreed that her evaluation was not accurate. She didn't change the comments, but did add one sentence at the end of the entire evaluation that unsuccessfully attempted to address the discrepancy.
- As a middle school principal, my Superintendent told me the new high school exit exam coming the following year was going to be highlighted in the media as an indictment of feeding middle schools and what did I plan to do about that? She offered no reflection, thoughts or ideas. Just the challenge. It was scary. I went to the high school district.

- Too general . . . Wait until the end to tell you what you should be doing, instead of ongoing assessment. . . .
- My "worst" experience was not receiving any evaluation in 2 different school districts as a principal.
- I got an excellent evaluation—but my evaluator and I never discussed any of the areas I was evaluated on.
- I was accused of several things without being given an opportunity to present my case. I was called abrasive and told that there was a "rap sheet" going around the district about me and that nobody wanted to work with me. It was very painful and handled very poorly.
- Not being evaluated in a timely manner, skipped a year.
- My evaluations are passive in nature and often grounded in rumor or speculation rather than facts or performance of leadership. The process lacks substance, support, or motivation for leadership growth.
- When a superior lied.
- My evaluator made it clear that everyone being evaluated was "satisfactory." There was no acknowledgement of my accomplishments because it might make others look bad.
- I know I am not perfect and sometimes my evaluations do not specify my area of weakness.
- I guess it would be—not being evaluated at all!
- Post-evaluation conference that literally consisted of . . ."You are doing a great job—keep up the good work!"
- I have been noted as not being able to make a timely decision.
- Not being evaluated.
- I haven't had a bad experience, just no feedback as to how to do an even better job.
- Not being evaluated for 15 years.
- It was positive, but did not note anything special or meaningful.
- Haven't had one!
- I was verbally told, "Not to worry . . . You're doing a great job." I almost forgot the time a principal had me complete an evaluation instrument for my position, and he signed it.
- Not being evaluated.
- Evaluation was vague. I'm glad it was good—but—I also know areas that I can improve on and would like specific feedback on those areas.
- No "formal" evaluation contact during the year. Form was given to me by appearing in my mailbox. I signed and returned it.
- Once per year—lots of build up and stress—would rather be evaluated 2–4 times/year.
- Had completed instrument in my mailbox with note attached—never actually sat down for pre- or post- and was never observed.
- Evaluated by someone with a very narrow agenda.
- Very little interaction with evaluator.
- Where I was called to the office to sign an evaluation but there was no dialogue at all concerning my performance.
- I've not had that experience.

- During an evaluation conference I was told that certain deficiencies needed to be addressed that had never ever been mentioned before. Had I known there was a problem, it would have been addressed.
- As administrative intern—principal said he "could fry me."
- Not having one for 2 years and then being held accountable for a performance I had no knowledge about.
- I was evaluated by someone who never visited my building except to see my goals and at the end of my goals.
- Initiative was totally from me—follow up was just an acknowledgement that I had met supervisor's criteria. It was not at all threatening and also not helpful—just another task.
- This year when my supervisor asked me to work with two of my co-workers to evaluate each other. We basically completed our own evaluations and then signed each other's forms.
- My evaluations have not been good or bad, just not meaningful tools for growth.
- No real problem in being evaluated.
- Being evaluated by a Principal that was totally incompetent.
- Characteristics were checked off as Satisfactory or Unsatisfactory—period.
- After carrying the majority of the responsibility for academic achievement the previous year (by a different administrator, who was promoted, by the way), I was told there wasn't a sufficient gain; therefore, I was only proficient in the area of "learning for excellence."
- Form completed in isolation by the board and then presented to me as a number. That number was what determined the rate of merit pay.
- No specific feedback from presentation of my evaluation to Board—I feel we should be allowed to participate in this presentation.
- The evaluation form was left on my desk and I was asked to sign and return it to my supervisor.
- I was handed the form to sign—there was no discussion.
- I have not had a bad experience during evaluation.
- The Stephen Covey Leadership Workshop evaluation as a leadership survey was not effective. Since a variety of people were surveyed and the result was a compilation, it was impossible to discern possible problems or to find out specific weaknesses.
- Brief, "you're great," sign here, when I felt like I had experienced a very unfulfilling year with very little new growth.
- Supervisor spends time during the evaluation. Completing the form. Then, nothing positive is mentioned. Therefore, an impersonal process—stated at the beginning that they were in a hurry.
- An evaluator who just goes through the process with no end in mind. It was just something that needed to be done.
- At this time I don't have a "worst experience" and I hope this never becomes a negative or non-productive process.
- No feedback.
- My other 9 evaluations as an administrator have been a joke. I write the goals with no discussion, and then at the end of the year I mark whether

or not goals were met and then evaluate and sign off on them. These have been my discussions.

- When I had to complete my own evaluation form and that was the evaluation! I value frequent specific reinforcement rather than summative evaluation.
- I was fortunate in not having one!
- This was when an evaluator was clearly not confident about his level of understanding, so he had me articulate what I felt the observation should reflect.

Resource C

Leadership Evaluation Survey

The Center for Performance Assessment is conducting research into the nature of leadership evaluations for a forthcoming book by Dr. Douglas Reeves, *Assessing Educational Leaders: Evaluating Performance for Improved Individual and Organizational Results* to be published by Corwin Press in 2003. Your responses are completely confidential and will be an important part of this research. Thank you for sharing your ideas.

1. Your current position (check all that apply to you):
   - ☐ Assistant principal
   - ☐ Principal
   - ☐ Department director
   - ☐ Assistant superintendent
   - ☐ Other central office administrative position (specify):_____
   - ☐ Other school administrative position (specify):_____
   - ☐ Superintendent
   - ☐ Board member
   - ☐ Other (specify):_____

2. How long have you been with your present organization?
   _____ years and _____ months

3. How long have you been in your present position?
   _____ years and _____ months

4. How long ago did you receive your last evaluation for your current position?
   _____ Have not received formal evaluation
   _____ years and _____ months ago

NOTE: The text above is from the questionnaire used in the National Leadership Survey.

5. Please reflect on that evaluation experience by noting your agreement or disagreement with the following statements: 1 = Strongly Agree (SA); 2 = Agree (A); 3 = No Opinion (NO); 4 = Disagree (D); 5 = Strongly Disagree (SD).

	1. SA	*2. A*	*3. NO*	*4. D*	*5. SD*
1. The leadership evaluations I have received helped me to improve my performance.	___	___	___	___	___
2. The leadership evaluations I have received improved my personal motivation.	___	___	___	___	___
3. The leadership evaluations I have received were directly related to the mission and vision of our school system.	___	___	___	___	___
4. The leadership evaluations I have received were related to student achievement results.	___	___	___	___	___
5. The leadership evaluations I have received are generally positive.	___	___	___	___	___
6. The leadership evaluations I have received were consistent with my original expectations for my job.	___	___	___	___	___
7. The leadership evaluations I have received were accurate.	___	___	___	___	___
8. The leadership evaluations I have received were specific—I knew exactly how to improve performance and exactly what performance I should continue.	___	___	___	___	___
9. The leadership evaluations I have received were based on clear standards that I knew would be the focus of my evaluation.	___	___	___	___	___
10. During my last leadership evaluation, I had the opportunity to make suggestions to improve organizational support for me and my colleagues.	___	___	___	___	___

Copyright 2009 by Douglas B. Reeves. All rights reserved. Reprinted from *Assessing Educational Leaders: Evaluating Performance for Improved Individual and Organizational Results* (2nd ed.), by Douglas B. Reeves. Reproduction authorized only for the local school site that has purchased this book.

6. Please briefly describe your most successful experience being evaluated as a leader:

_____

_____

_____

_____

_____

_____

_____

_____

_____

_____

7. Please briefly describe your worst experience being evaluated as a leader:

_____

_____

_____

_____

_____

_____

_____

_____

_____

_____

Copyright 2009 by Douglas B. Reeves. All rights reserved. Reprinted from *Assessing Educational Leaders: Evaluating Performance for Improved Individual and Organizational Results* (2nd ed.), by Douglas B. Reeves. Reproduction authorized only for the local school site that has purchased this book.

Resource D

The Gap Between What Leaders Know and What They Do

	Percentage Who "Strongly Agree" That They Perform This Function	Percentage Who "Strongly Agree" That This Function Is Important
DOMAIN ONE:		
Instructional Leadership		
A. *Visionary Leadership*		
1. Presents evidence that the vision is a shared vision	30 percent	60 percent
2. Uses the vision to guide and define decisions	31 percent	68 percent
3. Maintains a steady flow of two-way communications to keep the vision alive and important	27 percent	70 percent
B. *Curriculum Design and Development*		
4. Leads the faculty and community in a thorough understanding of the relationship between the learning needs of students and the NC Standard Course of Study	37 percent	63 percent
5. Ensures that there is an appropriate and logical alignment between the school's curriculum and the state's accountability program	58 percent	83 percent

	Percentage Who "Strongly Agree" That They Perform This Function	Percentage Who "Strongly Agree" That This Function Is Important
6. Ensures that appropriate differentiation in curriculum and instruction are available to those students with exceptional needs	38 percent	65 percent
C. *Instruction Effectiveness*		
7. Manages time to be an instructional leader as a priority	28 percent	68 percent
8. Provides targeted and challenging professional development activities designed to improve teachers' strengths in reaching all students	21 percent	62 percent
9. Arranges for teachers to teach in settings and circumstances that draw on their strengths and highest abilities	21 percent	53 percent
D. *Assessment and Evaluation*		
10. Uses the data collected from state and local testing and assessment programs to develop formative instructional strategies to improve the effectiveness of daily classroom instruction	40 percent	75 percent
11. Monitors student achievement throughout the year, using both classroom and testing data to assess progress	41 percent	73 percent
12. Monitors classroom performance on a regular basis, offering pathways to improve individual student performance through improved teaching practices	30 percent	67 percent
E. *Results Oriented*		
13. Monitors student achievement throughout the year, using both classroom and testing data to assess progress	43 percent	60 percent
14. Produces student achievement results that are commensurate with basic principles of the state's accountability system	48 percent	65 percent
15. Communicates the results of his/her leadership to appropriate audiences and constituencies	25 percent	46 percent

	Percentage Who "Strongly Agree" That They Perform This Function	Percentage Who "Strongly Agree" That This Function Is Important
DOMAIN TWO:		
Organizational Leadership		
A. *Climate*		
16. Provides and promotes a climate for learning that is safe and orderly	77 percent	91 percent
17. Creates an organizational climate that provides rewards and incentives for accomplishment	36 percent	41 percent
18. Assures that curricular, co-curricular, and extra-curricular programs are designed, appropriately implemented, evaluated, and refined	28 percent	36 percent
B. *Empowerment*		
19. Ensures that all faculty members are involved in the critical decisions that affect them	20 percent	52 percent
20. Involves all community stakeholders in the planning and development activities that affect their schools	12 percent	26 percent
21. Establishes partnerships with area businesses, institutions of higher education, and community groups to strengthen collaborative programs that support the accomplishment of school goals	15 percent	30 percent
C. *Communication*		
22. Keeps appropriate audiences and constituencies informed about the school and functions	22 percent	42 percent
23. Shares the school's achievement data with appropriate outside audiences and enlists their assistance to influence higher student achievement	20 percent	32 percent
24. Stays well-informed about professional issues and shares this information with appropriate groups	21 percent	33 percent

	Percentage Who "Strongly Agree" That They Perform This Function	Percentage Who "Strongly Agree" That This Function Is Important
D. *Continuous Improvement*		
25. Develops with faculty leadership a set of performance indicators that enable the school to monitor and benchmark its performance and progress among similar clusters of organizations	28 percent	48 percent
26. Uses student performance data to effect changes in school programs as well as the attitudes within the school family about needed changes	33 percent	68 percent
27. Possesses and maintains the energy necessary to meet the responsibilities and expectations of the position	40 percent	60 percent
DOMAIN THREE: **Moral/Ethical Leadership**		
A. *Commitment to Others*		
28. Creates and sustains a nurturing and caring environment	43 percent	74 percent
29. Maintains a learning environment designed to help others be as successful as they choose to be	40 percent	75 percent
B. *Professional Ethics*		
30. Demonstrates an adherence to values, beliefs, and attitudes that inspire others to higher levels of performance	32 percent	78 percent
31. Incorporates the qualities of fairness and honesty in administering all aspects of the school's management program	48 percent	86 percent
32. Protects the privacy rights and confidentiality of matters dealing with students and staff	68 percent	85 percent
C. *Respect for Diversity*		
33. Communicates a commitment to the dignity and contributions of all cultures	44 percent	68 percent

	Percentage Who "Strongly Agree" That They Perform This Function	Percentage Who "Strongly Agree" That This Function Is Important
34. Assures that all students have equal access to all parts of the school's curricular, co-curricular, and extra-curricular programs	53 percent	63 percent
35. Uses a wide range of opportunities to celebrate the diverse cultures represented in the school and its community	19 percent	38 percent
36. Ensures that established policies and procedures are in place and enforced equitably for all participants in the school	46 percent	68 percent
D. *Responsibility*		
37. Opens the school and its functions to public scrutiny, where appropriate	27 percent	35 percent
38. Fulfills his/her legal/contractual responsibilities and administers those same responsibilities for those in his/her supervision	59 percent	70 percent
DOMAIN FOUR: **Managerial Leadership**		
A. *Law and Policy*		
39. Shapes public policy to provide quality education for students	22 percent	38 percent
40. Ensures that established policies and procedures are in place, widely disseminated through faculty and student handbooks, and equitably enforced for all participants in the school	54 percent	69 percent
41. Provides both professional development and community engagement regarding new laws and/or new interpretations of existing laws and policies	21 percent	38 percent
B. *Resource Management*		
42. Uses fiscal resources efficiently and effectively to provide the materials and people needed to help the school be effective	44 percent	67 percent

	Percentage Who "Strongly Agree" That They Perform This Function	Percentage Who "Strongly Agree" That This Function Is Important
43. Uses space and time effectively to support both the instructional program and the ancillary functions of the school as well	47 percent	60 percent
44. Manages the school staff effectively, encouraging the contribution of their best efforts to the school's success	44 percent	70 percent
45. Provides for effective supervision of school support services and classified staff	40 percent	54 percent
C. *Personnel Management*		
46. Uses sound and effective principles for selecting new staff, both professional and classified	44 percent	88 percent
47. Includes appropriate faculty in recruitment, hiring, and mentoring opportunities	31 percent	49 percent
48. Ensures that new hires are properly brought into the school's culture successfully	28 percent	78 percent
49. Provides specific guidance for teachers trying to solve instructional problems	22 percent	68 percent
50. Helps new teachers gain expertise and confidence in their teaching	23 percent	72 percent
51. Appropriately uses the standards of performance evaluation to help both new and experienced teachers to develop as accomplished professionals	30 percent	65 percent
52. Constantly monitors the school's teacher turnover rate using comparative benchmark indicators from other schools similar to his/her own	12 percent	28 percent
D. *Information Management*		
53. Ensures that people who require information to perform effectively receive it in a timely manner	32 percent	56 percent
54. Uses technology to facilitate more effective access to school-generated data	21 percent	43 percent

	Percentage Who "Strongly Agree" That They Perform This Function	Percentage Who "Strongly Agree" That This Function Is Important
55. Submits accurate records and reports on time	38 percent	46 percent
E. *Student Behavior Management*		
56. Develops and monitors a safe school plan, anticipating potential trouble spots and dealing with them in advance	64 percent	85 percent
57. Develops and distributes student handbooks with information about rules, requirements, and expectations for student conduct and potential consequences	73 percent	75 percent
58. Handles student misconduct in a firm, fair, and consistent manner	59 percent	80 percent

DOMAIN ONE:

Instructional Leadership

F. *Visionary Leadership*		
3. Presents evidence that the vision is a shared vision	52 percent	67 percent
4. Uses the vision to guide and define decisions	60 percent	65 percent
18. Maintains a steady flow of two-way communications to keep the vision alive and important	59 percent	70 percent
G. *Curriculum Design and Development*		
19. Leads the faculty and community in a thorough understanding of the relationship between the learning needs of students and the NC Standard Course of Study	50 percent	66 percent
20. Ensures that there is an appropriate and logical alignment between the school's curriculum and the state's accountability program	67 percent	78 percent
21. Ensures that appropriate differentiation in curriculum and instruction are available to those students with exceptional needs	57 percent	68 percent
H. *Instruction Effectiveness*		
22. Manages time to be an instructional leader as a priority	45 percent	71 percent

	Percentage Who "Strongly Agree" That They Perform This Function	Percentage Who "Strongly Agree" That This Function Is Important
23. Provides targeted and challenging professional development activities designed to improve teachers' strengths in reaching all students	37 percent	56 percent
24. Arranges for teachers to teach in settings and circumstances that draw on their strengths and highest abilities	54 percent	61 percent
I. *Assessment and Evaluation*		
25. Uses the data collected from state and local testing and assessment programs to develop formative instructional strategies to improve the effectiveness of daily classroom instruction	58 percent	70 percent
26. Monitors student achievement throughout the year, using both classroom and testing data to assess progress	60 percent	68 percent
27. Monitors classroom performance on a regular basis, offering pathways to improve individual student performance through improved teaching practices	48 percent	64 percent
J. *Results Oriented*		
28. Monitors student achievement throughout the year, using both classroom and testing data to assess progress	55 percent	65 percent
29. Produces student achievement results that are commensurate with basic principles of the state's accountability system	57 percent	62 percent
30. Communicates the results of his/her leadership to appropriate audiences and constituencies	41 percent	45 percent
DOMAIN TWO: **Organizational Leadership** E. *Climate*		
31. Provides and promotes a climate for learning that is safe and orderly	92 percent	92 percent

	Percentage Who "Strongly Agree" That They Perform This Function	Percentage Who "Strongly Agree" That This Function Is Important
32. Creates an organizational climate that provides rewards and incentives for accomplishment	54 percent	57 percent
18. Assures that curricular, co-curricular, and extra-curricular programs are designed, appropriately implemented, evaluated, and refined	46 percent	47 percent
F. *Empowerment*		
59. Ensures that all faculty members are involved in the critical decisions that affect them	65 percent	67 percent
60. Involves all community stakeholders in the planning and development activities which affect their schools	23 percent	35 percent
61. Establishes partnerships with area businesses, institutions of higher education, and community groups to strengthen collaborative programs that support the accomplishment of school goals	27 percent	33 percent
G. *Communications*		
62. Keeps appropriate audiences and constituencies informed about the school and its functions	48 percent	54 percent
63. Shares the school's achievement data with appropriate outside audiences and enlists their assistance to influence higher student achievement	40 percent	41 percent
64. Stays well-informed about professional issues and shares this information with appropriate groups	43 percent	44 percent
H. *Continuous Improvement*		
65. Develops with faculty leadership a set of performance indicators which enable the school to monitor and benchmark its performance and progress among similar clusters of organizations	45 percent	52 percent

	Percentage Who "Strongly Agree" That They Perform This Function	Percentage Who "Strongly Agree" That This Function Is Important
66. Uses student performance data to effect changes in school programs as well as the attitudes within the school family about needed changes	58 percent	64 percent
67. Possesses and maintains the energy necessary to meet the responsibilities and expectations of the position	66 percent	71 percent

DOMAIN THREE:
Moral/Ethical Leadership

E. *Commitment to Others*

68. Creates and sustains a nurturing and caring environment	77 percent	81 percent
69. Maintains a learning environment designed to help others be as successful as they choose to be	78 percent	77 percent

F. *Professional Ethics*

70. Demonstrates an adherence to values, beliefs, and attitudes that inspire others to higher levels of performance	75 percent	76 percent
71. Incorporates the qualities of fairness and honesty in administering all aspects of the school's management program	88 percent	86 percent
72. Protects the privacy rights and confidentiality of matters dealing with students and staff	89 percent	89 percent

G. *Respect for Diversity*

73. Communicates a commitment to the dignity and contributions of all cultures	72 percent	73 percent
74. Assures that all students have equal access to all parts of the schools' curricular, co-curricular, and extra-curricular programs	80 percent	75 percent
75. Uses a wide range of opportunities to celebrate the diverse cultures represented in the school and its community	39 percent	49 percent

	Percentage Who "Strongly Agree" That They Perform This Function	*Percentage Who "Strongly Agree" That This Function Is Important*
76. Ensures that established policies and procedures are in place and enforced equitably for all participants in the school	78 percent	80 percent
H. *Responsibility*		
77. Opens the school and its functions to public scrutiny, where appropriate	63 percent	54 percent
78. Fulfills his/her legal/contractual responsibilities and administers those same responsibilities for those in his/her supervision	83 percent	79 percent

DOMAIN FOUR:
Managerial Leadership

F. *Law and Policy*		
79. Shapes public policy to provide quality education for students	44 percent	49 percent
80. Ensures that established policies and procedures are in place, widely disseminated through faculty and student handbooks, and equitably enforced for all participants in the school	76 percent	75 percent
81. Provides both professional development and community engagement regarding new laws and/or new interpretations of existing laws and policies	36 percent	40 percent
G. *Resource Management*		
82. Uses fiscal resources efficiently and effectively to provide the materials and people needed to help the school be effective	73 percent	74 percent
83. Uses space and time effectively to support both the instructional program and the ancillary functions of the school as well	73 percent	68 percent
84. Manages the school staff effectively, encouraging the contribution of their best efforts to the school's success	74 percent	75 percent

	Percentage Who "Strongly Agree" That They Perform This Function	Percentage Who "Strongly Agree" That This Function Is Important
85. Provides for effective supervision of school support services and classified staff	66 percent	65 percent
H. *Personnel Management*		
86. Uses sound and effective principles for selecting new staff, both professional and classified	83 percent	86 percent
87. Includes appropriate faculty in recruitment, hiring, and mentoring opportunities	61 percent	64 percent
88. Ensures that new hires are properly brought into the school's culture successfully	62 percent	73 percent
89. Provides specific guidance for teachers trying to solve instructional problems	63 percent	74 percent
90. Helps new teachers gain expertise and confidence in their teaching	66 percent	80 percent
91. Appropriately uses the standards of performance evaluation to help both new and experienced teachers develop as accomplished professionals	68 percent	69 percent
92. Constantly monitors the school's teacher turnover rate using comparative benchmark indicators from other schools similar to his/her own	38 percent	40 percent
I. *Information Management*		
93. Ensures that people who require information to perform effectively receive it in a timely manner	64 percent	69 percent
94. Uses technology to facilitate more effective access to school generated data	52 percent	55 percent
95. Submits accurate records and reports on time	74 percent	66 percent
J. *Student Behavior Management*		
96. Develops and monitors a safe school plan, anticipating potential trouble spots and dealing with them in advance	84 percent	87 percent

	Percentage Who "Strongly Agree" That They Perform This Function	*Percentage Who "Strongly Agree" That This Function Is Important*
97. Develops and distributes student handbooks with information about rules, requirements, and expectations for student conduct and potential consequences	91 percent	82 percent
98. Handles student misconduct in a firm, fair, and consistent manner	90 percent	91 percent

Resource E

Principal Evaluation Rubrics

Kim Marshall

Rationale and Suggestions for Implementation

1. These rubrics are organized around six domains covering all aspects of a principal's job performance:

    A. Diagnosis and Planning

    B. Priority Management and Communication

    C. Curriculum and Data

    D. Supervision and Professional Development

    E. Discipline and Parent Involvement

    F. Management and External Relations

    The rubrics use a four-level rating scale with the following labels:

    4—Expert

    3—Proficient

    2—Developing

    1—Novice

2. The rubrics are designed to give principals an end-of-the-year assessment of where they stand in all performance areas—and detailed guidance on how to improve. They are not checklists for school visits. To knowledgeably fill out the rubrics, a principal's supervisor needs to have been in the school frequently throughout the year; it is irresponsible to fill out the rubrics based on one visit.

3. The *Proficient* level describes solid, expected professional performance; no principal should be ashamed of scores at this level. The *Expert* level is reserved for truly outstanding leadership as described by very demanding

SOURCE: Copyright Kim Marshall 2007. Permission granted for educational purposes.

criteria; there will be relatively few scores at this level. *Needs Improvement* indicates that performance has real deficiencies—nobody should be content with scores at this level—and performance at the *Does Not Meet Standards* level is clearly unacceptable and needs to be changed immediately.

4. When scoring, take each of the 10 criteria and ripple up and down the four levels (for example, reading the descriptions for item "a." at Expert, Proficient, Developing, and Novice), find the level that best describes performance, and swipe the whole line with a highlighter. This creates a vivid graphic display of overall performance, areas for commendation, and areas that need work (see sample on pages, 184–185).

5. Evaluation conferences are greatly enhanced if the supervisor and principal fill out the rubrics in advance (using the highlighter approach), then meet and compare scores one page at a time. The supervisor has the final say, but the discussion should aim for consensus based on actual evidence of the fairest score for each criterion. Supervisors should go into the evaluation process with some humility because they can't possibly know everything about a principal's complex world. Similarly, principals should be open to feedback from someone with an outside perspective—all revolving around whether the school is producing learning gains for all students. Note that student achievement is not explicitly included in these rubrics, but clearly achievement scores are directly linked to a principal's leadership. The role of student results in evaluation will be for each district or governing board to decide.

6. Some supervisors sugarcoat criticism and give inflated scores for fear of hurting feelings. This does not help principals improve. The kindest thing a supervisor can do for an underperforming principal is give candid, evidence-based feedback and robust follow-up support. Honest scores for all the principals in a district can be aggregated into a spreadsheet that can give an overview of leadership development needs for the district (see page 186 for a sample).

A. DIAGNOSIS AND PLANNING

The principal:

4—Expert

a. Recruits a strong leadership team and develops its skills and commitment to a high level.

b. Involves stakeholders in a comprehensive diagnosis of the school's strengths and weaknesses.

c. Presents colleagues with the gap between current student data and a clear vision for future success.

d. Crafts a succinct, inspiring, results-oriented mission statement that becomes known by all.

e. Gets strong staff commitment on a bold, ambitious 4 to 5-year student achievement target.

f. Wins staff ownership for a robust, research-based theory of action for improving achievement.

g. Collaboratively crafts a lean, comprehensive, results-oriented strategic plan with annual goals.

h. Fosters a sense of urgency and responsibility among all stakeholders for achieving annual goals.

i. Masterfully wins over resistant staff members who feared change and/or harbored low expectations.

j. Regularly tracks progress, gives and takes feedback, and continuously improves performance.

· ·

3—Proficient

a. Recruits and develops a leadership team with a balance of skills.

b. Carefully assesses the school's strengths and areas for development.

c. Compares students' current achievement with on-track-to-college expectations.

d. Writes a memorable, succinct, results-oriented mission statement and shares it widely.

e. Builds staff support for a long-range student achievement target.

f. Reaches out to the research and develops a robust theory of action for improving achievement.

g. Gets input and writes a comprehensive, measurable strategic plan for the current year.

h. Builds ownership and support among stakeholders for achieving annual goals.

i. Skillfully manages resistance, low expectations, and fear of change.

j. Periodically measures progress, listens to feedback, and tweaks the strategic plan.

· ·

2—Developing

a. Enlists one or two like-minded colleagues to provide advice and support.

b. Makes a quick assessment of the school's strengths and weaknesses.

c. Lectures staff on how much better students need to do to be successful in life.

d. Distributes a wordy, vague, uninspiring, impossible-to-remember mission statement.

e. Expresses confidence that student achievement will improve each year through hard work.

f. Accepts teachers' current notions of how student achievement is improved.

g. Writes a cumbersome, non-accountable strategic plan.

h. Presents the annual plan to stakeholders and asks them to support it.

i. Works on persuading resistant staff members to get on board with the plan.

j. Occasionally focuses on key data points and prods colleagues to improve.

. . . .

1—Novice

a. Is a Lone Ranger working with little or no support from colleagues.

b. Is unable to gather much information on the school's strong and weak points.

c. Bemoans students' low achievement and shows fatalism about bringing about significant change.

d. Does not share a mission statement.

e. Takes one year at a time, urging teachers to improve their students' achievement.

f. Says that hard work improves achievement—but secretly doubts that progress can be made.

g. Recyles the previous year's cumbersome, non-accountable strategic plan.

h. Gets the necessary signatures for the annual plan, but there is little ownership or support.

i. Is discouraged and immobilized by staff resistance, fear of change, and low expectations.

j. Is too caught up in daily crises to focus on emerging data.

B. PRIORITY MANAGEMENT AND COMMUNICATION

The principal:

4—Expert

a. Plans for the year, month, week, and day, relentlessly getting the highest-leverage activities done.

b. Skillfully and eloquently communicates goals to all constituencies using a variety of channels.

c. Frequently solicits and uses feedback and help from staff, students, parents, and external partners.

d. Has a foolproof system for capturing key information, remembering, prioritizing, and following up.

e. Ensures that all staff know exactly what is expected for management procedures and discipline.

f. Has highly competent people in all key roles and delegates maximum responsibility to them.

g. Ensures that all key teams (e.g., leadership, grade-level, etc.) are scheduled to meet on a regular basis.

h. Takes the initiative so that time-wasting activities and crises are almost always prevented or deflected.

i. Deals quickly and decisively with the highest-priority e-mail and paperwork, delegating the rest.

j. Remains healthy and sane by tending to family, friends, fun, exercise, nutrition, sleep, and vacations.

3—Proficient

a. Plans for the year, month, week, and day, keeping the highest-leverage activities front and center.

b. Uses a variety of means (e.g., face-to-face, newsletters, Web sites) to communicate goals to others.

c. Regularly reaches out to staff, students, parents, and external partners for feedback and help.

d. Writes down important information, remembers, prioritizes, and almost always follows up.

e. Makes sure staff know what is expected for management procedures and discipline.

f. Delegates appropriate tasks to competent staff members and checks on progress.

g. Ensures that key teams (e.g., leadership, grade-level, student support) meet regularly.

h. Is effective at preventing or deflecting many time-wasting crises and activities.

i. Deals efficiently with e-mail, paperwork, and administrative chores.

j. Mostly balances work demands with family, friends, fun, health, exercise, sleep, and vacations.

2—Developing

a. Comes to work with a list of what needs to be accomplished that day but is often distracted from the tasks.

b. Has a limited communication repertoire and some key stakeholders are not aware of school goals.

c. Occasionally asks staff, students, parents, or external partners for feedback.

d. Writes things down but is swamped by events and sometimes doesn't follow up.

e. Often has to inform teachers of policies on management procedures and discipline.

f. Hesitates to delegate some tasks because key staffers are not that competent or trustworthy.

g. Needs to call key team meetings each month because they are not in people's calendars.

h. Tries to prevent them, but crises and time-wasters sometimes eat up large chunks of time.

i. Tries to stay on top of e-mail, paperwork, and administrative chores, but is often behind.

j. Finds that family, health, and vacations are suffering because of work demands.

. . . .

1—Novice

a. Has a list in his or her head of what needs to be accomplished each day, but often loses track.

b. Is not an effective communicator, and others are often left guessing about policies and direction.

c. Never reaches out to others for feedback or help.

d. Trusts his or her memory to retain important information, but often forgets and drops the ball.

e. Is constantly reminding staff of what they should be doing in management and discipline.

f. Must do almost everything him- or herself because staff people are not competent and can't be trusted.

g. Convenes grade-level, leadership, and other teams only when there is a crisis or an immediate need.

h. Finds that large portions of each day are consumed by crises and time-wasting activities.

i. Is way behind on e-mail, paperwork, and administrative chores, and they eat up large parts of the day.

j. Neglects family, rarely exercises, doesn't sleep enough, and is in poor health.

C. CURRICULUM AND DATA

The principal:

4—Expert

a. Provides clear, manageable, standards-aligned grade-level goals with exemplars of proficient work.

b. Ensures that all teams use previous-year summative data and fresh diagnostic data to plan instruction.

c. Gets each grade-level or subject team invested in reaching measurable, results-oriented annual goals.

d. Ensures that all teachers have top-notch curriculum materials—and training on how to use them.

e. Ensures that high-quality, aligned, common interim assessments are given by all teacher teams.

f. Orchestrates high-quality, low-stakes data or action planning meetings after each round of assessments.

g. Gets data meetings engaged in a no-blame search for root causes and constant hypothesis testing.

h. Gets teams invested in following up assessments with reteaching, enhancements, and remediation.

i. Uses data in all key strategic areas to monitor and drive continuous improvement toward goals.

j. Fosters morale and a sense of efficacy by getting colleagues to celebrate measurable student gains.

. . . .

3—Proficient

a. Tells teachers exactly what students should know and be able to do by the end of each grade level.

b. Provides teacher teams with previous-year test data and asks them to assess students' current levels.

c. Works with grade-level and subject-area teams to set measurable student goals for the current year.

d. Gets the best possible literacy and math curriculum materials into teachers' hands.

e. Orchestrates common interim assessments to monitor student learning at least four times a year.

f. Schedules time for teacher teams to score and analyze assessments and formulate action plans.

g. Ensures that data meetings go beyond what students got wrong and delve into why—the root causes.

h. After assessments, coordinates and supports improvements in teaching and effective remediation.

i. Gathers data on grades, attendance, behavior, and other variables to inform improvement efforts.

2—Developing

a. Refers teachers to district or national scope-and-sequence documents for curriculum direction.

b. Refers teachers to previous-year test data as a baseline for current-year instruction.

c. Urges grade-level or subject teams to set measurable student learning goals for the current year.

d. Works to procure good curriculum materials in literacy and math.

e. Suggests that teacher teams give common interim assessments to check on student learning.

f. Gives teachers common planning time to look at interim assessment results.

g. Urges teacher teams to focus on the areas in which students had the most difficulty.

h. Pushes teacher teams to use interim assessment data to help struggling students.

i. Monitors attendance and discipline data to inform decisions.

j. Congratulates staff on "small wins" and other successes.

• •

1—Novice

a. Leaves teachers without clear direction on student learning outcomes for each grade level.

b. Does not provide historical test data to teachers.

c. Urges teachers to improve student achievement, but without measurable outcome goals.

d. Urges teachers to make the best possible use of current curriculum materials.

e. Allows teachers to use their own classroom assessments to check on student learning.

f. Suggests that teachers use their classroom assessment results to modify and improve instruction.

g. Tells teachers to implement "data-driven instruction" to improve test scores.

h. Urges teachers to use test data to improve the performance of "bubble" (almost-proficient) students.

i. Keeps an eye on attendance and suspension rates.

j. Takes credit for improvements in school performance.

D. SUPERVISION AND PROFESSIONAL DEVELOPMENT

The principal:

4—Expert

a. In all-staff meetings, has teachers discuss results, learn best strategies, and build trust and respect.

b. Ensures that the whole staff is current on professional literature, constantly exploring best practices.

c. Orchestrates aligned, high-quality professional learning: coaching, workshops, school visits, and so forth.

d. Empowers teams to be engines of improvement, using data to drive constant refinements of teaching.

e. Gives teams the training, facilitation support, and resources they need to make their meetings work.

f. Ensures that teachers backwards-design high-quality, aligned units and discusses them with teams.

g. Visits 3–5 classrooms a day and gives helpful, face-to-face feedback to each teacher within 24 hours.

h. Courageously engages in difficult conversations with ineffective teachers, helping them improve.

i. Counsels out or dismisses all ineffective teachers, scrupulously following contractual requirements.

j. Recruits, hires, and supports highly effective teachers who share the school's vision.

. . . .

3—Proficient

a. Uses all-staff meetings to get teachers sharing strategies and becoming more cohesive.

b. Reads and shares research and fosters an ongoing, schoolwide discussion of best practices.

c. Organizes aligned, ongoing coaching and training that builds skills and a common language.

d. Orchestrates regular teacher team meetings as the prime locus for professional learning.

e. Provides teacher teams with facilitators so meetings are focused and substantive.

f. Has teacher teams cooperatively plan aligned curriculum units, reviews them, and gives feedback.

g. Makes unannounced visits to classrooms every day and gives helpful feedback to teachers.

h. Provides redirection and support to teachers who are not effective in classrooms.

i. Counsels out or dismisses most ineffective teachers, carefully following contractual requirements.

j. Recruits and hires effective teachers who share the school's mission.

. . . .

2—Developing

a. Uses staff meetings primarily to announce decisions, clarify policies, and listen to staff concerns.

b. Occasionally passes along interesting articles and ideas to colleagues.

c. Strives to make professional development workshops relevant and interactive.

d. Gives teacher teams common planning time to work together and share ideas.

e. Has teacher teams appoint a team leader to run meetings and file reports.

f. Reviews teachers' lesson plans with an eye to quality instruction and alignment with standards.

g. Tries to get into classrooms but is often distracted by other events; rarely gives teachers feedback.

h. Criticizes ineffective teachers but does not give them much help improving their performance.

i. Tries to dismiss one or two ineffective teachers, but is stymied by procedural errors.

j. Hires teachers who seem to fit his or her philosophy of teaching.

1—Novice

a. Rarely convenes staff members and uses those meetings for one-way lectures on policies.

b. Rarely reads professional literature or discusses best practices.

c. Organizes occasional professional development workshops at which teachers are passive listeners.

d. Urges teachers to share ideas, but does not give them common planning time to meet regularly.

e. Leaves teacher teams to fend for themselves in terms of leadership and direction.

f. Has teachers hand in lesson plans for inspection.

g. Only observes teachers in annual or biannual formal observation visits.

h. Shies away from giving honest feedback and redirection to teachers who are not performing well.

i. Does not initiate dismissal procedures, despite evidence that some teachers are ineffective.

j. Makes last-minute appointments to teaching vacancies based on candidates who are available.

E. DISCIPLINE AND PARENT INVOLVEMENT

The principal:

4—Expert

a. Gets staff to buy into clear, schoolwide student-behavior standards, routines, and consequences.

b. Deals effectively with anything that interferes with learning, and actively prevents recurrences.

c. Publicly celebrates kindness, effort, and improvement and builds students' pride in their school.

d. Ensures that staff are masters of positive discipline and sensitive handling of student issues.

e. Leads a proactive effort to get counseling, mentoring, and other supports for all high-risk students.

f. Makes families feel welcome and respected, responds to concerns, and maximizes their contributions.

g. Ensures that parents know weekly learning goals and involves them in helping their children learn.

h. Makes sure that parents get frequent, user-friendly progress reports with ideas for improvement.

i. Maximizes productive parent–teacher communication, especially on children's academic progress.

j. Provides effective safety-net programs for all students with inadequate home support.

3—Proficient

a. Sets expectations for student behavior and establishes schoolwide routines and consequences.

b. Deals effectively with disruptions to learning and looks for underlying causes.

c. Praises students who behave well and achieve at high levels, and works to build school spirit.

d. Uses a variety of approaches to build staff skills in discipline and handling student issues.

e. Identifies struggling students and organizes support services to meet their needs.

f. Makes parents feel welcome, listens to their concerns, and asks them to contribute to school goals.

g. Informs parents of monthly curriculum goals and ways they can support their children's learning.

h. Has teachers send home regular reports on students' progress and areas for improvement.

i. Works to improve parent–teacher communication and the quality of report card conferences.

j. Provides safety-net programs for most students whose parents do not provide adequate support.

2—Developing

a. Urges staff to demand good student behavior, but allows different standards in different classrooms.

b. Deals firmly with students who are disruptive in classrooms, but doesn't get to the root causes.

c. Reinforces good behavior and academic achievement and provides cheerleading for the school.

d. Organizes workshops and suggests articles and books on classroom management.

e. Tries to get crisis counseling for highly disruptive and troubled students.

f. Reaches out to parents, asks for their help, and tries to understand when they are critical.

g. Sends students home with information on the school's curriculum and general ideas on ways to help at home.

h. Makes sure that report cards are filled out correctly and given to all parents.

i. Schedules time for parents to speak to teachers about report cards.

j. Provides ad hoc, occasional support for students who are not adequately supported at home.

. . . .

1—Novice

a. Often tolerates discipline violations and enforces the rules inconsistently.

b. Tries to deal with disruptive students but is swamped by the number of problems.

c. Rarely praises students and fails to build school pride.

d. Urges teachers to get better at classroom management.

e. Works to expel or transfer out highly disruptive and troubled students.

f. Makes little effort to reach out to families and is defensive when parents express concerns.

g. Sends home an annual list of grade-level learning expectations.

h. Monitors the quality of report cards.

i. Allows report cards to be sent home with little opportunity for parent–teacher communication.

j. Is unable to provide assistance for students with inadequate home support.

F. MANAGEMENT AND EXTERNAL RELATIONS

The principal:

4—Expert

a. Implements proven macro strategies (e.g., looping, class size reduction) that boost student learning.

b. Creates an equitable schedule that maximizes learning, teacher collegiality, and smooth transitions.

c. Orchestrates smooth, friendly student entry, dismissal, meal times, transitions, and recesses each day.

d. Supervises staff to ensure effective, creative use of space and a clean, safe, and inviting campus.

e. Is transparent about how and why decisions were made, involving stakeholders whenever possible.

f. Deftly handles bureaucratic, contractual, and legal issues so staff can focus on student learning.

g. Skillfully manages the budget and finances to maximize student achievement and staff growth.

h. Fulfills all compliance and reporting requirements and creates new opportunities to support learning.

i. Builds warm relationships with key district staff and gets them excited about the school's mission.

j. Taps all possible human and financial resources to support the school's mission and strategic plan.

. . . .

3—Proficient

a. Suggests effective macro strategies (e.g., looping, team teaching) to improve student learning.

b. Creates a schedule that supports student learning, smooth transitions, and team meeting time.

c. Ensures safe and orderly student entry, dismissal, meals, class transitions, and recesses each day.

d. Supervises staff to ensure that the campus is clean, attractive, and safe.

e. Ensures that staff members know how and why key decisions are being made.

f. Manages bureaucratic, contractual, and legal issues so they rarely distract from teaching and learning.

g. Manages the school's budget and finances to support the strategic plan.

h. Fulfills compliance and reporting responsibilities to the district and beyond.

i. Schmoozes with district and external staffers so they will be helpful with paperwork and process.

j. Is resourceful in bringing additional human and financial resources into the school.

. . . .

2—Developing

a. Explores macro strategies that might improve achievement.

b. Creates a schedule that ensures smooth transitions during each week.

c. Tries to supervise student entry, dismissal, transitions, and meal times.

d. Works with custodial staff to keep the campus clean and safe, but there are occasional lapses.

e. Tries to be transparent about decision making, but stakeholders sometimes feel shut out.

f. Sometimes allows bureaucratic, contractual, and legal issues to distract teachers from their work.

g. Manages budget and finances with few errors, but misses opportunities to support the strategic plan.

h. Meets minimum compliance and reporting responsibilities with occasional lapses.

i. Is correct and professional with district and external staff but does not enlist their active support.

j. Occasionally raises additional funds or finds volunteers to help out.

· ·

1—Novice

a. Sticks with the status quo for fear of alienating teachers.

b. Creates a schedule with inequities, technical flaws, and little time for teacher teams to meet.

c. Rarely supervises student entry, dismissal, and common spaces, and there are frequent problems.

d. Leaves campus cleanliness and safety to custodial staff, and there are frequent lapses.

e. Makes decisions with little or no consultation, causing frequent resentment and morale problems.

f. Frequently mishandles bureaucratic, contractual, and legal issues in ways that disrupt learning.

g. Makes errors in managing the budget and finances and misses opportunities to further the mission.

h. Has difficulty keeping the school in compliance with district and other external requirements.

i. Is sometimes in conflict with district and external staff and does not get their full cooperation.

j. Is resigned to working with the standard school budget, which doesn't seem adequate.

EVALUATION SUMMARY PAGE

Principal's name: _____ School year: _____

School:_____

Evaluator: _____ Position: _____

Ratings on Individual Rubrics:

A. Diagnosis and Planning:

| Expert | Proficient | Developing | Novice |

B. Priority Management and Communication:

| Expert | Proficient | Developing | Novice |

C. Curriculum and Data:

| Expert | Proficient | Developing | Novice |

D. Supervision and Professional Development:

| Expert | Proficient | Developing | Novice |

E. Discipline and Parent Involvement:

| Expert | Proficient | Developing | Novice |

F. Management and External Relations:

| Expert | Proficient | Developing | Novice |

Overall Rating: Expert   Proficient   Developing   Novice

Overall Comments by Supervisor:

Overall Comments by Principal:

Supervisor's signature: _____ Date: _____

Principal's signature:_____ Date: _____

(The principal's signature indicates that he or she has seen and discussed the evaluation; it does not necessarily denote agreement with the report.)

SAMPLE PAGE USING HIGHLIGHTER APPROACH TO SCORING

The principal:

4—Expert

a. Gets staff to buy into clear, schoolwide student-behavior standards, routines, and consequences.

b. Deals effectively with anything that interferes with learning, and actively prevents recurrences.

c. Publicly celebrates kindness, effort, and improvement and builds students' pride in their school.

d. Ensures that staff are masters of positive discipline and sensitive handling of student issues.

e. Leads a proactive effort to get counseling, mentoring, and other supports for all high-risk students.

f. Makes families feel welcome and respected, responds to concerns, and maximizes their contributions.

g. Ensures that parents know weekly learning goals and involves them in helping their children learn.

h. Makes sure that parents get frequent, user-friendly progress reports with ideas for improvement.

i. Maximizes productive parent-teacher communication, especially on children's academic progress.

j. Provides effective safety-net programs for all students with inadequate home support.

3—Proficient

a. Sets expectations for student behavior and establishes schoolwide routines and consequences.

b. Deals effectively with disruptions to learning and looks for underlying causes.

c. Praises students who behave well and achieve at high levels, and works to build school spirit.

d. Uses a variety of approaches to build staff skills in discipline and handling student issues.

e. Identifies struggling students and organizes support services to meet their needs.

f. Makes parents feel welcome, listens to their concerns, and asks them to contribute to school goals.

g. Informs parents of monthly curriculum goals and ways they can support their children's learning.

h. Has teachers send home regular reports on students' progress and areas for improvement.

i. Works to improve parent–teacher communication and the quality of report card conferences.

j. Provides safety-net programs for most students whose parents do not provide adequate support.

2—Developing

a. Urges staff to demand good student behavior, but allows different standards in different classrooms.

b. Deals firmly with students who are disruptive in classrooms, but doesn't get to the root causes.

c. Reinforces good behavior and academic achievement and provides cheerleading for the school.

d. Organizes workshops and suggests articles and books on classroom management.

e. Tries to get crisis counseling for highly disruptive and troubled students.

f. Reaches out to parents, asks for their help, and tries to understand when they are critical.

g. Sends students home with information on the school's curriculum and general ideas on ways to help at home.

h. Makes sure that report cards are filled out correctly and given to all parents.

i. Schedules time for parents to speak to teachers about report cards.

j. Provides ad hoc, occasional support for students who are not adequately supported at home.

. . . .

1—Novice

a. Often tolerates discipline violations and enforces the rules inconsistently.

b. Tries to deal with disruptive students but is swamped by the number of problems.

c. Rarely praises students and fails to build school pride.

d. Urges teachers to get better at classroom management.

e. Works to expel or transfer out highly disruptive and troubled students.

f. Makes little effort to reach out to families and is defensive when parents express concerns.

g. Sends home an annual list of grade-level learning expectations.

h. Monitors the quality of report cards.

i. Allows report cards to be sent home with little opportunity for parent–teacher communication.

j. Is unable to provide assistance for students with inadequate home support.

Spreadsheet of Rubric Scores of 12 Principals for PD Purposes

	A. Diagnosis and Planning	B. Priority Management and Communication	C. Curriculum and Data	D. Supervision and Professional Development	E. Discipline and Parent Involvement	F. Management and External Relations	
Blenda Johnson	3	3	3	1	3	3	16
Henry Rodriguez	3	4	3	3	3	3	19
Henrietta Moreton	3	3	3	2	3	3	17
Priscilla Robb	4	4	4	4	4	4	24
Carlton Robinson	3	3	3	2	3	4	18
Kim Stavus	3	3	3	1	3	4	17
Brazil Moore	3	3	3	2	3	3	17
Marvin Marcus	4	4	4	4	4	4	24
Sartina Useem	3	3	3	2	3	3	17
David Boggs	3	3	3	1	3	3	16
Nancy Marshall	2	3	2	1	2	1	11
Totals	34	36	34	23	34	35	

Resource F

ASCENSION PARISH LEADERSHIP PROFESSIONAL GROWTH MATRIX[1]

Scoring by major domains and individual leadership dimensions occurs by adhering to the following protocol:

1. Assess or evaluate the administrator on whether the descriptions in the tables that follow can be observed as stated. Judgments about one dimension may not apply to the next, and administrators need to be careful to score each cell of each dimension of each domain individually and based on evidence of criteria statements.

2. Domain scores (e.g., 1.0 Student Achievement or 9.0 Professional Development) are determined by examining all the categories assessed and by determining which category represents the preponderance of evidence supporting and substantiating the designation. Definitions of *Exemplary, Proficient, Progressing, Not Meeting Standards,* and *Preponderance of Evidence* are provided on pages 209–210 following the Ascension Parish Leadership Professional Growth Matrix.

3. Dimension scores (e.g., 5.5 Communicates effectively for change) require demonstration of all the positive attributes contained in the narrative description, encouraging administrators to deepen their effectiveness and continuously improve.

Task Force End Statement

Ascension Parish was looking for an evaluation system that could be aligned to the continuous improvement model they were creating for school improvement. They also were cognizant of pending transitions across administrative levels and were interested in a professional growth model for administrators that reflected best practices and promoted collaborative relationships between supervisors and those supervised. They recognized the potential in AEL for greater focus, reciprocity, and the ability to be proactive in developing leaders. Finally, they were interested in a framework that would challenge the veteran and novice alike, recognize differences, and build on leadership strengths.

---

1. Used with permission from Patrice Pujol.

1.0 Student Achievement. Incorporates Louisiana Leadership Standard 4: School Improvement. *The administrator (Building Principal or Central Office) works with the school community to review data from multiple sources to establish challenging standards, monitor progress, and foster the continuous growth of all students.*

Leadership Dimension	Exemplary (Systemwide Impact in Addition to Proficient)	Proficient	Progressing	Not Meeting Standards
1.1 Improves student achievement	The administrator routinely shares examples of specific leadership, teaching, and curriculum strategies that are associated with improved student achievement. Others request assistance to implement successful new initiatives or refine leadership practices. There is a consistent record of improved student achievement on multiple indicators of student success, and explicit use of data indicates that the administrator has focused on improving performance for all students. Where new challenges emerge, the administrator highlights the need, creates effective interventions, and monitors and reports improved results.	The administrator's goals and strategies reflect a clear relationship between the actions of teachers and administrators and student achievement. The average achievement of the student population improves as does the achievement of each group of students identified as needing improvement.	The administrator provides some evidence of improvement, but insufficient evidence of changes in leadership, teaching, and curriculum are provided that create the improvements necessary to achieve student performance goals.	The administrator's goals are neither measurable nor specific. The administrator attributes limited gains more to student characteristics than to actions of teachers and administrators in the system. There are growing achievement gaps between student groups.
1.2 Uses student achievement data to make instructional leadership decisions	The administrator provides clear evidence of state, district, building, and classroom data to make specific and observable changes in teaching, curriculum, and leadership decisions. The administrator regularly shares with other administrators and teachers both successes and failures based on local data analysis.	The administrator makes changes in curriculum, teaching, and leadership practices based on data. Data is visible and both administrator and teachers refer to it in order to inform instructional decisions.	The administrator participates in data-driven decision making and professional development, but there is limited evidence of changes based on data.	The administrator makes few changes in schedule, instruction, curriculum, or leadership based on data. The data screams "change!" and the administrator's actions say "everything is just fine."

1.0 Student Achievement. Incorporates Louisiana Leadership Standard 4: School Improvement. *The administrator (Building Principal or Central Office) works with the school community to review data from multiple sources to establish challenging standards, monitor progress, and foster the continuous growth of all students.*

Leadership Dimension	Exemplary (Systemwide Impact in Addition to Proficient)	Proficient	Progressing	Not Meeting Standards
	Data is the focal point of both formal and informal leadership and faculty discussions.			
1.3 Understands student requirements and academic standards	The administrator conducts faculty meetings and staff development forums by focusing on student achievement, including periodic review of student work.	The administrator links standards and student performance by providing examples of proficient student work throughout the building.	The administrator posts standards-based student performance expectations and requires training appropriately, but the link between standards and student performance is not readily evident to faculty or students.	The administrator allows classroom curriculum to be a matter of individual discretion, and the administrator is hesitant to intrude or is indifferent to decisions in the classroom that are at variance from the requirements of academic standards.
1.4 Bases decisions on improved student achievement in teacher assignment, course content, schedule, and student curriculum	The administrator can specifically document examples of decisions in teaching, assignment, curriculum, assessment, and intervention that have been made on the basis of data analysis. The administrator has coached other school administrators in other schools to improve their data-analysis skills.	The administrator uses multiple data sources, including state, district, school, and classroom assessments, and has at least three years of data. The administrator systematically examines data at the subscale level to find strengths and challenges. The administrator empowers teaching and administrative staff to determine priorities from data. Data insights are regularly the subject of faculty meetings and professional development sessions.	The administrator is aware of state and district results, has discussed those results with staff, but has not linked specific decisions to the data.	The administrator is unaware of or indifferent to the data.

Leadership Dimension	Exemplary (Systemwide Impact in Addition to Proficient)	Proficient	Progressing	Not Meeting Standards
1.0 Student Achievement. Incorporates Louisiana Leadership Standard 4: School Improvement. *The administrator (Building Principal or Central Office) works with the school community to review data from multiple sources to establish challenging standards, monitor progress, and foster the continuous growth of all students.*				
1.5 Uses technology to improve teaching and learning	The administrator serves, beyond the scope of job responsibilities, as a model for technology implementation that adds value to the organization. The links between technology implementation and learning success are clear and public. The administrator coaches the entire staff on the results of the linkage between technology and organizational success, creating new ways to save resources and improve organizational effectiveness.	The administrator uses technology personally in a competent manner and links technology initiatives of the organization to specific teaching and learning objectives. The administrator makes technology decisions to optimize effectiveness, securing technical assistance for his own learning for routine use, delegating complex technology, and forming teams to study and recommend technology changes for students and staff.	The administrator is personally proficient in technology and an advocate for the use of instructional technology, but does not always differentiate between technology implementation and a clear impact on teaching and learning.	The administrator does not display personal competence in technology applications. The administrator does not link the installation of technology to specific teaching and learning objectives.

Leadership Dimension	Exemplary (Systemwide Impact in Addition to Proficient)	Proficient	Progressing	Not Meeting Standards
2.0 Professional Ethics. Incorporates Louisiana Leadership Standard 7: Professional Ethics. *The administrator (Building Principal or Central Office) demonstrates honesty, integrity, and fairness to guide school programs in an ethical manner.*				
2.1 Demonstrates integrity in word and deed.	This administrator's commitments to individuals, students, community members, and subordinate commitments have the same weight as the administrator's commitments to superiors, board members, or other people with visibility and authority. The administrator's commitment to integrity is recognized at all levels of the organization.	The administrator meets commitments (verbal, written, and implied), and negotiates exceptions where the commitment cannot be met.	The administrator generally meets commitments, but fails to negotiate exceptions where commitments cannot be met.	The administrator regards words "I'm working on it" or "I'm doing the best I can" as acceptable substitutes for commitments. This administrator often does not follow through with tasks, budgets, priorities, or performance.
2.2 Models emotional self-control to the school community	The administrator displays a commitment to self-control, empathy, and respect, even in the most difficult and confrontational situation, and provides assistance to colleagues in terms of emotional maturity.	The administrator deals with sensitive subjects and personal attacks with dignity and self-control. The administrator consistently defuses confrontational situations with emotional maturity, empathy, and respect.	The administrator occasionally raises her voice when angry or threatened, leading to a climate in which people are reluctant to raise sensitive issues.	The administrator has a pattern of losing his temper, which hampers the ability to interact effectively with staff, students, parents, or the community.
2.3 Complies with legal and ethical requirements in work relationships	Meets the letter and spirit of the law, avoiding both the fact and appearance of impropriety. Upholds the foundations of mutual respect for all stakeholders and the law throughout the organization.	The administrator meets all legal requirements for work relationships and takes swift and appropriate actions when inappropriate conduct is reported or observed.		The administrator's failure to protect work relationships is evident by permitting or engaging in inappropriate actions.

Leadership Dimension	Exemplary (Systemwide Impact in Addition to Proficient)	Proficient	Progressing	Not Meeting Standards
2.0 Professional Ethics. Incorporates Louisiana Leadership Standard 7: Professional Ethics. *The administrator (Building Principal or Central Office) demonstrates honesty, integrity, and fairness to guide school programs in an ethical manner.* **Incorporates Louisiana Leadership Standard 3: School Management.** *The administrator (Building Principal and Central Office) promotes the success of all students by ensuring management of the organization, operations, and resources for a safe and orderly learning environment.*				
2.4 Tolerates different points of view within the boundaries of the values and mission of the organization	The administrator actively seeks differences in perspective, encouraging different scenarios and curricula in the context of academic standards. Explicitly differentiates divergent thinking when it is constructive and facilitates a transition to convergent thinking to support organizational goals.	The administrator focuses on the achievement of mission and adherence to values, without penalizing differences in points of view that are within the framework of organizational requirements.	The administrator does not punish alternative points of view, but little or no development or encouragement of those views is evident.	The administrator suppresses other points of view and discourages disagreement or divergent thinking.
2.5 Honors the time and presence of others	The administrator consistently demonstrates an ability to effectively manage time and meetings by engaging others in the process, achieving meeting objectives, and beginning and ending on time. The administrator models respect for others by arriving early to all meetings. Colleagues can point to specific indicators of how they are afforded time, attention to their concerns, and respect during interactions with the administrator.	The administrator is on time and prepared, in regular attendance, participates fully, and is ready to listen and respect others in planned and unplanned meetings. The administrator is fluent with agenda items (knowledge of each topic) and is prepared to offer ideas and engage others in meaningful dialogue. Staff who report to the administrator indicate that they are afforded time, attention to their concerns, and respect during interactions with the administrator.	The administrator is generally on time and prepared, in regular attendance, participates fully, and is ready to listen and respect others in planned and unplanned meetings, with periodic exceptions (sidebar conversations, distracted during planned or unplanned meetings). The administrator is occasionally fluent with agenda items in terms of knowledge of each topic, but seldom offers ideas to engage others in meaningful dialogue.	The administrator is rarely on time and prepared, is absent at key meetings, and tends to engage in disrespectful behaviors that do not honor others (sidebar conversations, distracted during planned or unplanned meetings). The administrator may be attentive, but generally only in the presence of supervisors, and rarely takes the time to be fluent and knowledgeable regarding agenda items and topics of interest to the organization.

3.0 Resilience. Incorporates Louisiana Leadership Standard 1: Vision. *The administrator (Building Principal or Central Office) engages the educational community in developing and maintaining a student-centered vision for education, which forms the basis for school goals and guides the preparation of students as effective, lifelong learners in a pluralistic society.* **Incorporates Louisiana Leadership Standard 2: Teaching and Learning.** *The administrator (Building Principal or Central Office) uses knowledge of teaching and learning in working collaboratively with the faculty and staff to implement effective and innovative teaching practices that engage students in meaningful and challenging learning experiences.*

Leadership Dimension	Exemplary (Systemwide Impact in Addition to Proficient)	Proficient	Progressing	Not Meeting Standards
3.1 Constructively reacts to disappointment and barriers to success	The administrator models the acceptance of responsibility for failure. Nondefensive attitude in accepting feedback and discussing errors and failures with clear suggestions for systemwide learning resulting from such lessons.	The administrator readily acknowledges mistakes that inhibit her ability to meet professional and organizational obligations. Admits mistakes quickly, honestly, and openly. The administrator offers evidence of learning from past errors.	The administrator acknowledges mistakes that inhibit his ability to meet professional and organizational obligations only when confronted with evidence. Accepts evidence of mistakes when offered by others, and learns from those mistakes.	The administrator rarely acknowledges error. When confronted with evidence of mistakes, the administrator is defensive and resistant to learning from them.
3.2 Constructively handles disagreement with leadership and policy decisions	In disagreements with policy and leadership decisions, the administrator is able to articulate disagreement and advocate for a point of view based on best interests of organization. The administrator is willing to challenge executive authority and policymakers with evidence and constructive criticism, but once decisions are made, fully and enthusiastically supports and implements organizational decisions.	The administrator routinely accepts and implements leadership and policy decisions, and proactively articulates disagreements through designated chain of command.	The administrator sometimes challenges executive and policy leadership without bringing those concerns to appropriate executive and policy authorities. Sometimes implements unpopular policies because "I'm just following orders, but I don't like it"— unenthusiastically.	The administrator ignores or subverts executive and policy decisions that are unpopular or distasteful.

Leadership Dimension	Exemplary (Systemwide Impact in Addition to Proficient)	Proficient	Progressing	Not Meeting Standards
3.0 Resilience. Incorporates Louisiana Leadership Standard 1: Vision. *The administrator (Building Principal or Central Office) engages the educational community in developing and maintaining a student-centered vision for education, which forms the basis for school goals and guides the preparation of students as effective, lifelong learners in a pluralistic society.* **Incorporates Louisiana Leadership Standard 2: Teaching and Learning.** *The administrator (Building Principal or Central Office) uses knowledge of teaching and learning in working collaboratively with the faculty and staff to implement effective and innovative teaching practices that engage students in meaningful and challenging learning experiences.*				
3.3 Constructively handles dissent from subordinates	The administrator recognizes and acknowledges thoughtful dissent. Uses dissenting voices to learn and, as needed, acknowledges the administrator's error. Encourages dissent in which multiple voices are heard. Final decisions are broadly supported and implemented as a result.	The administrator listens to dissent to improve the quality of decision making, and broadens support prior to making final decisions.	The administrator tolerates dissent, but seldom invites it, sending a mixed message to staff about how dissent will be received.	The administrator creates a climate of fear and intimidation where she or he challenges or criticizes those who offer dissenting opinions.
3.4 Improves current performance on the basis of previous evaluations	Previous evaluations are combined with personal reflection to formulate an action plan that is reflected in the administrator's daily choices of priorities as well as in the organization's priorities. The influence of previous evaluations impacts not only the administrator, but the entire organization.	The administrator uses previous evaluations to reflect on projects, tasks, and priorities. Performance on each evaluation reflects specific measurable improvements along the performance continuum from Not Meeting Standards to Progressing to Proficient to Exemplary.	The administrator is aware of previous evaluations, but has not translated them into an action plan.	The administrator does not provide evidence of reference to previous leadership evaluations in the administrator's choices of tasks and priorities.

Leadership Dimension	Exemplary (Systemwide Impact in Addition to Proficient)	Proficient	Progressing	Not Meeting Standards
4.0 Decision Making. Incorporates Louisiana Leadership Standard 2: Teaching and Learning. *The administrator (Building Principal or Central Office) uses a knowledge of teaching and learning in working collaboratively with the faculty and staff to implement effective and innovative teaching practices that engage students in meaningful and challenging learning experiences.* **Incorporates Louisiana Leadership Standard 3: School Management.** *The administrator (Building Principal or Central Office) promotes the success of all students by ensuring management of the organization, operations, and resources for a safe and orderly learning environment.*				
4.1 Makes decisions based on achievement data regarding curriculum, teaching, and leadership improvements	The administrator's decision making is neither by consensus nor by leadership mandate, but consistently based on the data. Data is reflected in all decisions, ranging from course and classroom assignments to the discontinuance of programs. The administrator can cite specific examples of practices that have been changed, discontinued, and initiated based on data analysis. A variety of data sources, including qualitative and quantitative, are used. Data sources include state, district, school, and classroom. Inferences from data are shared widely outside the school community to identify and replicate the most effective practices.	The administrator's pattern of decision making reflects a clear reliance on student achievement data.	The administrator's decisions are based on data, but others are the result of personal preference and tradition.	The administrator rarely uses data for decisions; predominant decision-making methodology is popularity contest or mandate from the administrator.
4.2 Defines decision-making structures by clarifying decisions made by consensus, with consultation, and independently	The administrator communicates clear distinctions regarding the degree to which others will be involved in various types of decisions. The administrator uses data in such a compelling way that the vast majority of decisions are made in collaboration with colleagues and staff. Staff surveys are used to inform decisions, and staff report opportunities for input and a sense of empowerment and responsibility in the organization's (school, department, district) success.	The administrator clarifies decision-making method for all major decisions and shares decisions with the staff, routinely using data to support those decisions.	The administrator uses consensus and unilateral decision making, but it is unclear why decision-making structures change.	The administrator alternates from autocracy to democracy with no clear method for decision making.

4.0 Decision Making. Incorporates Louisiana Leadership Standard 2: Teaching and Learning. *The administrator (Building Principal or Central Office) uses a knowledge of teaching and learning in working collaboratively with the faculty and staff to implement effective and innovative teaching practices that engage students in meaningful and challenging learning experiences.* **Incorporates Louisiana Leadership Standard 3: School Management.** *The administrator (Building Principal or Central Office) promotes the success of all students by ensuring management of the organization, operations, and resources for a safe and orderly learning environment.*

Leadership Dimension	Exemplary (Systemwide Impact in Addition to Proficient)	Proficient	Progressing	Not Meeting Standards
4.3 Links decisions to vision, mission, and improvement plan priorities	The vision, mission, and improvement plans of the administrator and the organization are clearly visible to visitors, employees, and students, and can be described by direct reports, students, and stakeholders (community, parents). They are routinely referenced in making decisions, and guidelines for effective decision making are written to make decisions self-evident and reduce unnecessary confusion and delays.	The administrator's decisions are consistent with the vision, mission, and improvement plans of the organization.	The administrator's vision, mission, and improvement plans may be visible, but seldom associated with administrator decisions.	The administrator does not reference the organization's vision, mission, or plans for improvement. Links with organizational guideposts not visible.
4.4 Makes decisions based on care and concern for student welfare	The administrator models decision making in student welfare processes 1–4, and establishes one or more of the following procedures: (5) Feedback to determine effectiveness in honoring confidences and confidential information of students with the same commitment to protect the privacy and dignity afforded colleagues, faculty, and staff; (6) A transition planning process (entry, grade to grade, level to level, graduation) for *all* students; (7) School improvement goals that address urgent needs of students; (8) Annual review of all crisis, safety, health, FERPA (Family Education Rights and Privacy Act), engagement, newcomer, school improvement plans, and	The administrator makes decisions that represent high standards of care and concern for each student by clear implementation of items 1–2, and by establishing one or both of the following: (3) A welcome process for newcomers that establishes language supports for individual students whose ethnic background or language are not represented by large groups of students (adults and employees for district-level administrators); (4) An engagement process that promotes participation in all aspects of the school for targeted	The administrator makes decisions demonstrating care and concern for all students by (1) Impartial application of a schoolwide classroom management and discipline process consistent with Parish Board Policy and Louisiana Education statutes and guidelines; (2) Adhering to district policy for health and student records consistent with FERPA; (3) Annual review and rehearsal of a school	The administrator is apt to be arbitrary in administration of the district discipline policy, and has avoided establishing schoolwide classroom management procedures. Concern or attention is given to safety, health, or crisis management only when directed or reminded by others.

4.0 Decision Making. Incorporates Louisiana Leadership Standard 2: Teaching and Learning. *The administrator (Building Principal or Central Office) uses a knowledge of teaching and learning in working collaboratively with the faculty and staff to implement effective and innovative teaching practices that engage students in meaningful and challenging learning experiences.* **Incorporates Louisiana Leadership Standard 3: School Management.** *The administrator (Building Principal or Central Office) promotes the success of all students by ensuring management of the organization, operations, and resources for a safe and orderly learning environment.*

Leadership Dimension	Exemplary (Systemwide Impact in Addition to Proficient)	Proficient	Progressing	Not Meeting Standards
	commitment to confidentiality with leadership teams guided by input from students as to the effectiveness of student welfare procedures. Decision making in design of 5–8 will be informed by input and participation of faculty, students, and parents.	groups of students (employees and constituents if not school administrators). Decision making in design of 3–4 will be informed by input and participation of faculty, students, and parents.	or department health and crisis management plan.	
4.5 Evaluates decisions for effectiveness and revises where necessary	The administrator can provide clear and consistent evidence of decisions that have been changed based on new data. The administrator routinely reviews decisions and evaluates programs and practices in light of current data. There is a culture of candor in which those who interact with the administrator (at all levels) feel safe to discuss what is not working without fear of embarrassment or reprisal.	The administrator has established a pattern of evaluating and revising decisions based on new information.	The administrator has new information and will reconsider previous decisions, but does not have a clear record of making changes.	The administrator provides little or no evidence of reflection and reevaluation of previous decisions.

5.0 Communication. Incorporates Louisiana Leadership Standard 6: School Community Relations. *The administrator (Building Principal or Central Office) uses an understanding of the culture of the community to create and sustain mutually supportive school–community relations.* **Incorporates Louisiana Leadership Standard 1: Vision.** *The administrator (Building Principal or Central Office) engages the school community in developing and maintaining a student-centered vision for education that forms the basis for school goals and guides the preparation of students as effective, lifelong learners in a pluralistic society.*

Leadership Dimension	Exemplary (Systemwide Impact in Addition to Proficient)	Proficient	Progressing	Not Meeting Standards
5.1 Actively listens and analyzes input and feedback	The administrator models open communication. The administrator listens purposefully and actively. The administrator is able to "read" the situation and respond accordingly. The administrator maintains listening systems for major stakeholders (parents, teachers, students, community members, and staff), explicitly plans analysis and reflection of data, and establishes structures that facilitate action based on feedback and analysis.	The administrator's observations and documentation demonstrate that the administrator listens well, seeks mutual understanding, and welcomes sharing of information. The administrator has established an effective communication plan, communicates openly, and is receptive to ideas from a variety of sources and perspectives.	The administrator appears to listen to others, but often relies on personal interpretation of events rather than seeking out alternative perspectives and interpretation. Analysis of feedback occurs rarely.	The administrator hears what others say, but relies on personal interpretation. The administrator does not appear to communicate openly, omitting key details and attempting to resolve challenges without input or assistance.
5.2 Engages in two-way communication with students	The administrator has a functional system in place to listen to students. The listening strategies may include focus groups, surveys, student-advisory committees, and numerous one-on-one student conversations. Discussions with students reveal that they know that the administrator will listen to them and treat them with respect.	The administrator consistently demonstrates care and concern for students as individuals, greets many by name, and is proactive in talking with and listening to them. The administrator is particularly visible at the beginning and end of each day and during all other times when students are present.	The administrator knows many students by name and adjusts his schedule to communicate with students.	The administrator knows few student names and avoids student contact except where leadership presence is required. Many do not recognize her.

5.0 Communication. Incorporates Louisiana Leadership Standard 6: School Community Relations. *The administrator (Building Principal or Central Office) uses an understanding of the culture of the community to create and sustain mutually supportive school–community relations.* **Incorporates Louisiana Leadership Standard 1: Vision.** *The administrator (Building Principal or Central Office) engages the school community in developing and maintaining a student-centered vision for education that forms the basis for school goals and guides the preparation of students as effective, lifelong learners in a pluralistic society.*

Leadership Dimension	Exemplary (Systemwide Impact in Addition to Proficient)	Proficient	Progressing	Not Meeting Standards
5.3 Engages in two-way communication with faculty and staff	The administrator engages in "active listening" with faculty and staff. Her calendar reflects numerous individual and small-group meetings with staff at every level, not just with the direct reports. Bus drivers, cafeteria workers, first-year teachers all report confidence in their ability to gain a respectful hearing from the administrator.	The administrator's meetings and interactions with staff include open two-way discussions. Faculty members regularly have the opportunity for one-on-one meetings with the administrator. The administrator knows all staff members and makes an effort to recognize the individual contribution each one makes.	The administrator typically limits listening to questions during meetings with faculty and staff.	The administrator's faculty meetings consist of reading announcements with little or no interaction; access outside meetings is neither open nor encouraged.
5.4 Engages in two-way communication with parents and community	The administrator uses multiple forms of communication with parents and community stakeholders, including open forums, focus groups, surveys, personal visits, and extensive use of technology. Key decisions are informed by parent and stakeholder input. Survey data suggest parents and stakeholders view their opinions as valued in schools.	The administrator interacts frequently with parents and community members, using newsletters, personal briefings, personal visits and calls, and technology (voice mail, hotlines, e-mail, Web sites) where appropriate.	The administrator is accessible and responsive to parents and stakeholders, but they usually must initiate the communication.	The administrator provides parents and community members with little or no information on decision making

Leadership Dimension	Exemplary (Systemwide Impact in Addition to Proficient)	Proficient	Progressing	Not Meeting Standards
5.0 Communication. Incorporates Louisiana Leadership Standard 6: School Community Relations. *The administrator (Building Principal or Central Office) uses an understanding of the culture of the community to create and sustain mutually supportive school–community relations.* **Incorporates Louisiana Leadership Standard 1: Vision.** *The administrator (Building Principal or Central Office) engages the school community in developing and maintaining a student-centered vision for education that forms the basis for school goals and guides the preparation of students as effective, lifelong learners in a pluralistic society.*				
5.5 Communicates effectively for change	The administrator has established and implemented a process for faculty and staff to influence stakeholders and advocate for needed changes within the school. The administrator methodically considers proposals in light of the change process, and demonstrates an effective response to the emotional impact and perceived loss that accompanies change initiatives in schools.	The administrator routinely communicates the instructional program to staff and stakeholders, addressing positive elements and current challenges. Administrator influences stakeholders by persuasive argument, setting examples, or using expertise (proficiency in data management and presenting, disseminating information; in-depth knowledge of assessment, curriculum, instruction, and standards).	The administrator communicates need for change by stressing positive elements and minimizing challenges. Expertise is developing in key communication tools and strategies.	The administrator is content with the status quo, neither recognizing current needs for change nor examining data to identify the need for unknown improvements.

6.0 Faculty Development. Incorporates Louisiana Leadership Standard 5: Professional Development. *The administrator (Building Principal or Central Office) engages the educational community, faculty, and staff to plan and implement professional development activities that promote both individual and organizational growth and lead to improved teaching and learning.*

Leadership Dimension	Exemplary (Systemwide Impact in Addition to Proficient)	Proficient	Progressing	Not Meeting Standards
6.1 Understands faculty proficiencies and needs for further development	The administrator has demonstrated a record of differentiated professional development (PD) based on student and faculty needs. The administrator routinely shares professional development opportunities with other schools, departments, districts, and organizations.	The administrator makes sure faculty development (PD) reflects the prioritized needs of the school improvement plan and some effort has been made to differentiate and embed PD to meet the needs of all faculty coaching, mentoring, collaborative teams, and peer scoring.	The administrator is aware of the differentiated needs of faculty and staff members, but PD is only embedded in faculty meetings at this time rather than collaboration, study teams, and so on.	The administrator's plan for PD is typically "one size fits all," and there is little or no evidence of recognition of individual faculty needs or matching of faculty needs to students' achievement needs.
6.2 Leads professional development personally	The administrator is an active participant in teacher-led PD, demonstrating with a commitment of time and intellect that the administrator is a learner and is willing to regularly learn from colleagues. The administrator routinely shares learning experiences with other administrators and colleagues throughout the system.	The administrator devotes faculty meetings to PD, not announcements. The administrator personally leads PD at various times throughout the school year.	The administrator sometimes devotes faculty meetings to professional development and occasionally shares personal learning experiences with colleagues, but relies on others to lead each PD opportunity.	The administrator displays little or no evidence of new learning or sharing that learning with colleagues.

6.0 Faculty Development. Incorporates Louisiana Leadership Standard 5: Professional Development. *The administrator (Building Principal or Central Office) engages the educational community, faculty, and staff in planning and implementing professional development activities that promote both individual and organizational growth and lead to improved teaching and learning.*

Leadership Dimension	Exemplary (Systemwide Impact in Addition to Proficient)	Proficient	Progressing	Not Meeting Standards
6.3 Provides formal and informal feedback to staff or colleagues with the exclusive purpose of improving individual and organizational performance	The administrator uses a variety of creative ways to provide positive and corrective feedback. The entire organization reflects the administrator's focus on accurate, timely, and specific recognition. The administrator balances individual recognition with team and organization-wide recognition.	The administrator provides formal feedback consistent with the district personnel policies, and provides informal feedback to reinforce proficient performance and highlight the strengths of colleagues and staff. Corrective and positive feedback is linked to organizational goals and both the administrator and employees can cite examples of where feedback is used to improve individual and organizational performance.	The administrator adheres to the personnel policies in providing formal and informal feedback, although the feedback is just beginning to provide details that improve teaching or organizational performance.	The administrator's formal feedback is nonspecific. Informal feedback is rare and more likely to be associated with negative than positive behavior.
6.4 Models coaching and mentoring	The administrator is deliberate in establishing development structures that conform to the National Staff Development Council Standards.	The administrator engages in coaching to improve teaching and learning. The administrator is receptive to innovative teaching	The administrator is able to identify certain effective instructional strategies and completes observation	The administrator views classroom observations as an obligation to make

Leadership Dimension	Exemplary (Systemwide Impact in Addition to Proficient)	Proficient	Progressing	Not Meeting Standards
6.0 Faculty Development. Incorporates Louisiana Leadership Standard 5: Professional Development. *The administrator (Building Principal or Central Office) engages the educational community, faculty, and staff in planning and implementing professional development activities that promote both individual and organizational growth and lead to improved teaching and learning.*				
	The administrator coaches other administrators on successful observation strategies. The administrator is seen by his staff as capable of coaching them to improve yet willing to hold them accountable for performance that is not considered acceptable. Multiple examples exist that verify a standards-based professional learning community and action research is evident in context, process, and content.	strategies and practices and the willingness to facilitate new approaches to instruction through action research. The administrator actively coaches instructional staff for improvement of classroom practice. A system has been developed that provides for regular observation of classrooms. Observations are not just used for rating purposes; they are also used for coaching and professional development opportunities. The administrator has organized faculty into an effective learning and action research community where coaching and mentoring occurs formally and informally among the faculty.	process, but needs to develop strategies and practices to help teachers refine and improve their effectiveness.	sure teachers are teaching and students are on task. Evidence of coaching and mentoring, if any, does not specify effective teaching strategies or provide feedback that is either corrective or accurate.

7.0 Leadership Development. Incorporates Louisiana Leadership Standard 1: Vision. *The administrator (Building Principal or Central Office) engages the educational community in developing and maintaining a student-centered vision for education that forms the basis for school goals and guides the preparation of students as effective, lifelong learners in a pluralistic society.* **Incorporates Louisiana Leadership Standard 4: School Improvement.** *The administrator (Building Principal or Central Office) works with the school community to review data from multiple sources to establish challenging standards, monitor progress, and foster the continuous growth of all students.*

Leadership Dimension	Exemplary (Systemwide Impact in Addition to Proficient)	Proficient	Progressing	Not Meeting Standards
7.1 Mentors emerging administrators to assume key leadership responsibilities	The administrator has coached or mentored many individuals who have assumed administrative positions. Multiple administrators throughout the system cite this administrator as a mentor and reason for their success.	The administrator has personally mentored at least one emerging administrator to assume leadership responsibility at an administrative level.	The administrator provides some training to an emerging administrator who may, in time, be capable of independently assuming a leadership role.	The administrator provides no evidence of effort to develop others.
7.2 Identifies potential future administrators	The administrator routinely identifies and recruits new administrators. The administrator provides guidance and mentorship to new, developing, and emerging administrators even when they are outside of the administrator's personal span of leadership responsibilities. The administrator helps other administrators to identify and recruit potential leadership candidates.	The administrator uses a systematic identification process for administrators before recruiting subordinates to participate formally (training, internships, task force leadership).	The administrator understands personnel guidelines for new administrators, but has yet to develop a process to identify or engage potential administrators.	The administrator appears to be indifferent to the need for or benefit of leadership development within the system and within each school unit.
7.3 Delegates responsibility to subordinates	The administrator delegates to staff in formal and informal ways, consistently providing clear expectations and guidance as to desired outcomes. Faculty participates by facilitating meetings and leading committees and task forces; other employees, including noncertified staff, exercise authority and assume leadership roles as appropriate. The climate of trust and delegation in this organization contributes directly to the identification and empowerment of the next generation of leadership.	The administrator demonstrates a clear pattern of delegated decisions. The relationship of authority, responsibility, and delegation is evident in formal observations and evaluation, as well as meeting minutes and other schoolwide communications.	The administrator sometimes delegates, but also maintains decision-making authority that could be delegated to others.	The administrator reserves almost all decision-making authority. Subordinates are unwilling or unable to exercise independent judgment.

8.0 Time/Task/Project Management. Incorporates Louisiana Leadership Standard 3: School Management. *The administrator (Building Principal or Central Office) promotes the success of all students by ensuring management of the organization, operations, and resources for a safe and orderly learning environment.*

Leadership Dimension	Exemplary (Systemwide Impact in Addition to Proficient)	Proficient	Progressing	Not Meeting Standards
8.1 Organizes time and projects for effective leadership	The administrator maintains a daily prioritized task list. Personal organization allows administrator to consider innovations and be available to engage in leadership activities and collaborate with people at all levels. Calendar is free of conflicts and focused on priorities of the administrator and organization. Administrator's project management skills impact programs throughout the organization.	The administrator organization is evident by supporting documentation provided by the administrator. Project and task accomplishments are publicly celebrated and project challenges are open for input from a wide variety of sources.	The administrator's projects are managed using milestones and deadlines, but are infrequently updated. Impact is rarely documented.	The administrator provides little or no evidence of lists of milestones or deadlines in managing time and projects.
8.2 Provides fiscal stewardship by completing projects on schedule and within budget	The administrator regularly saves resources of time and money for the organization, and proactively redirects those resources to help the organization achieve its strategic priorities. Results indicate the positive impact of redirected resources in achieving strategic priorities. The administrator has established processes to use existing limited funds and increase capacity through grants, donations, and community resources.	The administrator uses knowledge of the budgeting process, categories, and funding sources to maximize all available dollars to achieve strategic priorities. The administrator has a documented history of managing complex projects, meets deadlines, and keeps budget commitments. The administrator uses a defined process to direct funds to increase student achievement based on best practice to effectively use resources, time, and instructional strategies.	The administrator sometimes meets project deadlines, but often at the expense of breaking the budget; or meets budget, but fails to meet deadlines.	The administrator has little or no record of keeping commitments for schedules and budgets.

Leadership Dimension	Exemplary (Systemwide Impact in Addition to Proficient)	Proficient	Progressing	Not Meeting Standards
8.0 Time/Task/Project Management. Incorporates Louisiana Leadership Standard 3: School Management. *The administrator (Building Principal or Central Office) promotes the success of all students by ensuring management of the organization, operations, and resources for a safe and orderly learning environment.*				
8.3 Manages facilities and district property	The administrator has a systematic program for facilities management (e.g., processes for safety, cleanliness, maintenance schedules). The system has been adopted or adapted by others.	All facilities supervised by the administrator are maintained and grounds, buildings, restrooms, lounges, public areas, and especially classrooms reflect the administrator's sense of order. A management system ensures all maintenance issues are handled in a timely manner, and facilitates custodial staff with daily duties.	The administrator maintains facilities to minimal standards. Custodial staff lacks direction and leadership.	Facilities are ignored to the point where safety issues arise.
8.4 Demonstrates proficiency in using technology for efficiency and effectiveness	The administrator creates new opportunities for effective technology implementation and models new learning methods.	The administrator personally uses e-mail, word processing, spreadsheets, presentation software, databases, and district software. Personal study and professional development pursuits reflect a commitment to continued learning and effectiveness with technology.	The administrator has mastered software required for proficient performance. Takes initiative to learn new technology.	Not technologically literate. Little or no evidence of taking personal initiative to learn new technology.

Leadership Dimension	Exemplary (Systemwide Impact in Addition to Proficient)	Proficient	Progressing	Not Meeting Standards
9.0 Professional Development. Incorporates Louisiana Leadership Standard 1: Vision. *The administrator (Building Principal or Central Office) engages the educational community in developing and maintaining a student-centered vision for education that forms the basis for school goals and guides the preparation of students as effective, lifelong learners in a pluralistic society.* **Incorporates Louisiana Leadership Standard 2: Teaching and Learning.** *The administrator (Building Principal or Central Office) uses a knowledge of teaching and learning in working collaboratively with the faculty and staff to implement effective and innovative teaching practices that engage students in meaningful and challenging learning experiences.*				
9.1 Understands research trends in education and leadership	The administrator promotes application of research trends, encouraging staff to participate in action research, provide case studies, and analyze local data to establish best practices and serve the interests of the profession beyond the obligations of his or her current position. Learning tools become part of the organization's culture and are locally initiated, not externally generated.	The administrator engages in professional development that is directly linked to organizational needs. Professional readings impact the administrator's performance. The administrator personally attends and actively participates in the professional development that is required of other administrators in the organization.	The administrator reads educational research and demonstrates interest in personal reading and learning. The administrator attends professional development with some evidence of application.	This administrator is not able to provide evidence of follow-up resulting from personal professional development for his or her school or department.
9.2 Creates a professional development focus	The administrator can identify specific professional development offerings of past years that have been systematically reviewed, eliminated, or modified because they failed to support organizational goals. The administrator has a process for prior review of new professional development programs and rigorously applies it to applications for time and funding. The administrator provides examples where requests for professional development failed to meet these criteria.	The administrator's professional development plan has no more than three or four areas of emphasis and each of those areas is linked to the organization's strategic objectives. Building principals attend and actively participate in the professional development required of teachers. Administrator embeds one or two focus areas for professional development in faculty meetings, grade-level meetings, and department meetings.	The administrator's professional development opportunities are somewhat related to the organizational objectives, but participant evaluations are the primary criteria for selection, so programs that are popular but ineffective tend to be the norm.	The administrator pursues topics superficially then chases the next fad. Faculty requests are routinely approved whether or not they are related to student achievement. The administrator's personal professional development agenda is based on whim and preference, not organizational needs.

Leadership Dimension	Exemplary (Systemwide Impact in Addition to Proficient)	Proficient	Progressing	Not Meeting Standards
9.0 Professional Development. Incorporates Louisiana Leadership Standard 1: Vision. *The administrator (Building Principal or Central Office) engages the educational community in developing and maintaining a student-centered vision for education that forms the basis for school goals and guides the preparation of students as effective, lifelong learners in a pluralistic society.* **Incorporates Louisiana Leadership Standard 2: Teaching and Learning.** *The administrator (Building Principal or Central Office) uses a knowledge of teaching and learning in working collaboratively with the faculty and staff to implement effective and innovative teaching practices that engage students in meaningful and challenging learning experiences.*				
9.3 Applies professional learning	The administrator applies each learning opportunity to improve the organization. This administrator creates forms, checklists, self-assessments, and other learning tools so that concepts learned in professional development are applied in the daily lives of teachers and administrators. The administrator regularly shares these application tools with others in order to maximize the impact of the administrator's personal learning experience.	The administrator applies professional learning to her position. Where learning has not been applied, this administrator rigorously analyzes the cause for this and does not continue investing time and money in professional programs that lack clear evidence of success when applied in the organization.	The administrator acknowledges some important learning experiences, but can give only a few specific examples of application to the organization.	When the administrator engages in professional development, the purpose appears to be merely collecting information rather than application to improvement. Professional development for others is viewed as an expense, rather than an investment.

Definitions

1. Performance Dimensions
   - *Exemplary.* This designation represents more than excellence or even achieving at higher levels than other administrators. Scores at this level represent performance that not only meets the rigorous and challenging expectations of proficient performance, but clearly demonstrate a systemwide impact that has influenced Ascension Parish schools in a way that will benefit staff and students for the foreseeable future. It does not represent perfection, but Exemplary means the administrator has gone beyond the requirements of his or her position to build capacity in others for the benefit of the entire organization.
   - *Proficient.* This represents a high degree of skill and accomplishment in the particular domain or dimension. This designation means the administrator has demonstrated excellence in meeting Ascension Parish's high expectations for performance. It means that the administrator consistently meets the expectations of the Parish in the dimension or domain. It is a designation that is not achieved automatically because someone achieved it last year, but something that requires dedication and focus each and every year of an administrator's career. Although veteran administrators are more apt to demonstrate proficiency in specific dimensions or domains just because of the cumulative effort and wisdom of their experience, the standards are challenging enough to require very high quality performance year after year, at levels set by the profession of administrative leaders in Ascension Parish.
   - *Progressing.* This designation represents performance that demonstrates appropriate effort but limited evidence that the skills and attributes have become established for the administrator. An administrator may be doing an excellent job of pursuing proficiency, but has yet to see the prescribed changes in faculty performance or communication structures or student achievement to warrant Proficient. It means the administrator is focused in the right direction but will need to demonstrate a number of attributes before achieving proficiency in those areas. It will be rare for any administrators, even expert veterans, to complete the cycle without some areas scored as Progressing. New administrators or those new to Ascension Parish will earn Progressing designations on some dimensions simply because it takes time and familiarity to lead faculties, staff, and students to make changes. This designation points administrators toward the standard of proficiency, providing focus and direction to their efforts and to continuous improvement.
   - *Not Meeting Standards.* This designation represents a level that is unacceptable and requires immediate attention and monitoring. It may mean that the administrator tries to do everything without delegating (see dimension 7.3) or it may mean the administrator has not viewed the need to develop potential leaders from within his or her

staff (dimension 7.2). Scoring at Not Meeting Standards for these dimensions does not mean the administrator needs to be removed from his or her position, but it does mean these areas need to be addressed now. On the other hand, some dimensions are much more serious when a Not Meeting Standards is observed, such as Dimension 2.5 (administrator honors the time and presence of others), where Not Meeting Standards may mean disrespectful behavior toward others and a pattern of being late and unprepared for meetings. These issues also need immediate intervention, but further demonstration of such behavior would certainly warrant progressive discipline that could lead to dismissal.

2. *Louisiana Leadership Standards.* The Matrix conforms very closely with the Louisiana Leadership Standards, as they are referenced within the Matrix. The Matrix addresses each standard with explicit, observable acts of leadership that actually provide clarity to the standard that is not there without the Matrix. Administrators can rest assured that pursuing proficiency on the Ascension Parish Leadership Professional Growth Matrix more than meets the expectations for leaders in Louisiana, providing very clear expectations and a guide for continuous improvement.

3. *Legal Aspects of Evaluation.* This Matrix does not replace all the existing legal elements of the evaluation process, including due process, progressive discipline, and notification. The Matrix does, however, provide a candid and transparent look at performance that benefits a marginal employee by providing accurate feedback early and avoiding the surprise (shock) of a post hoc evaluation conference at the end of the school year. The Matrix is about improvement and the framework ensures that everyone involved in the process knows where performance is now and where it needs to be in the future. The relationship of supervisor to supervisee is designed in the framework to change from a referee to a coach, and the relationship for the administrator being supervised changes from someone being judged to a participant in improvement.

4. *Preponderance of Evidence.* This is a professional judgment about the holistic performance on each of the nine domains based on the quality and relative strength of the scored dimensions.
   Preponderance of Evidence is not a numeric average, but an overall assessment of performance informed by the scores. For example, if a domain (e.g., 4.0 Decision Making) has four dimensions scored as Progressing, Exemplary, Not Meeting Standards, and Proficient, it would be poor professional judgment to consider that individual Proficient because of the Not Meeting Standards designation, and the behavior may be serious enough on the dimension that is Not Meeting Standards that even a total score of Progressing would be an inappropriate and even irresponsible assessment. A score of Progressing with immediate attention to the dimension not meeting standard is a much better professional judgment. At the same time, scores of Progressing,

Progressing, Progressing, Proficient, and Proficient in 1.0 Student Achievement may warrant a Proficient score because of the importance of dimensions 1.1 (describes gains and closing of learning gaps) and 1.2 (using data to make decisions about instruction). Hence, the framework relies on the administrator to candidly and continually self-assess his or her performance and the supervisor to be equally well-versed in best practices and educational research to determine preponderance of evidence.

Summary

The process is designed primarily for improvement:

- Improved performance for the administrator being supervised because the Matrix offers precise, identifiable, and measurable performance targets to pursue.
- Improved performance for the supervisor because of the obligation of reciprocity, or advocacy for the person being supervised to succeed.
- Improved performance for the school and system because the Matrix is transparent about its expectations for candor, integrity, collaboration, and respect for every student and every employee.
- Improved performance for teachers, because the Matrix clearly illustrates to faculty the unique and considerable challenges of leadership in schools today.
- Improved performance for the Board of Education because the characteristics of successful leadership provide the school system a unique window into practices that work and leadership practices that do not—a research goldmine regarding leadership that has been unavailable to school systems until now.

References

Ainsworth, L. (2003a). *Power standards: Identifying the standards that matter the most.* Englewood, CO: Advanced Learning Press.

Ainsworth, L. (2003b). *Unwrapping the standards: A simple process to make standards manageable.* Englewood, CO: Advanced Learning Press.

Bossidy, L., & Charan, R. (2002). *Execution: The discipline of getting things done.* New York: Crown Business.

Boyatzis, R. E., & McKee, A. (2005). *Resonant leadership: Renewing yourself and connecting with others through mindfulness, hope, and compassion.* Boston: Harvard Business School Press.

Christensen, D. (2001, December). Building state assessment from the classroom up: Why Nebraska has forsworn high-stakes testing in favor of district-tailored measures. *School Administrator,* pp. 27–31.

Collins, J. (2001). *Good to great: Why some companies make the leap . . . and others don't.* New York: HarperBusiness.

Cook, W. J. (2004). When the smoke clears. *Phi Delta Kappan, 86*(1), 73–75, 83.

Council of the Great City Schools. (2006). Urban school superintendents: Characteristics, tenure, and salary. *Urban Indicator, 8*(1), 1–10.

Danielson, C. (2002). *Teaching evaluation.* Alexandria, VA: ASCD.

Darling-Hammond, L. (1997). *The right to learn: A blueprint for creating schools that work.* San Francisco: Jossey-Bass.

Darling-Hammond, L. (2000). Teacher quality and student achievement: A review of state policy evidence. *Educational Policy Analysis Archives, 8*(1), 1–50.

Darling-Hammond, L., & Sykes, G. (Eds.). (1999). *Teaching as the learning profession: Handbook of policy and practice.* San Francisco: Jossey-Bass.

Davis, S., Darling-Hammond, L., LaPointe, M., & Meyerson, D. (2005). *School leadership study: Developing successful principals* (Review of Research). Stanford, CA: Stanford University, Stanford Educational Leadership Institute.

General Accounting Office. (2002, April). *Education needs to monitor states' scoring of assessments* (GAO-02–303). Washington, DC: Author.

Goldsmith, M., & Reiter, M. (2007). *What got you here won't get you there: How successful people become even more successful.* New York: Hyperion.

Goleman, D., Boyatziz, R., & McKee, A. (2002). *Primal leadership: Realizing the power of emotional intelligence.* Boston: Harvard Business School Press.

Goodlad, J. (1984). *A place called school.* New York: McGraw-Hill.

Hersey, P., Blanchard, K. H., & Johnson, D. E. (2000). *Management of organizational behavior: Utilizing human resources* (8th ed.). Upper Saddle River, NJ: Prentice Hall.

Interstate School Leaders Licensure Consortium. (1996, November 2). *Standards for school leaders.* Washington, DC: Council of Chief State School Officers.

Junger, S. (1998). *The perfect storm.* New York: Harper.

Marzano, R. J. (2003). *What works in schools: Translating research into action.* Alexandria, VA: Association for Supervision and Curriculum Development.

Marzano, R. J. (2007). *The art and science of teaching: A comprehensive framework for effective instruction.* Alexandria, VA: Association for Supervision and Curriculum Development.

Marzano, R. J. & Pickering, D. (2001). *Classroom instruction that works: Research-based strategies for increasing student achievement.* Alexandria, VA: ASCD.

North Carolina Center for School Leadership Development. (2001). *Principals and assistant principal's self-assessment.* Retrieved March 14, 2001, from www.ga.unc.edu/pep/resources.html

Peck, M. S. (1978). *The road less traveled: Beyond spiritual growth in an age of anxiety.* Cutchogue, NY: Buccaneer Books.

Peters, T., & Austin, N. (1986). *A passion for excellence.* New York: HarperBusiness.

Pfeffer, J., & Sutton, R. I. (2000). *The knowing-doing gap: How smart companies turn knowledge into action.* Boston: Harvard Business School Press.

Popham, J. (1999). *Testing! Testing! What every parent should know about school tests.* Boston: Allyn & Bacon.

Prichard Committee for Academic Excellence. (2005). *High achieving high schools* (Report). Retrieved April 16, 2008, from http://www.prichardcommittee.org/HS%20Report.pdf.

Quality Counts 2003: "If I Can't Learn From You." (2003, January). *Education Week.*

Reeves, D. B. (2001). *Holistic accountability: Serving students, schools, and community.* Thousand Oaks, CA: Corwin Press.

Reeves, D. B. (2002a). *The daily disciplines of leadership.* San Francisco: Jossey-Bass.

Reeves, D. B. (2002b). *Making standards work: How to implement standards-based performance assessments in the classroom, school, and district* (3rd ed.). Denver: Advanced Learning Press.

Reeves, D. B. (2003). *Accountability for learning: A constructive approach to educational accountability for teachers and school leaders.* Alexandria, VA: ASCD.

Reeves, D. B. (2006). *The learning leader: How to focus school improvement for better results.* Alexandria, VA: Association for Supervision and Curriculum Development.

Reeves, D. B. (2007, October). Coaching myths and realities, *Educational Leadership, 65*(2), 89–90.

Reeves, D. B. (2007, December–2008, January). Making strategic planning work. *Educational Leadership, 65*(4), 86–87.

Rosenthal, R., & Jacobson, L. (2003). *Pygmalion in the classroom: Teacher expectation and pupil's intellectual development.* Carmarthen, UK: Crown House.

Schmoker, M. J. (2004). Tipping point: From feckless reform to substantive instructional improvement. *Phi Delta Kappan, 85*(6), 424–432.

Sorcher, M., & Brant, J. (2002, February). Are you picking the right leaders? *Harvard Business Review,* pp. 78–85.

Stiggins, R. J. (2000). *Student-involved classroom assessment* (3rd ed.). Upper Saddle River, NJ: Prentice Hall.

Stiggins, R. J., Arter, J., Chappuis, J., & Chappuis, S. (2004). *Classroom assessment for student learning: Doing it right, using it well.* Portland, OR: Assessment Training Institute.

Tichy, N. M. (1997). *The leadership engine: How winning companies build leaders at every level.* New York: HarperCollins.

White, S. (2005a). *Beyond the numbers: Making data work for teachers & school leaders.* Englewood, CO: Advanced Learning Press.

White, S. (2005b). *Show me the proof! Tools and strategies to make data work for you.* Englewood, CO: Advanced Learning Press.

Wiggins, G. P. (1998). *Educative assessment: Designing assessments to inform and improve student performance.* San Francisco: Jossey-Bass.

Wiggins, G. P., & McTighe, J. (2005). *Understanding by design.* Alexandria, VA: Association for Supervision and Curriculum Development.

Index

CORWIN PRESS

The Corwin Press logo—a raven striding across an open book—represents the union of courage and learning. Corwin Press is committed to improving education for all learners by publishing books and other professional development resources for those serving the field of PreK–12 education. By providing practical, hands-on materials, Corwin Press continues to carry out the promise of its motto: **"Helping Educators Do Their Work Better."**